A Wild Impatience

Critical Systemic Practice and Research

Selected Papers

Gail Simon

everything is connected

everything is connected

everything is connected

First published 2020 by
Everything is Connected Press
9-11 Main Street, Farnhill, UK, BD20 9BJ

British Library Cataloguing in Publication Data

A.C.I.P. for this book is available from the British Library

ISBN 978-0-9930723-6-9 (pbk)
ISBN 978-0-9930723-7-6 (ebk)

A Wild Impatience. Critical Systemic Practice and Research. Selected Papers by Gail Simon

Cover image: Linocut by Gail Simon 1992

www.eicpress.com

everything is connected

everything is connected

A Wild Impatience. Critical Systemic Practice and Research. Selected Papers by Gail Simon

The writings that Gail Simon selected and collected in this book are like the different faces of a prism; each of them deepens a theme, an aspect of the therapeutic practice, and all together they offer a coherent multifaced view of the systemic approach to psychotherapy. The readers will hear the echoes of words spoken by the masters of the systemic approach (relational mind, curiosity, linguistic systems, context, embodied knowing) elaborated by Gail Simon in a practice concerned with power relations in society. Both clients and therapists are considered as individuals in relation with their local system in the context of wider systems. From this position she connects to the people experiencing oppression and, moving away from theories that individualize problems, she proposes alternative ways of doing therapy which challenge dominant discourses and subvert restrictive and unjust practices. Gail Simon writes in a conversation with the readers and shares with them her inner dialogues; her reflexive, transparent and collaborative style is an invitation to join and go further.

Laura Fruggeri, Professor of Social Psychology, University of Parma and Centro Bolognese di Terapia della Famiglia, Parma and Bologna, Italy

This is a fascinating book that brings together the full range of achievements of one of the foremost contributors to the development of systemic practice in the UK. It charts a series of progressions in theory, practice and through to intersect with research, much of it presaged in the first publication to be included "Incitement to Riot" (1998) which builds a plea for an extended post-modern approach that recognises wider systems and thereby becomes a basis for collective political action. Gail's willingness to challenge and propose constructive extensions to current thinking consolidates in her celebration of 'transgressiveness' while at the same time incorporating a very wide range of influences. Throughout, the book makes a call to recognise and implement the capacity of systemics for activism. Most recently it takes human systems beyond current limitations to address transmaterial worlding, extending the call for widening the applications of systemics to the whole of the natural world. The compilation here clearly shows that Gail is one of the foremost current theoreticians of both practice and practitioner research. It stands as a unique and original contribution with powerful implications while integrating all into a call to make a difference. This book has so much to offer it should be widely adopted for training, practice and research where it will surely have a major impact.

Professors Peter Stratton and Helga Hanks, Leeds Family Therapy Research Centre

I was lucky to have A Wild Impatience to read while the global pandemic forced me into quarantine. In this important and engaging collection of selected papers, Gail Simon invites the reader to engage with her inner dialogue, her professional evolution, and her practice as a transgressive activist. Each chapter is written with wit, intelligence, and engrossing clinical illustrations and vignettes, all superbly tailored to further articulate systemic constructionist theory and practice. Each chapter clearly illustrates the broader political/social aspects and implications of therapy and research. Each chapter also dissolves commonly held distinctions between professional practice and research, writing and speaking, talk and silence, dominant culture and marginalized communities. If one aims to work at the intersection of dominant discourses and social activism, there is no better book to use as a guide.

Sheila McNamee, PhD, Professor, University of New Hampshire, Founder and Vice President, Taos Institute

Gail Simon has always lived and practiced in the margins as it were and from here she has been fostering a different seeing and speaking, doing and being in her work as therapist, supervisor, writer, researcher and teacher. Her 'wild impatience' has been her greatest gift to us. Here is a life mapped out through systemic work of great creativity and integrity.

Imelda McCarthy PhD, Fifth Province Centre, Dublin

A life-giving book for systemic researchers and practitioners practising in complex system and uncertain world. Like her other writings, this book continues to blow me away in her ability to project systemic writing as a life-giving form that offers nurturing for anyone living or being in a complex situation, let alone not having the language to language their practice. Gail's writing is a bridge between the past and future of systemic practice and systemic thinking. This book will be a key textbook for our SYM Academy in Singapore. It's a book that can allow systemic practitioners and researchers to feel at home in helping those who are learning to situate their systemic practice and research. A key systemic purpose indeed!

Maimunah Mosli, Principal Family Therapist and Academy Director, PPIS, Singapore

Borrowing on the language of Adrienne Rich, Audrey Lorde and the solidarity of Gail's cultural ancestors, A Wild Impatience dances us into a journey of rigorous ethical investigation: a true reckoning with power. Gail's murmurations have accompanied me, worried me, unsettled me, but never abandoned me, as the writings are collectively steeped in an ethics of relational connection. With her hands in the dirt, Gail's offerings across decades of struggle, affinities, and points of connection humbly call for critique, for nurture, for resistance to oppression, and for organic systemic webs of connection and transformation.

Vikki Reynolds PhD, RCC activist/supervisor/adjunct professor. Vancouver, Canada

everything is connected

For Gwyn,
without whom these papers would have made the sound of one hand clapping

everything is connected

Contents

everything is connected

About the author

Gail Simon was born in 1956 in Yorkshire in the north of England into a family of German-Russian-Polish Jewish heritage. At school she bumped along the bottom streams not feeling very connected with dominant culture of an English grammar school. Sixth form and Jewish Sunday school were better intellectual playgrounds as was her degree in sociology and social work, and later in systemic therapy.

Gail worked as a social worker, family therapist and counsellor in statutory and independent organisations in the London Boroughs of Brent, Camden, Hackney, Islington and Haringey during the 1980s and 1990s. In 1989, Gail co-founded The Pink Practice, a lesbian, gay, queer, bisexual, transgender and intersex systemic therapy practice in central London where she continues to supervise.

From early on in social work, and to a degree as a result of her own experience in psychotherapy, Gail wanted to work as a psychotherapist. After several years of training in both psychoanalytic and family therapy, Gail trained at KCC in the early 1990s and where she completed her doctorate in 2011 on Writing (as) Systemic Practice. Gail has trained counsellors across a range of modalities but mainly in systemic social constructionist therapy. Teaching research to counsellors and therapists is something Gail pioneered in developing qualitative research methods for relational practitioners and is an active member of the European Congress of Qualitative Inquiry.

Gail is programme director for the Professional Doctorate in Systemic Practice at the University of Bedfordshire where she teaches and supervises systemic doctoral researchers. She is founding editor of *Murmurations: Journal of Transformative Systemic Practice.* She is happiest when out in the countryside with her partner and dog and when developing new theory and practice with colleagues.

Permissions

Part 1

Simon, Gail (2017). Indigenous and other ways (Denkzettel). *Journal of Feminist Dissent,* 2, 40-56. This work was licensed under a Creative Commons Attribution 4.0 International License.

Simon, Gail (1998). Incitement to Riot? Individual Identity and Group Membership: Some Reflections on the Politics of a Post-Modernist Therapy. *Human Systems Journal of Systemic Consultation and Management,* 9, 1, 33-50. Permission to re-print granted by Prof. Peter Stratton, Editor.

Simon, Gail & Whitfield, Gwyn (2010). Transgressive Lives, Transgressive Practices. *Context.* October 2010. Association for Systemic Family Therapy Publications. Permission for this re-print granted by Brian Cade, Editor.

Simon, Gail (2010). Self Supervision, Surveillance and Transgression. *Journal of Family Therapy*, 32, 3, 308–325. Licence to reprint granted by Wiley Publishers.

Simon, Gail (2014). Beyond the Spoken Word. In *Creative Positions in Adult Mental Health. Outside-In : Inside Out.* Eds. Partridge, Karen & McNab, Sue. London: Karnac. Licence to reprint granted by Karnac Books.

Simon, Gail (2016). Thinking Systems. Mind as relational activity. Opportunities for communicating within relationships. In *Re-thinking Autism: critical approaches in a global context.* Eds. Mallett, Rebecca; Runswick-Cole, Kathrine & Timimi, Sami. London: Jessica Kingsley Publishers. Licence to reprint granted by Jessica Kingsley Publishers.

Part 2

Simon, Gail (2010). Dublin Description. A methodological poem. In *Writing (as) Systemic Practice.* Unpublished dissertaion.

Simon, Gail (2014). Systemic Inquiry as a Form of Qualitative Inquiry. In *Systemic Inquiry. Innovations in Reflexive Practice Research.* Eds. Simon, Gail & Chard, Alex. Farnhill, UK: Everything is Connected Press. Permission to re-print granted by Everything is Connected Press.

Simon, Gail (2012). Praction Research: A Model of Systemic Inquiry. *Human Systems Journal of Systemic Consultation and Management,* 23, 1, 103-124. Permission to re-print granted by Prof. Peter Stratton, Editor.

Simon, Gail (2013). Relational Ethnography: Writing and Reading in and about Research Relationships. *Forum Qualitative Sozialforschung / Forum: Qualitative Social Research*, 14, 1. Copyright (c) 2012 Gail Simon. This work was licensed under a Creative Commons Attribution 4.0 International License.

Simon, Gail (2016). Ventriloquation and ghost writing as responses to oppression. *Counselling & Psychotherapy Research Journal,* 17, 1, 16-24. Licence to reprint granted by Wiley Publishers.

Simon, Gail (2018). Eight Criteria for Quality in Systemic Practitioner Research. *Murmurations: Journal of Transformative Systemic Practice,* 1, 2, 40-62. This work was licensed under a Creative Commons Attribution 4.0 International License.

Simon, Gail & Salter, Leah (2019). Transmaterial Worlding. An ecosystemic approach to therapy. *Murmurations: Journal of Transformative Systemic Practice*, 2, 2, 1-18. This work was licensed under a Creative Commons Attribution 4.0 International License.

Preface

By Julia Jude, DProf

Here is a collection of articles written in different moments of time. I was surprised to find that the chapters transcended the eras that they were created in and remain relevant. A Wild Impatience offers one author's commitment to share a medley of systemic encounters which traversed the social landscape with her ancestors, friends, colleagues, and encounters with others: human and non-human along the way. I was drawn to the title of the book and pleased to be greeted by "Denkzettel" and "Incitement to Riot" which speaks to the frustration of unheard voice and silent stories. These silent stories reside in our bodies, mind, heart, skin, hands and clothes; in our gestures, relationships, environment - voices that no longer want to be neutralised or domesticated.

The first section is a collage of systemic reflexive practice and experiences, untamed voices with aromatic breaths. Incitement to Riot was published in 1998. It holds an invitation to inquire under the belly of theory, to explore how we might liberate ourselves from ready-made responses and knowledges that have kept us ignorant. This section starts with a slow climb into unfamiliar zones. Taking in systemic history, theories and alternative writing forms, the chapters traverse the professional and personal. There is an appreciative curiosity in this commitment of writing. The writings make visible transgressive cuts that disrupt taken for granted descriptions without foreclosing the possibilities of building new connections and openings for doubt.

The second section of the book, "Going Further Again", establishes systemic research methods as a soft tool for the exploration of our experiences. It provides an alternative way of engagement but not at a distance; not one that requires measurements, "objective" evidence and categorisation. This form of knowing is being put to rest and asked to stand aside; instead, it is replaced by raw methods and situated ways of knowing. This shifts the movement of theories to enter a space that speaks to action, responsibility and seeing our environment as a condition for knowledge. It demonstrates that the muting of voices can be reversed if we are prepared to allow others to show their methods.

The chapters depict endless travel and movement with no preconceived destination in sight. Characterised by questions, struggle, and renewal of ideas, there is a specific focus on inventing new systemic practices that imbue a range of possibilities that allow local, regional, national and global stories to be occupied but which resist the pull to create small islands that diminish and limit the possibility of new and unimagined stories.

This book propels us to want more from our frames of knowledge. It urges us to go beyond in to the yet not known. There is a plea to the systemic community not to allow systemic ideas to be regulated in the memory lanes of museum galleries, and to avoid becoming too comfortable with tools that we have inherited. There is a reminder that systemic tools are not innocent and do not protect us from becoming infected with the virus of enforced compliance that dominates and blights the lives of marginalised groups.

We end with "Transmaterial Worlding" which disposes of borders and barriers. It feeds on connection and co-construction, nestles in homes of the unheard, and demands that we re-imagine our relationship with our environment.

Wild Impatience marks out the route towards an unfinished journey. It shows that systemic ideas can travel near and far. It's a celebration of systemic movement which invites the reader to wander into unknown dialogical zones which at first sight might appear inaccessible but descends into spaces of debate which offer stepping stones toward new bonds. A Wild Impatience creates new ways to engage with injustice on which the culture of yesterday is rooted. It refuses to settle and to be permanently defined. It is a call to the systemic community to continue wandering, travelling, performing acts of resistance with the systemic baton.

Backwords and Forewords

This collection traverses many green lanes. A green lane is a track, usually hundreds of years old, connecting places, reminders of long, slow, often difficult journeys. In the north of England where I have lived a lot of my life, a green lane is typically marked on each side of by the presence of dry-stone walls over which one is sometimes able to see a long view across a valley or simply an immediate slope of grass field. You can see how these dry-stone walls create pattern both as part of the valley's markings and in marking out the valleys. From a distance, the walls look a uniform light grey. Close up, they are full of colours and shapes from lichen, moss, strands of sheep wool, and occasional bird droppings. Each stone is unique. It has its own story and a particular job to do in the wall, carefully chosen by an expert eye. Writing this now, I realise now how much happens when I'm out walking, moving between the microscopic detail of lichen on a single stone among thousands, and learning what else is present from how my dog's nose and ears react, from how my own ears react. An elusive horizon reveals itself with each pace I take.

These tracks enabled people to make progress over distance, often across tricky terrain which benefitted from a metalled track. They did not start out as waymarked trails for weekend hikers. Signposts and enclosed lanes do not in themselves guarantee a predictable journey.

Writing is like this. There is no map. You set out with a hunch, a sense of direction, you get lost, try different avenues until pointers and connections start to appear. It's rarely a linear process, and certainly far from straightforward. You have to be able to trust the getting lost, the time spent meandering, resting, and not panic about whether you will get back to the last known point or, indeed, your end point. Given the right conditions, tales tell themselves. Theories and practice meet and ignite new sparks. Discomfort must be listened to. It will have something new to say. You have to hold your nerve.

I've been wondering what other writers hope for when preparing an introduction to a collection of their writings. Perhaps they plan to offer a coherent overview of what they have produced. Perhaps they want to explain how they have arrived at the present moment by showing where they have been, whom they have met along the way, and how they have traversed tricky terrain. There is no straight line, no single path, no single story that binds these writings.

Sometimes, having lived as a systemic social constructionist for a few decades, the idea of having just one identity and a single story sounds calmly appealing. For a moment, I imagine how it could simplify my life and people's wide-ranging expectations of me. I wouldn't feel like an overly condensed CV, separated by developmental, political, professional and paradigmatic eras, urban and rural geographies, cultural identities and histories, a chronology of workplaces, trainings, and houses in which I have lived, and alongside many people. Of course a single story, and a single identity would be constraining, impossible, life-sapping. Perhaps one thread that runs through my work is the need to be many-in-one and live parallel lives. I have heard this from other second generation Jewish Holocaust survivors. I live across many communities, distinct, sometimes overlapping, which provide me with a wide range of differently situated and critical perspectives, histories, ways of being and doing separately and together.

Feeling allied with one or more community can offer camaraderie and validity but it also heightens a sense of responsibility in advocating for particular ways of seeing or doing. Writing from within and across communities requires transparency and context. And as I am part of the context, I need to show myself, my various selves with enough detail to honour the reader's intelligence so they can share the responsibility by forming their own opinions about the matters addressed in these texts. This is as necessary in reflexive therapeutic texts as it is in reflexive research writings. How else can we expect a reader to become a reflexive, discerning reader and a conversational partner?

Writing each of these papers was a response to a need I had to formulate something that had been troubling me and where I found a gap in the literature. I wrote the paper I couldn't find. For me, writing is a shout out to colleagues to join me in trying to understand and challenge dominant ideologies and how their constraining material and narrative structures work. Writing is a way of dropping or throwing pebbles into a dialogical pond. One hopes the ripples will merge with those of other people and create a third intra-active movement that disrupts more than the surface so enabling us to go further together.

I haven't changed any of the texts in this book though there are some sentences I would prefer to have changed. What bothers me is that much of what I have written still remains relevant for contemporary systemic practice.

A worry that persists is that critical thinking and innovative practice in the systemic profession is being compromised through standardised training programmes and assimilation into mainstream institutions. Systemic social constructionist therapy is not just another profession to help people in relationships. Systemic social constructionist theory offers a critique of how society works, how power relations play and replay to feed some and deprive others. Our profession theorises change in and across all manner of systems, demonstrating how change can happen or be restricted, who benefits and who is disadvantaged. Our clusters of transdisciplinary theories recognise the power of disruption and the possibilities arising out of deconstructing ideology and its influence of theory and practice. Systemic therapy is an activity but it is also a movement. Mistaking it as simply a profession, institutionalises us and paralyses us. We become inducted into someone else's parameters while apparently adhering to our own theory and practice; the wisdom and values of systemic practice become contained in a watertight consulting room bound and prevented from spilling out onto the streets of our societies.

The chapters in the first section on systemic practice may appear disconnected: what has autism got to do with queerness or silence with supervision? You may want to make your own connections but for me, the common threads running through these works are to do with opening oneself in such a way as to resist falling into dominant narratives about what counts as good practice. My shift into writing about research is simply an extension of these threads. The research chapters have been a response to rebalance the attention away from outcome research to process or practitioner research. The systemic professions have needed to develop or rediscover ways of studying, describing and understanding what we do. We need to expand, with confidence, creativity and competence, ways of sharing that level and complexity of understanding with others. Postpositivist qualitative research opens ways for us to do this.

***

Sometimes I tell people my first training in systemic family therapy was in my family home. No big surprise. That must be the case for most people in the helping professions. By the time it was just my mum and my brother and me, we were back in Yorkshire after a few years in London. Things were clearer. My dad had moved to Florida. I was twelve years old when we returned to my hometown and to my grandmother's house. It was good to be back in my hometown but it took about a day at school to realise I was being treated as an outsider. That was unexpected. By now I spoke with a London accent. I was one of only three Jewish kids in a school of thirteen hundred children. In the small Harrogate Jewish community I felt on the periphery coming from a one parent, low-income family. Having said that, the shul (synagogue) was a hundred times better than the one I grudgingly attended in London. The cheder (hard ch) was much smaller in Harrogate with only twenty kids. I really liked going there on Sunday mornings. We had classes, there were lots of quizzes, we did Purim plays, make sukkot, and played football in the breaks with the teachers. We put on cool events for charity. I was given as much responsibility as I wanted and much free rein for ideas and activities. I learned a lot too. It wasn't always stuff I agreed with but it was all interesting. There was an extensive lunar calendar of festivals with their rituals, many different tunes, ancient and modern history, the Hebrew and Yiddish languages, the celebration of learning and the solemnity of witnessing and remembering those lost, the belonging to a trans-generational English and European community, and the centrality of study around understanding and meaning making.

As I got into my later teens, I asked more difficult questions about the religious texts. I was never a believer but I loved the intellectual engagement that religious studies involved. The weekly portions of the Chumash, the five Books of Moses with the seemingly random, weekly haftorah all read by men in the shul on Shabbos nevertheless made for engaging reading. There was nothing else to do given women were not allowed to participate in the service. I understood little Hebrew but the commentaries which filled half of each page were more interesting. I followed the Hebrew as it was recited, read the English translation to get the gist of the narrative and then I delved into the many reflections on what different rabbis said about the etymology, about the possible meanings of the text and the implications of these messages and metaphors for how people were expected to live their lives. On Yom Kippur, every year I read the English translation "and man will not lie with man, nor man with beast". I knew I was reading ancient texts which were in my world being replaced by those of CHE, the Campaign for Homosexual Equality.

Fortunately, my cheder teachers beamed with appreciation at my questions. They didn't try to give me answers but told me where to look. This is how I remember it anyway. They gave me a class to teach. They put my critical thinking down to my lineage as a descendent of the respected scholar Rabbi Akiba Eger. It was a useful story, I suppose, in that they interpreted my actions as evidence of intellectual ability. That was a useful counter-narrative as my grammar school did not see me as intellectual.

I was sensitive about the imbalance of wealth in my hometown and all that went with that. I was angered by the need for women to sit upstairs in the synagogue and not counting as part of the minyan with the start of the service being delayed until a tenth chap arrived. Those minutes waiting were not wasted in irritation. Frustration churned into articulation. It was the early 1970s and, like many women, I wore my feminism with pride and loudly. The synagogue responded to my increasingly challenging questions by creating the first eshet chayil in Harrogate so the teenage girls could have a watered down and communal version of a barmitzvah. I participated but felt conflicted as there was no intellectual challenge in it and it felt like a biological conveyer belt. The community encouraged dating with boys from the community but I shrugged that off. On some level I understood that the older people wanted to see the Jewish community survive and grow again after its decimation during the holocaust of the second world war. But it was clear I wasn't interested in boys and they gave me some space or gave up, perhaps relieved as I wasn't from the right kind of family anyway.

I graduated from synagogue to hockey and the ranger guides. These were good places to develop responsibility, teamwork and discussion about one's place in the world. My first positive story about lesbians came from a time in the school library when I looked up lesbian in Encyclopaedia Britannica and found long tracts about Sappho and the island of Lesbos. I continued my research in the Harrogate library. I read Sappho's poetry and about her life in a community of women. This was encouraging as I also wrote poetry and wanted to live in a community of women. It helped me survive the hurt when I encountered homophobia aimed at me or others in school and in parts of my extended family. By sixth form, I had friends and teachers who encouraged me to go further and I felt more confident in myself and my future. But my interest in relationships with women was not going to happen in a small conservative town. I knew who and what I was. I just didn't know quite how to get where I needed to go. Failing one of my A levels meant I got there more quickly. And then I graduated with some urgency to being a lesbian and moved to London. 1975.

I learned critical theory at what was then North East London Polytechnic. I studied sociology and social work which gave rise to two enduring interests: critical thinking and the place of power in professional practice. Firstly, critical thinking was unavoidable. You just needed to observe that the lecturers were all at war with each other over the different schools of Marxism and then listen to their lectures in that context. It was fascinating and located the arguments within relationships between people in both spoken and written language. I loved studying sociology through those lenses. The second tension was between sociology and social work. I agreed that social workers could be agents of social control so how was I going to do social work without acting on behalf of a state with interests counter to those of the community it served. I flirted with the question of whether bourgeois aspirations could sit alongside socialist revolutionary praxis. And I felt the gap between psychoanalytic theory and socio-economic led practical need.

In all my adult education, I have wanted to do more than simply pass an essay, I wanted to be stretched and enjoy the experience of creating them. This involved taking some risks in both style and content. In a second year paper on power relations, I focused entirely on the plot, characters and orchestration of the opera Fidelio. And I remember writing a paper on expressionism when at art school in the early 1990s while also completing systemic training at KCC. I wrote the whole art history essay as a long list of systemic questions broken into sections with different hypotheses. It situated expressionist painting in political, social and other relational contexts to explore intent and decision making. I got a very non-systemic response back from the tutor. But the point is that when I have to write something, I don't want it to be a waste of my time, an act of box ticking. Writing is an opportunity and I want it to take me further, to make connections between the complexities and aesthetics of theory and practice and life.

***

When I was looking for a psychotherapy training through the nineteen eighties, I was aware of informal exclusionary criteria for some programmes. If you were not gender "normal", heterosexual - a "healthily matured" individual you were excluded from training in the psychotherapeutic profession in the UK. This heteronormative and Eurocentric prejudice was typical of many psychotherapeutic modalities, especially, but not only, psychoanalytic. This is not simply a matter of equality but of theoretical narratives that formed in-house truths. As an applicant you had to choose. You either undertook therapy to convert or "progress" to heterosexuality (if that indeed worked) or you kept quiet about your life choices and sexual orientation and managed disagreements with the theory in a unemotional fashion so as to display intellectual acuity but not be disruptive or, indeed, suspected. I didn't pursue a psychoanalytic training beyond the first three years as this culture was at odds with my lifestyle, politics and philosophy. By this point, I had also experienced five years of intensive psychoanalysis and had a critique of this way of working compared to other modalities, in particular systemic family therapy which I first met in 1978.

I have encountered homophobia and anti-semitism in in various forms across most areas of my life, directly or indirectly, whether I witness it or not. Of course, "phobia" is the wrong term. People are frightened of people in oppressed and minority groups for the simple reason that equality of power means everyone has to give up something for someone else that they don't want to give up. The truth is that in this world some lives matter more than others. The Black Lives Matter movement names this inequality in its title. We are provoked to engage with the questions, "Why do some lives matter more than others?" and "What is my part in supporting these daily, draining and deadly practices?" and "How can I generate sustainable motivation to open myself to consciousness of my prejudice, to new ways of seeing, being and doing and encourage others to do so too?" Being female and Queer and Jewish and committed to challenging prejudice offers some but limited awareness of what it means to be an ally. But as a white woman, I have to work hard to avoid being involved in the reproduction of oppressive practices. Everyone with whatever kind of privilege has to learn more about the lives of others, about transgenerational pain, to challenge the subtlety of dysconscious systematic oppression and the lenses through which we are encouraged to see and evaluate worth in people. The pain of generations of systemic oppression and murder does not go away. It lives in the air we breathe, infects our daily practice and recreates oppression. As systemic practitioners, we can explore how homeostasis works in our institutions, societies and professional practice.

***

When I wrote my first peer reviewed paper, *Incitement to Riot? Individual Identity and Group Membership: Some Reflections on the Politics of a Post-Modernist Therapy*, I couldn't get started and I kept stalling. It took years to get it ready for publication. I felt alone with these theories and practices.

At some point Gwyn asked, but who are you writing this for? Then I realised the audience in my mind's eye was too different from me. So I didn't expect them to get it. And that was making the process of communicating difficult. But when I imagined a group of lesbian practitioner academics like myself, I felt I was speaking with colleagues, peers, sisters, people who would also be concerned about these issues. I found a way of going on. Years later, when writing my doctorate and teaching writing to therapists and researchers, I advised them to write with friends in their ears, critical, appreciative allies, people who get what you're addressing and want you to go further than you realise you can go.

The work of my lesbian foremother and sister, Adrienne Rich, has been important to me in articulating the limits of language and what poetry can speak to and show of the marginalised intimacies of everyday life. In the first year of my doctorate I wrote a paper using titles from Adrienne Rich's books of poetry. It was called after Rich's 1981 book of poems, *A Wild Patience Has Taken Me This Far.* In the introduction, I wrote (for the male assessors) *"The headings in this paper are taken from collections of poetry by Adrienne Rich, a significant other in my landscape. I felt the need to have some help with the personal and political poetics of this paper. In the final stages of preparing this paper, I was re-minded by reading this paper, and wrote it again with lesbian feminist academic craftswomen at my side, reading my words, seeing them as perhaps our words."*

In this same first year doctoral paper, I proposed that *"many people from oppressed minority backgrounds may connect with the idea of a 'wild patience' when working in the territory of a dominant culture"*. Like many, I may have been seen as patient while agreeing to a polite interface with dominant cultures – and wild for not succeeding in this endeavour – but inside me I have felt a wild *im*patience. It has taken a great deal of energy to manage at times. It splits into an impatience that must endure in order to stay alive and stay true to one's multiple group identities, and a patience in order to be eligible to stay alive and participate in a limited way in other territories. To participate in culturally *nice* conversations where there are unacknowledged hierarchies of power played out through how trainees are assessed, how Queer people are understood, how people from Black,

Indigenous and Minority Ethnic communities are framed, how bold women are met, how older people, and autistic people are treated is infuriating and upsetting. Writing has allowed me to channel some of these frustrations and use language to challenge and disrupt professional narratives and practices of power. I am at home in the systemic community because it welcomes diversity. But I am not at home in the systemic community because, like all communities, diversity is understood as like adding mustard to a sandwich – *yes, we can include that too, and it will add some heat.* But it doesn't change anything at a structural level. It just adds some heat that may become unpalatable if laid on too thick and challenges a familiar balance of power. The Black Lesbian Feminist, Audrey Lorde, offered a profound and blunt critique in title of her paper, *The Master's Tools Will Never Dismantle The Master's House*. Her uncompromising outspokenness is something I have aspired to though I worry at times that I have become part of what I want to critique. When I pick up that groups of trainees or workshop participants are preparing themselves to be nice to me hearing I am a lesbian, I make a point of telling them that I am not a *nice* lesbian. I wonder now why I have never said I'm not a nice Jewish lesbian. Perhaps I thought it would be too much discomfort for these audiences. John Shotter, with whom I had the honour of studying during my doctorate and whose work I read for many years before and afterwards, said that *"if our ways of talking are constrained in any way - if, for instance, only certain ways of talking are considered legitimate and not others - then our understanding, and apparently our experience of ourselves, will be constrained also"*. Such constraints act in insidious ways. It has been important to find a both-and position of being a reasonable community member and ensure there is space around me (and others) to be disruptive where necessary. Lorde said that *"Difference must be not merely tolerated, but seen as a fund of necessary polarities between which our creativity can spark like a dialectic"*. She knowingly created discomfort when she spoke of the necessity for an integrated feminism which took into account Black experience and history, the history and experience of sexuality and other experiences and characteristics which are subject to structural and systemic oppression. The connections between different forms of oppression were not incidental but integral to meaningful change. Lorde was one of the first people to address what is now framed as intersectionality and perhaps this is what I was also creating in the *Incitement to Riot* paper: a case for recognising the diverse specifics of each person's situation which locate them then in an imagined but real community of others who exist somewhere and who would understand what they were experiencing. This practice of decentring of the therapist to foreground existing knowledge in people coming for therapy was an important political shift that reflected what was happening in the field of systemic therapy. Influences on my practice included Imelda McCarthy, Nollaig Byrne, John Burnham, Laura Fruggeri, Gianfranco Cecchin, Luigi Boscolo, Desa Markovic, Susan Lang, Peter Lang, Christine Oliver, Karl Tomm, Glenda Fredman, Vernon Cronen, Barnett Pearce, Harlene Andersen, Harry Goolishian, Michael White, David Epston to name a few of those connected with the KCC School of Systemic Practice where Gwyn and I did our systemic trainings in the early nineties.

The KCC systemic social constructionist ethos of foregrounding the knowledge and expertise of all parties involved in therapy, supervision and training reflected our existing ethical stance in The Pink Practice. The Pink Practice is a lesbian, gay, bi, trans, queer therapy practice in London which Gwyn Whitfield and I co-founded in 1989. We were members of the queer community working as therapists within our own community. We were visible, we were out and we were peers. While we supported the LGBTQI communities, we also needed to find support from people close and far, from our own communities and from academic texts, from the performing and literary arts to challenge the theoretical, liberal humanist, monocultural and heteronormative prejudices within the psychotherapies. And when we couldn't find them, we had to be the writers who made sense of what we were doing.

***

For a while, when I was assembling these papers, I worried they were not going to reflect the queer side of my life and work. But now I see they are all about queering, meaning subverting or challenging, oppressive practices and their supporting discursive structures. Actually, the first piece I wrote in 1999 for the family therapy magazine, Context, challenged the use of the term family therapy as *"too steeped in restrictive discourses and political intent"*.

In a sense all the papers pivot off the *Incitement to Riot* paper, which, by the way, came out of my final 1993 dissertation at KCC – I was examined by Imelda McCarthy and John Burnham. All the papers challenge dominant discourses and propose alternative ways of doing practice which subvert restrictive practices and theories.

My systemic social constructionist growing up took place during a critical time when *Human Systems: Journal of Consultation, Management and Training* was spectacular in bringing chilli hot off-the-shelf reading matter from leading figures in the systemic fields. It also created leading figures in the systemic field. By having its own journal, KCC encouraged its students and tutors, systemic relatives to write and be read by friends. It created community. I am grateful to founding editor, Peter Stratton and co-editor, Helga Hanks for finding space for some of my papers in this journal.

Perhaps this is why co-founding the journal *Murmurations: Journal of Transformative Systemic Practice* with Birgitte Pedersen and Liz Day has been important to me in creating opportunities for the systemic social constructionist community to write, to respond, to be fired up, share learning, and to feel connected to each other. Interestingly, I can see an early indication of my publishing politics at the end of the Incitement to Riot paper, I subverted the protocol of requesting readers not to copy the paper without the author's permission and instead wrote, *"Feel free to photocopy this paper without the author's permission"*. I understood then the importance of published papers being a form of dialogue with anticipated and imagined others out there who would be looking for just that paper. My doctoral thesis, *Writing (as) Systemic Practice*, took that further. I wrote all of it with dialogical intent and in a variety of literary forms. I started Everything is Connected Press to gain some control over pricing, and therefore accessibility, of systemic texts.

***

One of the challenges in putting together a collection of one's writings is how to honour the people who have taken me further and offered me courage over the years. In my mind's eye, I see myself situated in historical and contemporary landscapes surrounded by amazing women pioneers, brave people whose daily lives have been a form of action research to improve the lives of others, to challenge injustice in ways which developed their own aesthetic. I have learned to be proud of where I come from and how I am born out of lesbian feminist communities, Jewish social justice movements, made up of poets-artists-activists-writers-theorists offering me intellectual, ethical and aesthetic invitations. I am following on from them and feel encouraged by them. They act as the rule of a margin, reference points for my values, and when the going is tough, I know they are there.

Those whose voices I need to hear often are close to me, close enough for me to see their eyes and as well as their cues. They speak in specifics, through metaphor, and wise sayings with facial expressions and bodily responses. They open my world through their poetry, or theory, or other art forms, or over meals and talk. They are alive to me whether living or dead. They must always be close by. When I forget them, I rely on finding them or them finding me. I make sense of the world through my responses to it, and my responses to their responses. It pains me when I find a crack of disagreement with what they say. But it happens sometimes. And I know that it needs to happen and why. These are my sisters, my foremothers, my heart-cousins, heroes and guides. Part of my job is to carry on with what they started. To live eyes wide open in worlds not everyone can enter.

***

A single paper by Rosanne Leppington, *From Constructivism to Social Constructionism – and Doing Critical Therapy* - a wonderful 1991 discovery from Human Systems journal - has acted as a pivotal text for me throughout my writing. It storied in a unique manner the important shift to systemic social constructionist practice. It was my go-to text along with the paradigm shifting, *Therapy as Social Construction* (1992) edited by Sheila McNamee and Kenneth Gergen. What the Leppington paper did was to make visible reflexive connections between the influence of our unacknowledged ideologies and their hidden taken-for-granted norms, how our theories and methods are also ideological products so creating very particular genres of data and truth. I reference and build on her work in most of these writings in a range of ways. Perhaps the most difficult of them (for me) is in the paper, *Praction Research: a model of systemic inquiry,* when I finally elaborated on the Leppington model and deconstructed some fundamental principles of Coordinated Management of Meaning's levels of context for what I call spheres of influence. This still sits uncomfortably with me. It's unsettling to undertake major structural alterations on works that are already stable – even if there is a good reason for doing so. I had a similar experience when writing *Transmaterial Worlding. Beyond Human Systems* with Leah Salter when we found ourselves re-constructing some fundamental social constructionist ideas to be more inclusive of who and what mattered, who/what counted as matter and how systemic practice adds a method of mattering to social construction.

***

I extend a humble thanks to all the people I have worked with in therapy, in teaching, through therapy or research supervision, and as colleagues over the years. If there is a powerful way to learn it is through listening to others. Many people with whom I have worked and studied are not named here but their contributions have been instrumental by issuing invitations, reading drafts, and being good conversational partners.

I feel I owe a tremendous and heartfelt debt to the people whose words I draw on in these texts. Such courageous contemporaries and ancestors some of whom now take me beyond human systems into the posthuman and new materialist theorists, to new forms of social justice activism, and the subversive yet respectful playing fields of qualitative inquiry.

I'm grateful to many people who have encouraged or inspired or challenged me along the way. I could say many similar things about each of these people but I will pick just a couple for each. I value the incisiveness, courage and sincerity of my great friend and mentor, Imelda McCarthy. I thank my friend and colleague Sheila McNamee for her humour, wisdom, and friendship. Caroline Dalal was kind enough to be my first reader with useful feedback when I was nervous about sending the Incitement to Riot paper to Human Systems. Desa Markovic was for many years a trusted supervisor and consultant to many areas of my work. Her astute comments and human connection with ethics stay with me. I have enjoyed a kind of rabbinic discussion with John Burnham through his writings while also being inspired by his framing and inventing of much systemic theory and practice. A random but surprisingly precious gift came decades later when Joanna Michopoulou presented the Incitement to Riot paper at a seminar in the most fascinating manner. I was blown away. Liz Day and Birgitte Pedersen bring joy, energy and creative thinking to our shared lives as the editorial team of *Murmurations: Journal of Transformative Systemic Practice* and its mission to get the systemic practice community reading journals again and writing for them. Thanks and appreciation to the inspirational students and team of colleagues on the Professional Doctorate in Systemic Practice at the University of Bedfordshire from whom I learn so much, in particular, Liz Day, Birgitte Pedersen, Julia Jude, Leah Salter. Love and *Skole!* for the encouragement and camaraderie of friends and colleagues Lisen Kebbe, Anne Hedvig Vedeler and Ann-Margreth Olsson while we accompanied each other through our doctoral journeys and in our lives since. Two people in particular are no longer talking aloud in real time but whose voices I still hear anyway: John Shotter and Peter Lang. I especially thank the following people who provide me with encouragement and opportunities for reflecting: Helena Pugh, Vicky Klein, Naz Nizami, Gill Goodwillie, Janine Lees, Amanda Middleton, Ann Jinks, Mai Mosli, Sophia Simmonds, Nathan Simmonds and Gary Simmonds, all of whom, for sure, take me further. There have been two particular creative thinkers and writing companions who, over the years, have inspired me in their noticings and accompanied me up hill, down dale and at my desk: our border collies, first Treacle and now Moss.

I also wish to recognise the women in my family who showed resilience and courage across generations of Jewish and not Jewish experience. From them I have learned things that cannot be taught. And much of my appreciation of this learning comes into a sharper focus as I gain more experience with age. Last in this context but foremost in my life, I can say that Gwyn's opinions and responses are always worth listening to. I have often found myself wishing I had recorded what she had just said because the point she was making and its articulation were so striking and arresting. I know some of my words here are Gwyn's. I don't always know which so I will just say that her intellectual and political astuteness, thoughtfulness and generosity run as an invisible thread through these writings.

Gail Simon, Yorkshire

August 2020

PART ONE

A WILD IMPATIENCE HAS TAKEN ME FURTHER

everything is connected

ONE

Indigenous and other ways Denkzettel

Some contextual stories

I had a long psychoanalysis when I was a young woman. The therapeutic relationship was a warm, collaborative inquiry but I did not succumb to the threat that making non-mainstream gender normative relationship choices would affect my long term mental health. I remained a lesbian and felt well.

One afternoon, during this period of therapy and while training as a social worker, I was entertaining myself in the psychoanalytic section of Swiss Cottage library when I came across a book by Marion Kaplan on the history of the Jüdischer Frauenbund (Jewish Women's Society) in early twentieth century Germany. I learned that Anna O, the 'subject' of the famous late nineteenth century case study by Sigmund Freud and Joseph Breuer was, in fact, an extraordinary political activist, Bertha Pappenheim who challenged fundamentalist narratives as they were played out in everyday life within early twentieth century German society, within Jewish society. Bertha Pappenheim and her colleagues led the development of extensive national resources for unmarried mothers and unemployed women.

In 1989, with Gwyn Whitfield, I started The Pink Practice, a lesbian, gay, bisexual, transgender and queer therapy project in the UK. It was a form of activism – to make something available, visible, so people who were LGBTQI could see a therapist secure in the knowledge that only theory would be deconstructed as part of the therapy - not people's sexual or gender identity. Systemic social constructionism was an important theoretical and philosophical ally. It pulled the rug out from under gender normative development theories. We used it to show how power in society and in professional relationships is played out through linguistic and institutionalised rules and structures. As community activists, we are still ready to support the subversion of dominant narratives if they are not in a person's or a community's best interest. "Good practice" means being in a state of readiness to develop new and transgressive practices if a different kind of talk or action is needed that has yet to be professionally sanctioned.

In this piece of writing, I string together some *Denkzettel*, thought-notes, a term created by Pappenheim. These are episodes, memories, stories I have heard and found. I am interested in not just *what* we know, but *how* we know, and what gets passed on across time, place and generations. And *who* picks this up – because not everyone picks up everything. But there is, for me, this string, a string of pearls and pebbles, grit and thorns, perfectly strung together as if for me, perhaps by me. I don't know. So, I share these *Denkzettel* with you, dear reader, and trust you will know what to do with them in your world.

Indigenous and other ways (Denkzettel)

People sometimes think

that *indigenous*

refers to being,

to biology,

to inherent knowledges,

and not

to the more fluid practices

of becoming,

looking after that

which is precious

historical

vulnerable to eradication.

* * *

Many things come to mind.

Firstly,

when people ask me what

being Jewish

means to me,

a thousand images,

a thousand feelings

flash before my eyes,

mostly untellable, unsayable, uncommunicable,

all

positioning me

an imagined

left or right

of the asker.

In my mind's eye,

I am holding the small

square

black and white photo
(greyscale actually)
of Edith Klatchko, my mother's cousin
and her daughter - Féschen
aged five
between her mother and her mother's boyfriend
all holding hands
for the photographer
on a wide,
wide street
in Riga.
1938.

I see the Negev.
(I have never been there.
I cannot go).
And stories of places,
people,
sites,
tribes
and tribalism,
turning points that made their way into history
creating narrative foundation stones

for education

for survival

and ways of knowing -

long since critiqued by me

and others.

Many others,

too numerous to honour in this moment -

this nanosecond of an unfolding life

beyond my body -

or yours...

I see a moment in Swiss Cottage Library

when, in the psychoanalytic section, my hand reached up

and took down

the biography

of the real "Anna O"

- Bertha Pappenheim.

When I realised

who she was

who she really was

I sat down on a library bench

Read till the library shut,

amazed, shocked

angry, relieved to realise that
Anna O
the famous case study
was a work of fiction -
that the description of her
said more
about the describers
than she who was
being described.
Storytellers, biographers for theory
resembling nothing
of the truth of a life lived
ethically
proudly
courageously
knowingly.

This woman is where I come from
whom I have followed.
She is, was
a pioneer
a social worker
a thorn in the side

a truth teller.

She spoke out

at conferences.

She did not lie.

She told problematic truths

as theatre.

She told the male Jewish authorities the fucking truth

about white slavery

the abduction of poor white women

of poor white Jewish women.

And the men

were scared.

Scared

of what was happening around them

to the community,

the threat of Nazis trafficking Jews to their deaths.

Yet Bold and Brave and in their face

She, Bertha Pappenheim,

(for this name needs saying

as often as we can

to douse the fictionalised Anna O.

Those professional theories

live on to keep other women down)

She, Bertha Pappenheim,

pointed to, evidenced,

the oppression of women

of communities;

she pointed

to lies told,

to the systems that support them;

she pointed

to the men

whom she was addressing

who, behind her back, said

"Back to the doctor!

Back to Breuer, to Freud!

to whoever will get her and her uppity

friends

out of our hair!

We have a job to do."

But the holocaust came anyway.

Despite their best efforts.

And I am here

speaking my truths

because *some* of my family didn't die then,

they didn't perish then.

Not all of them anyway.

They tried to get away.

They tried every which way.

In fact, the eleventh hour came and went,

And they got out.

Just.

And how did they get out?

Because Tante Lulu,

[A family friend who got out earlier

from Berlin

to Bradford,

from a city built on sand

to a city built on Millstone Grit

- cities I know well in this life –]

because Tante Lulu

wrote

letters.

She wrote letters.

She wrote letters at regular intervals

to the Jewish Board of Deputies.

She wrote the facts.

She emphasised the time frame.

She kept writing.

And after several months

- time dangerously spent -

my mother aged 11,

her 13 year old brother

and my grandparents came

to Bradford

to run a hostel

for unaccompanied minors,

refugees,

teenagers who had said goodbye to their parents

and grandparents,

and siblings too,

all knowing

deep down

it was

forever.

And so it was.

* * *

In a folded nineteen sixties newspaper cutting

I read last year,

a Telegraph and Argus interview,

Jewish Chronicle maybe,

with Tante Lulu,

she casually reported that she trained as a young woman

in social work

with Bertha Pappenheim...

Tante Lulu trained with Bertha Pappenheim...

My family was saved by the learning of women that

persistence

is what you do.

You never give up.

You don't hide

your Jewishness.

You don't hide

your humanity.

You don't sidestep

your commitment.

This I learned

and I already knew.

* * *

Indigenous knowing

is not about biology,

it is about history

or herstory;

it is about learning from those

who walked the walk

who trod paths

sometimes in one direction only

sometimes not even walked,

taken

there

out of sight

disappeared…

We know those facts, those figures

but

what

did

they

know

that we

choose

to forget?

What did

they hope

we would remember

and *act on*?

They believe in us

they

the children across the world,

they

the people of all genders

in whatever countries

they whose languages

have been eradicated

whose tongues cut out

whose bodies assaulted

whose lives terminated

secretly

publicly.

Indigenous knowledge

is not just about knowing

it is not about surviving

it is about

living

with a critical awareness

of what has gone before

what is going on

what will happen.
We act
because of our indigenous knowing.
We try to prevent
because of our indigenous knowing.
This knowing
is not in our genes,
it is in our conscience,
in our courage
not to protect old ways
or restricted customs
but human rights
safety
freedoms
possibilities
to right power imbalances
to correct unfairness
to challenge stereotypes
and laws created to constrain and restrain
the best of human energies.

Indigenous knowing is not about creating silos for population groups.
Blood

flows.

It runs

wild through/

beyond the contours

of human life

into confluences

of great

majestic even

scary rivers,

the small feeding into the large

shaping the landscape

cutting it

into left and right banks

and the confusion of tribalised

territories.

The essence of ourselves -

our tributaries

made us so,

separated us

with the land.

And the short-term history

eats our long-term memory

so when we are told to count the grain in our back yard,

sometimes we count;

and when we are taught to sharpen the tips of our weapons,

sometimes we reach for our knives.

Someone here asks

"Who are 'we' paleface?"

And they are right

to ask;

they are right

to challenge

the lumped-together-ness

of all.

And yet are we not also an 'all',

a collective,

with responsibility for each other?

References

Kaplan, Marion (1979). The Jewish Feminist Movement in Germany: The Campaigns of the Jüdischer Frauenbund, 1904-1938. Westport, CT: Greenwood Press.

Librowicz, Luise (1965). Hannah Karminski, Letter to the Editor, Association of Jewish Refugees Newsletter, June 1965, p.15.

TWO

Incitement to Riot?

Individual Identity and Group Membership

Some Reflections on the Politics of a Post-Modernist Therapy

> After all, what is reality anyway? Nothin' but a collective hunch. My space chums think reality was once a primitive method of crowd control that got out of hand.
>
> Jane Wagner, 1986, p.18
>
> The Search for Signs of Intelligent Life in the Universe

Introduction

The hypothesis in this paper is that therapy, including social constructionist practices, undermines or, at least, does not contribute sufficiently to a notion of group identity, potential group strength and the possibility of group action. I would suggest that this undermining takes place in the therapeutic conversation by the *system in focus* most frequently being constructed as involving only smaller, more local systems of the individual, family or work place etc.

I suggest we need to examine how are we limiting the stories and experience which clients and therapists draw on if the larger, specific groups, of which people are also members, are left out of the conversation. Are we overlooking the significance of that membership for the individual and undermining that individual's potential for participating in collective action and other discourses?

Given the level of abstraction involved in these concerns, I show, later in this paper, how I have experimented in practice with creating hypothetical or imaginary situations with clients in which they access multiple voices evoking the experiences, advice etc. of others. I call these voices hypothetical audiences. I have developed the use of wider system questions to facilitate such conversations.

In the interests of space in this paper, I have limited the discussion to the role of the therapist and have not focused on the co-constructive element in the therapy which I regard as central to social constructionist practice.

From Home Town to Cyberspace: Stories of Group Membership

My interest in group membership has been fuelled by my experience of growing up in a small town with an absence of others with whom I could identify. As a lesbian, as a jew, as an unconventional woman, I recognise the value in being able to identify the existence of others like myself. I have found strength in this identification and experienced the creativity of groups producing and participating in political debate.

In my experience of groupwork, both as a therapist and as a client, I have experienced how powerful groups can be in bringing forth accounts of experience in broader social contexts, particularly of commonalities and especially where encouraging a critique of dominant culture in groups, in societies.

The civil rights and protest movements of the 1960s gave rise to a notion of the validity of subjective experience and drew attention to the wider socio-political contexts as discriminating against certain groups of people. The consciousness-raising and self-help groups of the 1970s and '80s developed this shift and encouraged people, particularly women, to create their own accounts of the problems they were experiencing. In the context of these groups and movements, descriptions emerged which spoke both of individualised and shared struggles. People started to develop politicised accounts of personal difficulties, locating them in the contexts of gender, sexuality, class and race politics. People were not solely individuals with personal problems but peers, social critics and agents of change amongst other things.

A more current example of the potential uses of groups can be witnessed on the internet which offers the possibility of bringing together groups of people with similar interests or concerns who would otherwise not necessarily be able to create a sense of community. For example, there are newsgroups for people who have been sexually abused in which people can write openly about their experiences and the effects of their experiences and get feedback, advice or information about resources from other people who have also been abused. Another example is that of a mailing list for lesbian and gay narrative therapists who are geographically scattered and isolated which offers many people the possibility of entering into an international discourse about practices and theories and of "meeting" the occasional person with whom they feel they have something in common [Examples changed to protect identity.]

Contextualising Theory

The postmodernist paradigm lends itself well to exploring the themes of individual identity and group membership because of its emphasis on the centrality of subjectivity in what becomes established as "truth", "knowledge" or "reality". Descriptions of experience from within or between people are valued more highly than those generated by outside experts or those acting on behalf of others.

In practising a social constructionist therapy, I am interested in exploring the narratives through which people's ideas about themselves, their choices, their "realities", are constructed. In addition, I find social constructionism to be a useful methodology for examining the practices of therapy. By focusing on the ideology behind the methodology we can examine what ideas therapist and client are bringing to bear on a subject. I understand "reality" as something we construct socially when we "'actually live in language', (which is to avoid saying that individuals live in a real world and simply use language as a tool to denote and do things.)" (Leppington,

1991, p.55). Through language we can, to varying degrees, bring forth or reproduce our realities.

Social constructionism can be a useful framework in which to use and critique ideas from other discourses and from other paradigms. Ideas, for example, from a Marxist discourse might make a unique contribution but overlook the importance of language and yet the ideas need not be discarded. In this paper and in the context of my clinical work, I find it useful to draw on postmodernist and modernist theories arising out of the discourses of social constructionist therapy, literary criticism, critical art theory, cultural studies and sociology which appear to me to create contexts for each other. As Frazer and Williams (1993) remark, "The communitarian subject is exposed not just to one predominant cultural discourse but to multiple discourses" (cited in Williams 1995, p.155).

It may be useful here to contextualise social constructionist practice by exploring some of the ideological influences of both postmodernism and liberal humanism as I see them.

The Politics of Postmodernism and Some Expectations of "Change"

Postmodernism is steeped in political debate. It has been described as a-political, anti-political, politically ambiguous or politically ambivalent (Rosenau 1992). This relates largely to how the postmodernist idea of relativity is often misunderstood to mean "all ideas are of equal value" and is taken up by different groups to justify conflicting points of view at a moral level. Postmodernism may lack a particular political identity but this does not mean it can be politically "neutral". White (1991) has said that not everything is relative, not all stories are equal. Some stories are better than others in terms of the effect on an individual or society. I understand postmodernism is more of a paradigm for critiquing paradigms as well as a perspective in its own right. It does not have a theory of change as do many other paradigms such as Marxism. What it has is a theory of the reproduction of culture and, by implication, power relations and a status quo.

Jacques Derrida's ideas of deconstruction (1981) have been treated by the left as revolutionary with the possibility of destabilising the status quo, challenging modernist and hegemonic discourses and opening the way for marginalised groups and those oppressed by capitalism. Postmodernism has been seen by the right as overthrowing traditional methods without providing an alternative and as promoting a value relativism which does not distinguish between right and wrong. Some right wing theorists support postmodernism for having a value relativism which can break down specific political allegiances across groups (Rosenau 1992).

One criticism by Marxists of postmodernism is that, in paying strict attention to discourse, it can be seen "to set up language as an alternative to the social problems which plague society." (Eagleton 1983). Leppington (1991) uses the drawing by Escher of ants to visually convey the relational impact between ideas, practice and data in a reflexive figure of eight - but the image itself *does not change*: the ants are on a treadmill. There is no suggestion of any alteration in the environment of the ants. Is that their choice? An implication of this might be that it is our language, our accounts of what is happening that need to change and not our material environment.

The Construction of the Individual: A Liberal Humanist Creation

Liberal Humanism emphasises the rights of the individual above all else and has an "all people must be treated equally" philosophy. It has been criticised for denying differences between people (Kitzinger 1989, Eagleton 1983) and the contexts in which they live. Social constructionists encourage the recognition, valuing and generation of meaning of differences between people and across varying contexts but how do we recognise and challenge the structures which maintain inequalities based on difference? Are we running the risk of modelling an inactive response to social inequality by accepting differences in individuals without reference to the experience in a larger socio-political context?

Kitzinger (1989) describes an example of this with reference to the apparently accepting attitude of liberal humanists towards lesbian individuals. She points out that this acceptance is conditional upon lesbians being quiet about their experience, unchallenging, not too different from heterosexual women etc. Difference is underplayed with liberal humanism stressing "the essential personhood of the lesbian and the relatively trivial nature of her sexual preference" (Kitzinger 1989). The lesbian is assured of her relative social acceptability so long as she does not challenge the dominant heterosexual group nor define herself in a way that does not fit with the idea of the (acceptable) individual lesbian.

In short, difference can be acceptable in the individual. It is more threatening if demonstrated by groups or if the individual does not conform with being a "nice" version of a lesbian, black man, person with HIV etc. Individuals from oppressed or minority groups are unlikely to communicate parts of their identity which may be experienced as threatening to a therapist perceived to be from a more dominant cultural group.

I am proposing that a liberal humanist ideology is, in part, responsible for our focus on smaller systems. Let us consider further the hypothesis that therapy, including social constructionist and narrative therapies, might be contributing to the maintenance of ruling classes and dominant oppressive structures through the separating of the individual from the group, for fear of its potential strength or threat, and by constructing the individual as a local site for treatment. Philippi (1991) draws attention to the political significance of focusing on the individual:

> Site marks the cross-roads of relations of power and their effectiveness on the level of the real, on the subject's very body; the site becomes a specific point of collision of forces - social, political, cultural - which can be distinguished from the ...... [institution] ..... where they are enacted.

Kitzinger (1989) asserts that liberal humanism takes identity and experience out of the public and political arena and relocates it in the personal zone.

If we are to review where we focus - on the notion of the individual or on society - perhaps we can consider Leppington's suggestion (1991) of a shift in focus from the individual to the social context. "The question then is not 'How does the individual rational consciousness account for the social world?' but *'How, in a social world, to account for the culturally specific notions of the individual?'*" (Leppington 1991, p.57) [my italics].

Such a shift is obviously not straightforward. Even in leaving behind modernist discourses, Eagleton (1983) proposes that literary theory, for example, reveals an "unconscious complicity" with them. I would suggest these influences are still affecting social constructionist therapy practices.

> It assumes, in the main, that at the centre of the world is the contemplative individual self ..... this individual is in personal relationship with others ...... but it is noticeable how often such individual consciousness, set in its small circle of relationships, ends up as a touchstone of all else.
>
> Eagleton 1983, p.171

Therapy and the Reproduction of the Status Quo

Focusing on the Smaller System

When I was studying sociology and social work in the late 1970's, the thinking was that social workers were tools of the state, agents of social control. The role of psychotherapists was similarly regarded, namely, by treating the symptoms of individuals or of individual families the therapist was seen as ignoring the social and political causes of their distress. Further, by developing a particular story with the individual or family of their own pathology being the sole or main cause of their difficulties, the therapist decontextualised and, by implication, depoliticised the client's plight. I do not believe that all therapists are, by virtue of being therapists, inclined to act to maintain the status quo but I believe that therapy is often practised without sufficient recognition of the political impact of dominant ideologies.

Most social constructionist and narrative therapists have adopted a framework which is less likely to participate in a discourse of "pathology" and take into account the various social contexts in which people are living, particularly with regard to race and gender, and some also recognise the oppressive discourses which maintain an imbalance of power. However, the system in focus in the therapy does tend to be only known, nameable others from within a person's immediate social or professional circles. The accounts, then, that emerge are likely to be drawn from the "knowledge" and descriptions of experience available to the individual, their smaller system and the therapist.

"Leave it to the politicians......."

Recently, while addressing these issues at a conference, I heard the following questions: "Is it really the job of psychotherapists to concern themselves with the way society works?" and "Shouldn't our focus be our [sic] client?". There are ethical questions for us to consider here. Should we, as therapists, have an analysis of how society works for and against peoples? Is life what you make (of) it? Where do our responsibilities as therapists begin and end? Where do our responsibilities as human beings begin and end? Are therapists and human beings one and the same thing? Are they compatible identities?

It is interesting to speculate as to how the implied dualism of either acting for the individual (or smaller system) *or* acting for the state or larger system has come about. I do not see this dilemma as being connected with a question of who is commissioning the work so much as raising a question about where therapists see therapy as located.

I locate the practice of therapy in the context of our communities. I understand therapy as occurring, not "on the margin of society" (which would suggest a modernist notion of objectivity), but within social contexts which participate in power relations and which cannot be free of prejudices. We will all have investments in maintaining certain accounts and structures but as therapists we particularly need to address how we exercise reflexivity about our most fundamental ideological assumptions of which we are often least mindful; assumptions which will be influencing our practice and by implication what gets brought forth through therapeutic conversation. What might be some of the implications of reviewing our relationship with these ideas? Would we feel comfortable enough to remain therapists or heterosexual, retain certain gender specific behaviours or cultural norms? Could we feel safe, protected and part of a solution; that we were always likely to be on the "right" side of the law?

Critical Therapy

In proposing a shift from knowledge to ethics, Leppington (1991) suggests that all actions in the world are moral actions and therefore have political implications. Languaging, conversing, communicating are considered political acts in that they have social repercussions. "Words are deeds and action is discourse, both construct and express reality." Therapy is not exempt (Leppington, 1991, p.66). White (Allen & White, 1993) remarks "Without doubt, the psychologies and psychotherapies play an entirely significant role in the reproduction of the dominant culture" and Eagleton, speaking of literary criticism, makes the comment "The idea that there are non-political forms of criticism is simply a myth which furthers certain uses of literature all the more effectively." (1983, p.182). Substitute "therapy" for "literature".

Ethical Dilemmas in Questioning

Social constructionist and systemic therapists are constantly faced with decisions about the implications of where to focus in the therapeutic conversation. I want to illustrate with a case example some of the political implications certain questions. (I am not intending here to pay attention to the context for the conversation, who is asking, the hypothesising, the client's expectations from the conversation etc.)

Case Example I

David [2], a forty five year old man who has been unemployed for two years complains of social isolation. His colleagues served a social purpose and he now sees no-one socially outside of his mother and his brother. He feels very bitter about being unemployed and wants another job but feels his prospects are very poor.

David - So what am I going to do? I'm not going to find another job at my age.

Response 1

Therapist - *If you were never going to find another job, what do you think you would do instead?*

['Job' is reframed as merely an activity; the right to work/earn is not taken into account.]

Response 2

Therapist - *What does having a job mean to you?*

[Deconstruction of 'job'; possible implication that unemployment is not a 'real' issue; localising of meaning within the individual.]

Response 3

Therapist - *If you were never to find another job, who, out of all the people you know would be most affected?*

[Implication of coming to terms with unemployment. Reference to smaller system voices only.]

Response 4

Therapist - *If you weren't to think of yourself as 'unemployed', how would you describe yourself?*

[The deconstruction of 'unemployment' could trivialise its significance; an invitation to an individualised description.]

Response 5

Therapist - *Can you think of other situations in which you have felt pessimistic about your prospects?*

[May be empowering but is individualising; implication that his worry is not a 'real' problem.]

Response 6

Therapist - *Perhaps you should join the Socialist Workers' Party in their fight for jobs or help the Labour Party by stuffing envelopes for their campaign against unemployment.*

[Similar to Response 1 in focusing on alternative activities and making suggestions which do not necessarily address his concerns.]

Response 7

Therapist - *If we were having this conversation as a group of marchers on a demonstration about unemployment on the way to the Houses of Parliament, what might we be saying to each other about the effect of unemployment on social isolation?*

[Wider context introduced for conversation. Relocating of David's individual concerns into a wider context.]

Response 8

Therapist - *If, in the next room, there were a hundred or so other men in their mid forties who had also been unemployed for a while, what sort of advice might they give you?*

[The individual's experience is being relocated in a wider system of hypothetical others.]

The last two questions allow for reference to a collective experience by creating a hypothetical audience or virtual group and manage to avoid imposing solutions or attempting to deconstruct the client's concerns.

Critical Therapy prompts us to constantly review the thinking that shapes our practices in therapeutic contexts. Connerton (1978) described critical theory as "resistant to summary; not least, because almost its only unchanging basic thesis is that it is itself changeable." Such an approach invites and encourages reflexivity and *account-ability*: how we account for our actions as therapists, how our accounts in turn influence what we notice and treat as meaningful, what we include and exclude.

Leppington (1991) proposes a way of thinking about practice by looking at the reflexive and recursive relationship between our methodological assumptions, which are incalculably influenced by dominant cultural ideology and epistemology (ways of thinking about what we think we know), theory, method and data (what we do, learn and feedback).

Fig. 1 - Liberal Humanist

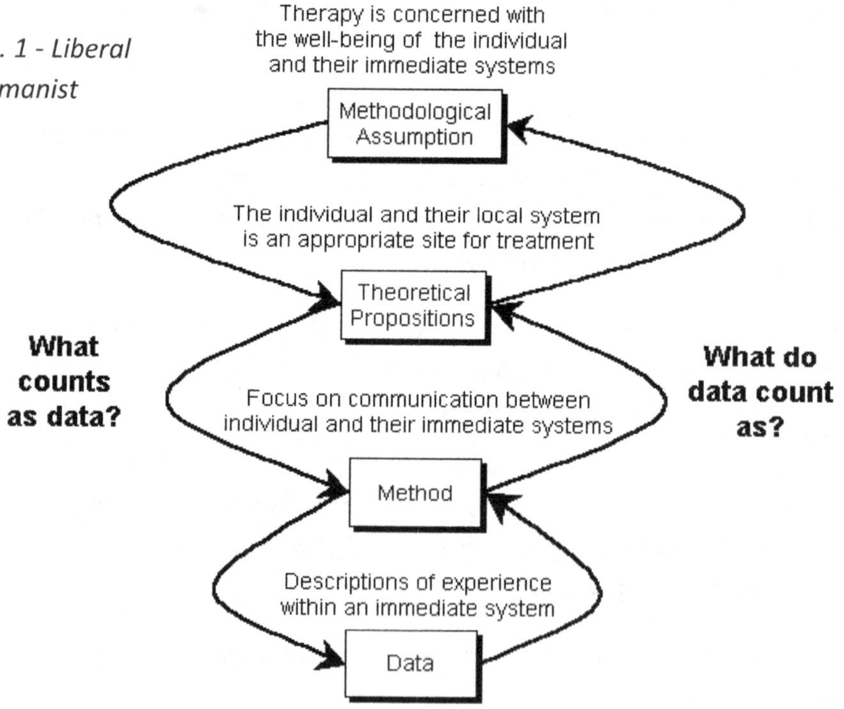

This diagram demonstrates a relationship between these components which allows for change - *encourages* change - at any level, at any point in the therapeutic process although change at a methodological level may be the hardest to change as it is influenced by our ideologies. Each level acts as a context for each other.

Fig. 2 - Critical Therapy

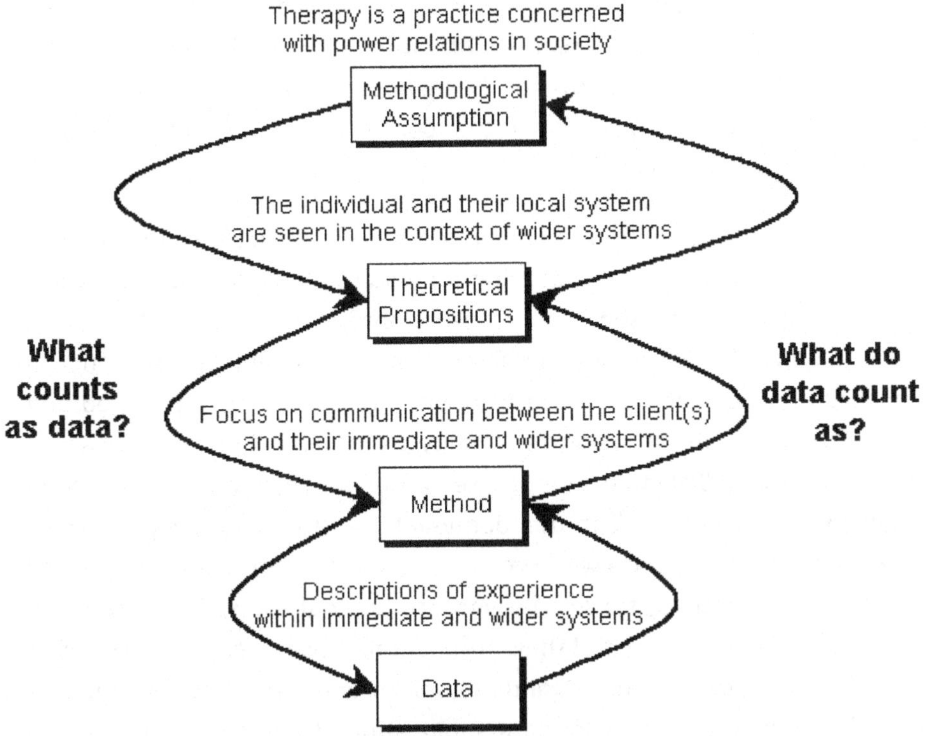

These examples based on Leppington's diagram, (1991) illustrate some differences between the influence on therapeutic practice of a liberal humanist ideology and a more radical ideology.

In discussing the relationship between these different levels, Leppington (1991) proposes taking an ironic stance to one's work and to the conversation by asking questions of oneself:

What are the stories I am drawing on?

What might be some consequences of my ideas?

How are they influencing what is being brought forth or not being brought forth?

As Weingarten (1992) points out, the therapist "is constantly selecting aspects of the conversation to amplify or diminish" and "that this process of selection is guided by a number of variables including the therapist's experiences gained by virtue of being located in a particular racial, gendered and class position in the wider socio-political context within which therapy takes place."

There are problems in identifying what one is overlooking, not bringing forth. Leppington suggests exploring a person's "final vocabulary" which shows itself in half finished sentences or phrases like "You know what I mean". White (1991), is also interested in what might be "present" in conversation but not said and asks how certain ideas are privileged and come to dominate a person's "reality". He uses Derrida's ideas of deconstruction (1981) to explore these absent voices, why they have been silenced and make explicit the dominant narratives in people's lives. "Deconstruction has to do with procedures that subvert taken-for-granted realities and practices; those so-called 'truths' that are split off from the conditions and the context of their production, those disembodied ways of speaking that hide their biases and prejudices, and those familiar practices of self and of relationship that are subjugating of persons' lives." (White 1991, p.27)

I am using the term "deconstruction" in this paper to refer to a questioning process which explores taken-for-granted descriptions *associated with particular voices* and which encourages openness and curiosity to enquire about meaning, how it is attributed, its contexts and its exceptions. By using a hypothetical audience, one can create additional contexts in which further or preferred descriptions of self can emerge. White (1991) sees an integral part of a politicised therapeutic practice as going beyond the deconstructing of ideas and going on to "develop alternative and preferred practices of self and relationship - counter practices." (1991, p.36)

Hypothetical Audiences and Wider System Questions

I have created the term of hypothetical audience to describe a group of other people who may not be physically present but who undoubtedly exist and on whose stories the therapist and client may be able to draw.

Hypothetical audiences can be used to bring forth multiple descriptions or offer support for personal views which do not find support in their immediate systems.

The hypothetical audience can take many different forms. The therapist can invite the client to participate in an imaginary scenario with a group of others of whom the client might ask questions.

The use of the hypothetical audience has proved useful in a practice context where

- *a client has a strong attachment to a decontextualised description of their own difficulties*

and/or where

- *clients sometimes present as isolated with no peer group or community on whose experience or advice they might draw.*

Using a Hypothetical Audience and Wider System Questions with Clients

When co-constructing a hypothetical audience with a client, I have found it most fruitful to "invite" a group of people who might directly relate to the client's situation. The audience will still contain different points of view. Selecting a more general or very different audience has often proved too difficult for the client to identify with and can exacerbate any sense of isolation. Being very specific seems to help the client to identify with or conceptualise of such a group; for example, a hundred other mothers with children under five who have been living in poor temporary accommodation for over six months; a hundred other men in their fifties who have been made redundant for whom work was their life; a hundred other single gay men who have considered coming out to their parents as gay since finding they were HIV positive.

It is also an intervention with the client to create such a group. Individuals become mindful of themselves as members of a group that does exist albeit not immediately or visibly.

Inviting a large number of people allows for the possibility of more variation in audience response. I have found that the first responses which clients bring forth "from" their audience are usually their most familiar and least supportive voice - what Michael White might refer to as the dominant description (1991): "They would think I am crap", "They would think I should try harder", "They would be shocked". It is important to enquire beyond these initial voices to invite the alternative descriptions of *other voices not yet heard*.

A shift can also be seen here from an idea of interviewing a *named* 'internalised other' (Tomm, 1991) to exploring 'internalised discourses' (Allen & White, 1993).

Case Illustration II

Clara, a woman in her late twenties from near Dublin, was approaching the end of her four years in therapy and was still very much under the influence of an individualised description of her struggles which she had been recruited into and which did not include systems greater than her family and colleagues. Working here as the therapist, I thought I would see what other descriptions might be brought forth with a wider audience.

Clara - I don't know. I must be mad.

Therapist - I wonder what a hundred other young women, also from or near Dublin, living in London, would think of your struggles over the past four years? What sense would they make of it?

C - [Pause] I don't know. [Looks puzzled]

T - Well, if someone had made a movie of your life over the last four years or so, including our conversations, edited clips, a two hour movie maybe and had shown it to these other women from Ireland, in their late twenties, what sort of comment would they be making on coming out after the film?

C - Women from Ireland?

T - Women from Ireland who now live in London.

C - Oh. They'd know what I'd been through. They'd understand the isolation and not understanding how things work here, living in poor accommodations, feeling lost and confused. [Pause] I don't know. They'd probably think I was mad.

T - All of them?

C - Yes. No.

T - Out of a hundred women from Ireland of about your age, now living in London, how many would think you were mad and how many would understand your experience differently?

C - [Contemplative pause] Maybe sixty would understand what I had been through. The others might think I was mad. But they might have it yet to come. They might be trying to fit in and suffering like the rest of...... like I used to.

This conversation begins to locate the client's experience within wider systems: a cultural context, a religious context, a political context of immigration, ethnic prejudice. The conversation strengthened the client's positive identification with others from a similar background to herself with an analysis which highlights the plights and strengths of Irish People in London and more generally, of immigrants received by the English. By relocating her experience from the personal to the political or social arena, she loosens her attachment to the personalised story of inadequacy and madness. It was interesting for me to see a shift in the client's posture which seemed to indicate more confidence. She also sounded more confident and contemplative.

In the past, in enquiring about the meaning of the word "mad", I called on the voices in her smaller, known systems. It might have been useful to have interviewed the movie goers about their interpretations of the word "mad" and so used a wider system to deconstruct the term.

The following examples demonstrate the use of wider system questions in bringing forth other audiences which offer further contexts for exploring the meanings of personal experience.

Case Illustration III

Bimla and Rachel, age 29 and 32, had been together three years when they came to counselling. They were having regular arguments which were exhausting them, leaving them feel the only alternative was to split up. Their problems were compounded by living in a small town and not having friends who understood some of the issues they had to deal with in a racially mixed relationship.

I asked them some wider system questions to help them find validity for their experiences in a group beyond their immediate friends, families and therapist. (Simon, 1996)

- If we could, by magic, skip to the next town in this county, what do you think the chances are of us finding another racially mixed lesbian couple in a similar position to yourselves?

- Supposing we hold a conference now for all the lesbian and gay couples in a similar position to you from smaller towns across the U.K., what kinds of things do you think these couples would be putting on the agenda?

- What effect would it have on you two, as a couple, to be surrounded by so many other racially mixed lesbian or gay couples in a similar position to yourselves?

- Imagine you have two or three days at this conference and you are now returning to your home town, to your friends, what do you think you might, if anything, do differently?

By using a hypothetical audience (the conference of other couples) with wider system questions we are drawing on a range of experience which might not otherwise find a voice or an audience and, hence, validation. Another advantage to using these questions is that the counsellor does not need to be an "expert" in the area of the clients' concerns - on the other hand, in many situations some "knowledge" of other groups is necessary in order to know what questions to ask. In this instance, the couple find their own solutions and at the same time relocate their experience into a more public or political arena.

Shotter (1989) writes, "I act not simply 'out of' my own plans and desires but in some sense also 'into' the opportunities offered to me to act, or else my attempts to communicate will fail or be sanctioned in some way." (1989, p.144). He stresses the importance of audience in bringing forth different "you's" and emphasises the co-constructive nature of the relationship between "you" and an audience whose expectations organise the emergent "you". These accounts, says Shotter (1989), are "constitutive of our actual relations to one another, and to the extent that we constitute ourselves in our relations to others, constitutive of ourselves." (1989, p.136) Identity is something which is performed to and brought forth in conjunction with an audience.

Obviously different questions bring out different voices. For example:

- If you were at a meeting now with tens, hundreds and thousands of others and they were saying, in turn, just what you had been saying to me now

  - what effect would that have on you?

- how might you understand differently what you have been saying?

- what might the range of opinions be?

- what do you think you would remember most five years down the line from the experience of hearing hundreds and hundreds of people say the same as you said?

- If you were reading a book of accounts written by mothers who had brought up a severely disabled child, what difference, if any, do you think it would make for you if you came across a story which was just like yours?

- If we imagined for a moment that our conversation was being witnessed, with your consent, by a room filled with other gay men who had also been arrested for "soliciting" a while ago, what advice do you think they would be giving you for coping with this arrest and its effects on your life?

- If we were to go out onto the streets and interview other African Caribbean young men about what they would do if their girlfriends got pregnant, what do you think the range of opinions would be? And if we then interviewed them individually, do you think they would say anything different to what they had said in public amongst their friends?

Or in instances where diversity in opinion is hard to bring forth:

- I think I can see a couple of women at the back of the room who seem to be holding back. What do they think?

Appraising Some Issues, Identifying Some Questions...

- *What are the social and political implications of a therapeutic discourse which places the emphasis on language?*

Brad Keeney was asked by Stephen Madigan whether he saw the individual as an isolated unit 'pulling themselves up by their bootstraps' or whether Keeney thought that empowerment happened "in a community of conversation"? Keeney replied, "Nothing so abstract. Just a community, one's family, one's clan, one's tribe etc." He locates the individual in a larger system, asking, "What is your part at the community table? What is your offering to the whole?" (Keeney in Madigan, 1994, p.53)

- What is your account of the link between change at a level of the individual or smaller system in therapy and change at a level of society or larger group?

- *What is the relationship between group identity and group action in a postmodernist discourse?*

Butler asks, "Can the visibility of identity suffice as a political strategy or can it only be the starting point for a strategic intervention which calls for a transformation of policy?" (1991, p.376).

Perhaps it is important for therapists to re-examine their own membership to groups - actual and virtual, present or hypothetical.

- How does your group membership show itself and to whom?
- How would you like it show itself?
- Do you count only the actual groups or hypothetical groups too?
- What purposes does your group membership serve?
- What are your accounts for how group action comes about, its effectiveness or otherwise?
- Do you believe change can occur using the methods of protest and representation available through existing structures or do you feel more drastic action is sometimes required?
- For what kinds of people or issues would you/do you support or encourage or participate in alternative forms of protest?

- How constrained might you feel from participating publicly in alternative forms of protest by virtue of "being" a therapist?
- *To what degree does focusing on the re-description of individual circumstances contribute to change at a level of society?*

One thing systemic and social constructionist therapists have not yet developed is an analysis of change at a level of the larger system, of society. I feel strongly that we should concern ourselves with this issue so we can have a coherent analysis of change at both a level of the smaller system - the individual, the family, the workplace - and at a level of wider systems. The ethical implications of actions between human beings are a central concern for postmodernist therapists. I have suggested the use of *wider system questions* using *hypothetical audiences* as one response to this issue. But this is a small contribution and the question remains of how else systemic, social constructionist and narrative therapy might go on to contribute to a notion of group membership, group responsibility and group action with a view to changing institutionalised *discourses and practices* which maintain an oppressive status quo.

I understand postmodernist therapy as the practice of inciting people to riot - against oppressive discourses and the structures or institutions which thrive on them. "Riot" is often used to refer to an idea of "mindless", uncontrollable or "anti-social" group behaviour and "incitement", in a therapeutic context, reminds me of the revised ideas about maintaining neutrality or non-directive therapy. But "to incite" can be taken to mean to provoke, arouse, call forth and "riot" to mean disorder, confusion or revolt. The practice of deconstructing dominant, oppressive discourses is no less than a calling forth of disorder as part of a process of change which can create the conditions for other alternative and challenging voices, practices of power and structures to emerge.

Acknowledgement

Gwyn Whitfield at the Pink Practice, Leeds and London, and Shoshana Simons for comments and support.

Feel free to photocopy this paper without the author's permission.

References

Butler, J. (1991). Imitation and Gender Subordination. In *Inside/Out Lesbian Theories, Gay Theories*. Ed. Fuss, D. New York, NY: Routledge.

Connerton, P. (1978). *Critical Sociology*. London: Penguin.

Cronen, V. & Pearce, W.B. (1980). *Communication, Action and Meaning: The Creation of Social Realities.* New York, NY: Praeger.

Derrida, J. (1981). *Positions.* University of Chicago Press.

Eagleton, T. (1983). *Literary Theory*. Oxford: Basil Blackwell Publisher.

Foucault, M. (1984[1976]). *The History of Sexuality: An Introduction.* London: Peregrine.

Foucault, M. (1977). *Language, Counter-Memory, Practice*. Ithaca, NY: Cornell University Press.

Foucault, M. (1979). *Discipline and Punish: The Birth of Prison.* London: Peregrine.

Foucault, M. (1980). *Power/Knowledge: Selected Interviews and Other Writings.* New York, NY: Pantheon.

Williams L. (1996). Neither Liberal Nor Communitarian: Feminism, Political Theory, Possibility. Review of The Politics of Community: A Feminist Critique of the Liberal Communitarian Debate. *C THEORY*.

Keeney, B. & Madigan, S. (1994). A Conversation with Brad Keeney. In Power and Politics in Practice. *Dulwich Centre Newsletter*, No. 1.

Kitzinger, C. (1987). The Social Construction of Lesbianism. London: Sage.

Kitzinger, C. (1989). Liberal Humanism as an Ideology of Control: The Regulation of Lesbian Identities. *Texts of Identity*. Eds. Shotter, J. & Gergen, K. London: Sage.

Leppington, R. (1991). From Constructivism to Social Constructionism and Doing Critical Therapy. *Human Systems: Journal of Systemic Consultation and Management*, 2.2

Pearce, W. B. (1989). *Communication and the Human Condition.*

Carbondale, IL: Southern Illinois University Press.

Philippi, D. (1994). Invisible Sites. *Siteworks.*

Polkinghorne, D. E. (1992). Postmodern Epistemology of Practice. In *Psychology and Postmodernism*, Ed. Kvale S. London: Sage.

Rose, N. (1989). Individualising Psychology. In *Texts of Identity*. Eds. Shotter, J. & Gergen, K. London: Sage.

Rosenau, P.N. (1992). *Post-Modernism and the Social Sciences.* Princeton, NJ: Princeton University Press.

Shotter, J. (1989). Social Accountability and the Social Construction of "You". In *Texts of Identity*. Eds. Shotter, J. & Gergen, K. London: Sage.

Simon, G. (1996). Working with Lesbian, Gay and Bisexual Couples. In *Pink Therapy.* Eds. Davies, D. & Neal, C. Buckingham, UK: Open University Press.

Simon, G. & Whitfield, G. (1995). *A Discourse-in-Progress: Gay Affirmative Practice and A Critical Therapy*. Paper presented at Association of Lesbian, Gay and Bisexual Psychologies Conference 16th & 17th September 1995, University of Nottingham.

Sarup M. (1993). *An Introductory Guide to Poststructuralism and Postmodernism.* Second Edition. London: Harvester Wheatsheaf.

Tomm, K. (1991). *Ethical Postures in Therapy: Facilitating Client's Empowerment. Workshop* at the Kensington Consultation Centre.

Weingarten, K. (1992). A Consideration of Intimate and Non-Intimate Interactions in Therapy. *Family Process,* 31, 1, 45-59.

White, M. (1988). Externalising the Problem. *Dulwich Centre Newsletter.* Australia.

White, M. (1991). Deconstruction and Therapy. *Dulwich Centre Newsletter*, 3, 21-40.

THREE

Transgressive Lives / Transgressive Practices

Gwyn Whitfield and Gail Simon

Editorial, special issue of Context, celebrating 20 years of The Pink Practice and queer systemic therapy

June 1990: Lesbian and Gay Pride in Camberwell Park. We set up a stall and formally launched the first independent lesbian, gay and bisexual counselling practice in London. Why? Well, we kept getting phone calls from people saying, "I've heard, um, that you're a therapist who, um, works with lesbian and gay people? Is that right? That you're gay?" And people told us how difficult it was to find a gay or gay-sensitive therapist. Worse, we heard terrible tales of therapists situating people's sexual orientation at the heart of highly pathologising hypotheses – ones which they were married to with an unswerving monogamous loyalty! We're using the past tense here but unfortunately this is still common across many psychotherapeutic modalities.

As survivors of psychoanalytic therapy and having failed to develop into healthy heterosexual adults, we decided to deviate from mainstream psychoanalytic theories. We abandoned that backbone of analytic theory, the developmental model, which described 'healthy' maturational processes and outcomes. We became interested in how people get pathologised, how their own experience is undermined and subjugated, how some stories dominate and present themselves as common sense or professional knowledge. There felt to be an uncomfortable fit between socio-legal oppression and psychotherapy theory-in-practice bullying tactics. Reading texts like Adrienne Rich's "Compulsory Heterosexuality and Lesbian Existence" (Rich 1986) and connecting with other critical thinking lesbian therapists like Shoshana Simons (see her account in this edition) helped us stay connected to what we knew to be true for us.

As lesbian therapists working in the lesbian and gay communities of which we were and are also members, we wondered how to position ourselves and our knowing. We asked ourselves which therapeutic theories we were using and why. We were mindful of what impact these ideas and practices were having on each of us, on people coming for therapy, on the therapeutic relationship *and on the broader lesbian and gay communities*.

In the eighties there was, as many of you might recall, much discussion of power in relationships be it professional or partner relationships, in workplace teams and so on. Conversations and learning, sometimes painful, sometimes joyous, happened between people of different sexualities, ethnicities, ages, abilities, gender, class and more. The lesbian and gay communities have a history of connecting their own struggles with those of other peoples. *Lesbians and Gay Men support the Miners*! was a familiar sight outside Hackney Town Hall in the mid eighties. *Lesbians and Gay Men Against Apartheid!* banners were always present at anti-apartheid marches in London and elsewhere at that time. The campaign *Gay Men Fighting Aids* did not mean 'we are only looking out for ourselves'. Yes, it was in response to a slow reaction from the medical establishment but it was also an attempt to utilise the tragic experience of us losing so many beautiful men in our own community as a springboard to generate changes in policies on an international scale which would educate, resource and protect others and encourage medical progress.

Solidarity between oppressed and marginalised groups was at the heart of the politicised lesbian and gay communities in the 1980s. And as a community we continue to address our own inclusiveness and speak about a Lesbian, Gay, Bisexual, Transgender and Queer community where Trans advocates choice and determination of gender stories and identities, where Queer proudly embraces a range of sexual and gender identities and practices which transcend, critique and corrupt inherited binaries.

This sense of us at The Pink Practice being part of a community which is connected to other communities, particularly people experiencing oppression, drove us away from theory which *individualised* problems. We could hear how people coming to therapy had already been inducted into very closed, undermining stories about themselves by the normative pop-psychology discourses. So when we heard about the shift in systemic therapy moving from a modernist, method led approach to a post-modern critique of theories as stories, as products of culture, time and place we immersed ourselves in systemic practice. In 1989, Gwyn joined the first ever intake of the training in *Systemic Therapy with Individuals* at the Kensington Consultation Centre which positively undermined the story of the individual as the site for the identification and treatment of pathology. A year later, Gail followed her tracks into KCC and trained in *Systemic Therapy with Individuals, Couples and Families.*

The theory of Co-ordinated Management of Meaning (Cronen and Pearce 1980, Pearce 1999/2004) encouraged a recognition of multiple levels of separate and interconnected influencing contexts. It offered us ways of storying what it might mean to be, for example, from a particular ethnic group and class and be gay, be of a particular age *and* work as a housing officer. We could use this theory to explore with people what other choices there might be for them and explore relational consequences of those choices. Social Constructionism provided us with a means of critiquing theory. Michael White's paper "Deconstruction and Therapy" (White 1991) was hugely supportive. He drew on the work of our gay brothers, Derrida and Foucault, to describe how oppressive practices can function and suggested some means of subverting them through therapy. Heroines have included Rozanne Leppington for her paper 'From Constructivism to Social Constructionism and Doing Critical Therapy' (Leppington 1991) and Celia Kitzinger for her book 'The Social Construction of Lesbianism' (Kitzinger 1988), a fine text – both of these works acted as theoretical, political and philosophical cornerstones for our practice. Judith Butler helped keep us sane with her thoughts on the construction of gender and positioning in relationships (Butler 1990) as did Patti Lather with her politicised theory, courage and complexity (Lather 1994). John Shotter understood something about the affordances and limitations of what we can create with each other, of each other in speech. In his chapter 'The Social Accountability of You' he says "I act not simply 'out of' my own plans and desires, unrestricted by the social circumstances of my performances, but in some sense also 'in to' the opportunities offered to me to act, or else my attempts to communicate will fail or be sanctioned in some way." (Shotter 1989 p.144). John Burnham and Gianfranco Cecchin theorised the importance of a playful and lively relationship with theory (Burnham 1992, 1993; Cecchin et al 1993). The emergence of this permission within a broader professional community felt like an invitation to participate fully, openly and with an expectation of dialogue as opposed to top-down theoretical monologue – and with it, possibility. Having colleagues writing about repositioning expertise (Anderson & Goolishian 1992), making visible one's own thoughts and experience (Roberts 1995), addressing issues of power and possibility (Byrne and McCarthy 1999), and understanding something about living change on the margins and the inherently transgressive nature of systemic practice (Markovic/ Radovanovic 1993) has helped us elaborate what we were already trying to do through politicised intuition. These theories have supported us in creating contextually responsive rule-creating practice.

At The Pink Practice we developed questioning styles to contextualise people's individual struggles using what we called *wider system questions* with *hypothetical audiences* (Simon 1998, 2010). We felt that systemic therapy focused too much – and still does – on close family systems and not enough on other quite specific groupings and communities of which people are members – for example, a gay second generation Greek Cypriot builder working for the family business who is the eldest son with aging parents. We need to remember that there are others out there who would identify with this description, who can offer understanding and suggestions. They can become consultants to people through the therapy, albeit in a virtual way.

We have needed to develop therapeutic practices which are useful to the people with whom we are working and not worry about upholding the foundations of an imagined institution. In that sense we have felt much ethical responsibility for how theory and practice play themselves out.

Overall, we have shied away from invitations to offer “How To” courses, *how to work with lesbians, gay men etc* as we have been concerned to avoid presenting ourselves as insider experts with a fixed knowledge which might exclude other people’s knowledge. It can so easily thingify both ourselves as ‘representatives’ - of what exactly? It can fix in language the very mixed group of people who live in evolving communities with emergent practices and identities and ways of speaking about them. Instead we have offered “Working Across Difference” trainings which help practitioners to get beyond any paralysing liberal guilt and rather explore limiting stories, develop confidence and care in their conversations with others and experiment with questions which situate people in wider, culturally complex systems. We have invited therapists to have confidence in exploring the many overlapping, sometimes less noticed or contradictory circumstances in which people live. Our message has always been that one needs to know how to work with one’s own not knowing and use it to find ways of drawing on knowledge which people already have. Having said that, it has been useful at times to just share examples and stories with people about what others have done in similar situations.
These two examples illustrate how we have at times used therapy as a means of relocating the experience of the individual, couple or family into a broader *community of conversation*.

One Story

A young woman told her Pink Practice therapist about a really profound thought she had that day. Her therapist could see she was still reeling from the effects of it as she was speaking. The therapist asked her to repeat what she had said so she could write it down. It felt important to capture it in some way. The therapist felt inspired by the experience the woman was describing and suggested that it might be moving or useful to others. She asked “How would you feel if I asked you to write that thought on the whiteboard and, um, leave it there for others to experience?” It was a bit of a risky suggestion. She hadn't discussed this with a colleague who also used the room. "I was aware" she said, "of being quite impetuous. Hmm, maybe intuitive is a kinder word! I was also aware that I was transgressing one of the principles of several therapeutic approaches: to keep any information from any one client out of the sight of other clients. But it felt like something to celebrate, something worth putting out there."

But then in subsequent consultations with other clients, we found ourselves asking people, "We're doing this thing of inviting people to write on the whiteboard an important thought or feeling they have been having in the last week or so. If something occurs to you that you want to share, feel free to put it up there or just forget about it if you can't think of anything or you don't want to do it." It was especially important to create some choice so people did not feel pressured to do something they were not comfortable with. And it helped to provide an explanation for what was already written on the whiteboard so people did not think it was a careless left over from someone else's session. Anyway, by the end of the week we had a long list of really amazing reflections. For us as solitary practitioners working with all these compartmentalised conversations with people, it felt not only liberating to break down some of the knowledge boundaries but also was an exciting opportunity to connect people. Most people were keen to participate and they connected to something on the board which was meaningful to them. One or two people just ignored it. One person contributed by translating something someone else had written in Italian into English. That was moving.

It was interesting to see how people took to it as if it was a natural thing to happen. It seemed to feel more unnatural for us as therapists than for the people coming to therapy. And we were moved by the things people wrote and moved also by the time people took to read the words of others. Many people pointed at someone else's reflection and said how they connected to it. It seemed like an opportunity to be alongside someone they had never met and feel understood, supported in a shared experience. Perhaps they felt that their contribution might be make sense to someone else. This one white board acted to unite all these disparate conversations and create a sense of participating in a resourceful, supportive and creative community.

Another Story

A fairly isolated lesbian couple wanted to move to London which was going to be more lesbian friendly and a better cultural fit with their particular ethnic backgrounds than where they were currently living. They had no knowledge of the different areas of London. Their therapist suggested that she could ask everyone else who came for therapy at The Pink Practice what suggestions they had about suitable areas of London to live in for couples in their situation. They looked surprised at the offer and were keen to take it up. For a month, their therapist carried round in her diary a folded piece of paper and she ended each and every session with this question. People took the request very seriously, gave it some thought, put their suggestions in order of consideration, offered the thinking behind their ideas. When she met with the couple a month later, she handed them a rather battered piece of paper for them to take away with all the suggestions from the other people. They were blown away by it. It looked to the therapist as though the couple was starting to feel more part of a LGBTQ community before they had even decided on an area.

These kinds of activities decentre us as therapists. Our words, our thoughts mix with other voices so that people coming to therapy have more of a choice about which words to read or hear. We enjoyed seeing how this kind of process could connect people in a lateral way. It foregrounds a person's situatedness in a community of real people beyond the consulting room. We are led by the idea of *therapist-as-connector* (Simon 1998, 2010). We see these activities as forms of activism which offer opportunities for challenging oppressive practice wherever it occurs and which require our vigilance against complacency, against tokenism and modernist monological truth discourses.

While we are writing, we are remembering, many years ago now, an annual meeting of the register of therapists at the Kensington Consultation Centre.

We were, as a community, reviewing the Code of Ethics for Systemic Therapists. There was one particular clause which pronounced "Thou shalt not bring thy profession into Disrepute." It was at the time when there was much public challenging of Section 28 and some lesbians had the day before abseiled into the house of lords. We were clear that in the event that we needed to act as a lesbian or as a woman first, then we might act in a way that could be considered 'to bring the profession into disrepute'. We like to think that the systemic therapy community does appreciate that therapists are members of other communities with their own priorities which at times may clash with professional concerns. On the other hand, to not act, meaning to act in a way which contradicts one's ethics might in itself render our ethics-led profession disreputable.

Gwyn Whitfield and Gail Simon
*The **P**ink **P**ractice*

We would like to recognise the special contribution of our supervisors over the years who have supported our work at The Pink Practice: Caroline Dalal, Desa Markovic and John Burnham. And of our fellow community members. And each other.

References

Anderson, Harlene & Goolishian, Harold (1992). The client is the expert: a not knowing approach to therapy. In *The Social Construction of Therapy*. Eds. Gergen, Kenneth J. and McNamee, Sheila. London: Sage

Burnham, John (1992). Approach, method, technique: making distinctions and creating connections. *Human Systems: Journal of Systemic Consultation and Management,* 3, 1, 3–26.

Burnham, John (1993). Systemic supervision: the evolution of reflexivity in the context of the supervisory relationship. *Human Systems: Journal of Systemic Consultation and Management,* 4, 3-4, 349–381.

Butler, Judith (1990). *Gender Trouble: Feminism and the Subversion of Identity. New York: Routledge.*

Byrne, Nollaig O'Reilly & McCarthy, Imelda Colgan (1999). Feminism, Politics and Power in Therapeutic Discourse: Fragments from the Fifth Province. In *Deconstructing Psychotherapy*. Ed. Parker, Ian. London: Sage.

Cecchin, Gianfranco, Ray, Wendel and Lane, Gerry (1993). *Irreverence: A Strategy for Therapists' Survival*. London: Karnac.

Cronen, Vernon & Pearce, W. Barnett (1980). *Communication, Action and Meaning: The Creation of Social Realities*. New York, NY: Praeger.

Foucault, Michel (1975). *Discipline and Punish: the Birth of the Prison*. New York, NY: Random House.

Kitzinger, Celia (1987). *The Social Construction of Lesbianism*. London: Sage.

Lather, Patti (1994). *Getting Smart: Feminist Research and Pedagogy Within/in the Postmodern* (Critical Social Thought). London: Routledge.

Leppington, Rozanne (1991). From Constructivism to Social Constructionism and Doing Critical Therapy. *Human Systems Journal of Systemic Consultation and Management*, 2, 2, 217-31.

Pearce Associates (1999, rev. 2004). *Using CMM*. http://www.pearceassociates.com/essays/cmm_seminar.pdf

Markovic (Radovanovic), Desa (1993). Knowing systemic rules. *Human Systems: Journal of Systemic Consultation and Management*, 4, 3-4, 235–258.

Rich, Adrienne (1986). Compulsory Heterosexuality and Lesbian Existence. In *Blood, Bread, and Poetry: Selected Prose, 1979–1985*. NY: Norton.

Roberts, Janine (1995). Transparency and Self-Disclosure in Family Therapy: Dangers and Possibilities. *Family Process*, 44, 1, 45–63.

Shotter, John (1989). Social Accountability and the Social Construction of "You". *Texts of Identity*. Eds. Shotter, J. & Gergen, K. J. London: Sage.

Simon, Gail (1998). Incitement to Riot? Individual Identity and Group Membership: Some Reflections on the Politics of a Post-Modernist Therapy. *Human Systems: Journal of Systemic Consultation and Management*, 9, 1, 33-49.

Simon, Gail (2010). Critical Thinking: A first step towards good practice in training. In C. Lago & B. Smith (Eds.) *Anti- Discriminatory Counselling and Psychotherapy Practice.* London: Sage.

White, Michael (1991). Deconstruction and Therapy. *Dulwich Centre Newsletter*, 2, 21-40.

FOUR

Self-supervision, Surveillance and Transgression

Transgression: a living practice

It has often seemed to me that systemic practice is a bit of an oddity in more rule bound professional cultures. In my work as a systemic supervisor in statutory and independent settings, I have noticed the amazement and confusion for trainees, supervisees and other systemically inclined colleagues as they explore the spontaneous and innovative practices arising out of systemic therapy. Through supervision, people seem to become more curious as to what the relationship is between dominant organisational values and systemic practice and between systemic and other therapeutic ways of working. Some have become frustrated when a fixed description of systemic therapy has not emerged. My own experiences of belonging to oppressed and marginalised groups, theoretically, professionally and politically, have influenced my inclination to work with people to create theory out of their lived experiences and develop theory-in-the-moment as a transient, living way of being. Any examples I use, have either been highly disguised and/or I have agreement from the participants to use the example.

This is a paper about systemic supervision which, as with all areas of systemic practice, I have come to think of as often being transgressive. By ***transgressive*** I mean Breaking New Ground, promoting critical thinking, creating permissions that do not already exist from within the systemic texts. Maybe we could even think of *systemic supervision as a* ***transgressive partnership***. The experience of discussing my 'own' work with systemic consultants or supervisors is that we spend a great deal of time not only developing systemic accounts of my practice but also extending the boundaries of what counts as systemic practice. Like many people I often act first and later on I wonder "Now how on earth does that connect with systemic thinking?" and "*What* would my supervisor say about this?" But, it seems, I can never guess. I am always surprised. I never feel my practice, or the communities in which I practice, are disqualified in any way. Instead my gestures and forays are understood as context specific, a needed response to particular cultural circumstances. The experience leaves me feeling part of a comfortable and inspiring, ground-breaking partnership interested only in making systemic practice more useful to people.

I sometimes wonder if supervisees and supervisors from oppressed or marginalised groups might have a more vigorous and rigorous inner dialogue with inner supervisory voices about appropriate behaviours than those who identify with majority or dominant group norms. They may be living with voices from both dominant *and* counter cultures. In having gone through a process of recognising that they are different in some ways from a mainstream culture, out lesbians, gay men and other queer identified people, for example, ***have learnt to be transgressive*** – to achieve some degree of coherence between their private and public worlds. In order to be a lesbian, I have no choice but to be transgressive in a world dominated by images, values and embodied practices of heterosexuality. As a Jew living in a predominantly Christian culture, recognising or not recognising Christmas or Easter could be seen, either way, a transgressive act.

My experience is that it is unusual for these worlds to come together in a supervision context and that transgressive practices and other mindful deviations associated with culture, gender, age or lifestyle, for example, are often not welcome or appreciated within psychotherapy training courses or counselling organisations. There often exists a form of unspoken censorship by the host culture which can lead to self surveillance and private assessment by people from oppressed and marginalised cultural groups as they try to anticipate what the consequences might be of expressing or even acting on ideas from outside the mainstream culture.

It is this more problematic aspect of self surveillance, cultural dissonance and power in training courses and in the workplace which I want to discuss further.

Becoming Systemic

Systemic practice has been changing so fast that its character, its practices, its place in the psychotherapies is becoming more difficult to describe. It is a constantly evolving practice. And that seems to be part of our ethical commitment: to explore the relationships between different levels of context – be it about the most minute detail in how we respond to another person, different conversational practices or ideological influences (Leppington 1991; Burnham 1992). In our commitment to challenging our own prejudices, we listen out for the novel, for exceptions, that which is unique, "the difference that makes a difference" (Bateson 1972) or, as John Shotter would say "the difference that makes a difference *that matters*" (Shotter 2007). In so doing, we are always taking the ethical position of being prepared to change how we go on in relationship with others, how we go on in our relationship with theory and, in fact, with our most deeply held assumptions. The potential for change between every level of context makes systemic practice a very hard to capture and fast 'science'.

We could borrow from Foucault who felt the term "being gay" was too static, too fixed. He proposed that it is more a matter of *becoming gay,* that gayness was an activity, something which required a performance and came to life in the act of *doing* being gay (Foucault 1981). Perhaps we are always in the process of *becoming systemic* - the activities we engage in develop our story of what counts as systemic. We are involved - less in a process of defining or refining - but in naming and situating and responding to discursive activities.

bell hooks suggests that by creating an environment in which people can be encouraged to develop a questioning relationship with theory, we are teaching them to become critical thinkers (hooks 1994). Instead of absorbing knowledge in what she and Paolo Freire (Freire 1972) describe as the banking system (passively take in, store, get out and use as needed), bell hooks encourages teaching as a transgressive act with its outcome, meaning and uses always being in the hands of the trainees.

Watching You Watching Me Watching You

I have been particularly interested in how often supervisees, whether in training or qualified, reveal a restrictive inner dialogue. This connects with the frequent examples I have noticed of people coming to therapy using apologetic and self pathologising language. Perhaps it is not so surprising that many of the inner supervisory voices reported are restrictive and critical given the modernist culture in which we live, work and study. Trainees, in particular, have to demonstrate "knowing", to reproduce and speak about theory in a way which is recognisable to others. When practitioners cannot, *in the moment*, recognise and name what they are doing as "systemic" - as is often the case - then a regulatory voice can dominate inner dialogue. Many readers will recognise comments such as

> "But how is *that* systemic?"
>
> "I don't know *what* you will think of this...."
>
> "I have no idea what I was doing here."
>
> "I'm afraid I wasn't being very *systemic* when I..."
>
> "Are we *allowed* to..."
>
> "I was thinking, What Would Gail Say..."

I find Foucault's idea about Panopticism helpful in offering a partial explanation for some of these critical, fretful inner voices (Foucault 1991). Foucault drew on Jeremy Bentham's design of a prison to illustrate how members of the public internalise an invisible monitoring authority and go on to police themselves. Bentham's panopticon was designed to be an opposite of the dark cell, the dungeon. In his design, cells were well lit - from front **and** back - and positioned around a single watch tower enabling the supervisor, the prison guard to see all prisoners simultaneously. The inmates would have no knowledge of whether there was anyone watching *at that moment* but they would assume that they were being observed and therefore be affected by the idea that an authority figure was always present.

> He who is subjected to a field of visibility, and who knows it, assumes responsibility for the constraints of power; he makes them play spontaneously upon himself; he inscribes in himself the power relation in which he simultaneously plays both roles; he becomes the principle of his own subjection.
>
> (Foucault, Discipline and Punish 1991, p.202)

Interesting then to speculate about the effect of live supervision in systemic therapy, audio recordings, one way screens, video cameras and note taking. It is often the case that the design and seating arrangement, the view through the screen or cameras in the interview room is often to provide an optimum view for the team.

> This enclosed, segmented space, observed at every point, in which the individuals are inserted in a fixed place, in which the slightest movements are supervised, in which all events are recorded, in which an uninterrupted work of writing links the centre and periphery, in which power is exercised without division, according to a continuous hierarchical figure, in which each individual is constantly located, examined and distributed among the living beings, the sick and the dead - all this constitutes a compact model of the disciplinary mechanism.
>
> (Foucault, Discipline and Punish, 1991, p.197)

The Urban Panopticon of CCTV culture (Koskela 2003) in which most of us now live is very different from the leisure video culture which gave rise to the use of recording and live supervision in family therapy. Given the prevalence of monitoring in most public places, perhaps we need to take into account possible changes in meaning and effect of recording and watching practices despite our care with language?

Cutting the Power

In liberal circles, in our effort to be welcoming and inclusive, we may either not know or we might forget the oppressive aspects of everyday life for people living in a host or dominant culture not in their own image. It is not just difference about which we are speaking but practices of power in institutions and their discourses...

> practices that systematically form the objects of which they speak
>
> (Foucault, 1972, p.49)

Foucault drew attention to ***power*** having been visibly enacted in earlier societies but twenty first century Western society is less that of *spectacle* and more of *surveillance.* Foucault defines surveillance as a process of supervision that imposes discipline. It is, he says, the *physics of power* and becomes central.

I want to suggest that members or representatives of non-dominant cultures and communities may choose *to appear* to comply with power with an "anticipatory conformity" (Zuboff 1988*).* We may or may not try *to act* in accordance with what the central power expects from us but our choices may be influenced by the need *to be observed* putting one's own cultural values to one side in order to get ahead in one's job or pass a course. In situations where we feel secure that we are not being observed, we may act differently. Otherwise, we might resemble *"docile bodies"* (Foucault 1991), but our docility would only be apparent, a mask that we carried as long as we thought we were being observed. To put it differently, we would internalise *power's eye* (Foucault 1991) but we would not

> identify with its values.... Self- surveillance would be, in fact, experienced as surveillance of an internalized, but identified, other upon us.
>
> (Vazl and Bruno, 2003, p.276)

> On the other hand, self-surveillance is part of the necessary care of the self, with this care assuming the form of an effort to constitute oneself as a normal citizen.
>
> (Vazl and Bruno, 2003, p.279)

Perhaps this links to the point made by Viv Gross (2007) about the usefulness of a person assessing the risk in outing an aspect of themselves.

Reconnecting the Power

Let's get back to restrictive comments and questions from supervisees which I mentioned earlier. My first response to those questions is usually to "think systemically" with them about their practice and see if we can together develop an account which brings their practice or dilemma back into a systemic framework, a systemic way of talking. However, I have been reviewing this strategy and have been thinking of systemic practice as a common language which both facilitates the communication of the supervisee and supervisor and which links us to a wider regulatory discourse against which we can assess good or safe practice. This is more pronounced when supervising practitioners in a training context, an assessment context.

Mostly using a systemic framework appears to work well but when working with people from marginalised groups I have felt that at times one or both of us are strangers in another's country. This is not necessarily a terrible thing - I think we could assume that thousands and thousands of people are at any moment having meaningful conversations in a language which is not their first language - but I have found that by recognising and foregrounding the culture, the language, the customs of the supervisee – and perhaps supervisor – over my first port of call - systemic theory - that other explanations for practice dilemmas emerge. In short, systemic theory in supervision is a means to an end but not always the best starting point. Who I am and what I bring explains, to a significant degree, my choice of theoretical approach – not the other way around and these other parts of my life experience create a context for my use of systemic ways of thinking.

Here is an example where culture was not successfully foregrounded in the supervision until other events from outside influenced the supervisory conversation.

> *One supervisor with whom I was working, a woman of white British origin, was under pressure to pass on more intensive work to a less experienced colleague, a woman recently arrived from an Eastern European country. The supervisor was struggling to find evidence of the level of competence needed in their one to one supervision sessions – in fact she had crossed over into looking out for inadequacies. When the team recruited some additional women from the same Eastern European country, she noticed this same colleague come up with some very interesting ideas in the fortnightly team case discussion.*
>
> *The supervisor used her supervision with me to explore how she could work with the colleague on making her abilities more visible in their conversations. In a team discussion months later the three women from Eastern Europe spoke openly about their frustration of their qualifications not being recognised in the UK and how their struggle with the English language seemed to have the effect of them being seen as less intelligent. They said this made them more irritable, impatient and try to sound more expert that they sometimes felt themselves to be.*

Had there not been, in this instance, a number of similar others, the story of an individual's inadequacy may have been further developed. In wanting to be supportive to the supervisor, I had been starting to participate in the pathologising of the individual worker. What do we need to see, feel, find out about with people from oppressed and marginalised groups to build trust in the supervisory relationship? The challenge may be in putting curiosity (Cecchin 1987) and not knowing (Anderson & Goolishian 1987) to work in a way which reflexively addresses how one's own prejudices may influence what does and doesn't get brought forth in supervision.

We don't have to ***know*** about the experiences and lives of others but we do need to know how to bring in the voices of others and make connections across context (Simon 1996, 1998). What we can do is believe that people are not 'bad' or 'inadequate', they are not 'difficult' or 'resistant' but that they are acting out of self-preservation until the relational context is safe enough for them to emerge with confidence – and see if and how and with what effect, these two worlds in which people live might collide.

Some questions which might have been useful for the supervisor to ask her colleague:

- If you were working with families back in your home town, what would you be doing similarly / differently? What freedoms or constraints would there be?
- With whom would you talk about your work?
- Who would be appreciative of your skills? What would they enjoy about your practice?
- What would the you of back home be most proud of what you did in this session?
- What would your previous supervisor tell me about how your practice has developed?

- If you were going to a support group for therapists from your country of origin, what would you be telling them about what works well about our supervisory relationship and what doesn't work so well?
- What has working in another language taught you about your practice?
- What do you think they would suggest we do to preserve the good things and to improve any areas of difficulty?
- What do I need to know about you in order to work with you in a way that respects your integrity? What would be unhelpful?
- What do you need from me so that our working relationship does justice to your abilities and your ambitions?

It is not that these questions are in themselves novel but there is a need to recognise when there are cultural chasms and try not to fill them with the more pathologising language of some of our theoretical relatives. In fact, *when pathologising language creeps into our speech, we could understand its presence as an indication of a need to bridge a culture gap, differences in lived experience and other kinds of knowing.*

And here is an example where cultural issues and matters of power were foregrounded and addressed:

> *As a supervisor in a training team in which there was the only black member of the course, I noticed the rest of the group – including myself – cutting across this person. We were always interrupting with little awareness of our behaviour. After I had got my own behaviour in check and immersed myself in the discomfort of not knowing what to do, I decided to share my observations with the group. The black worker welcomed these observations and elaborated with their own perceptions which they had until that point chosen not to discuss with the team. So the discomfort was*

shared and over an uncomfortable couple of weeks, the team worked through some reflections crucial to their future functioning as a cohesive team. This team was also an important microcosm of the course which supported this trainee.

As the supervisor, I had reasons to feel anxious about my intervention – to some degree because naming issues is no guarantee that they will come to a fruitful resolution but mainly because I felt my efforts to manage issues of power in the group would not be recognised by the agency in which I was working. I felt I needed to keep the process to myself and my own supervisor until it had progressed somewhat. I did "go public" about this once things has progressed but for the most part I felt my colleagues did not appreciate the importance of the intervention, the risk and the skill involved.

Supervisors need to feel supported to deal with matters of challenging power and not out on a cultural limb. But if they are in a minority themselves – either in the views they hold or in terms of their own lifestyle - it can add to any risk, strain and isolation for that person.

Authorising Theory

A therapist felt his supervisor seemed to be overly interested in a gay client's attachment patterns with his mother as a way of explaining his difficulties. The supervisee felt the supervisor's hypothesis was pathologising, drawing on stereotypical ideas about gay men reinforced by psychoanalytic theory. For a while the supervisee questioned themselves asking if they were perhaps being "oversensitive" but as time went on they found they chose not to discuss any gay clients with that supervisor.

This kind of silent questioning of oneself as a first check point, this anticipatory conformity referred to above, is something that will be familiar to many people from minority or oppressed groups. It is more than self reflexivity or an ethical stance. It is a comparative positioning of dominant norms with critical thinking.

I did much of my professional growing up in psychotherapeutic discourses which pathologised lesbians and gay men. It is only recently that psychoanalytic training institutions have agreed to take on lesbian and gay trainees though some are still reluctant. ***This has not just been a matter of equal opportunities. It is a matter of whose theory or knowledge is imported, whose language, whose authority we bring to our intimate working relationships and how.*** When we practice equal opportunities we need to ask if we are importing bodies or culture.

> *In the 1980s, I was part of initiating a lesbian therapists' supervision group. There were some psychodynamically oriented members (as was I at the time) who were struggling with psychoanalytic explanations of the "abnormal sexuality" of lesbians and gay men. After many months of not finding a satisfactory explanation, some of the group members suggested asking a respected liberal heterosexual therapist if they could offer an alternative psychoanalytic explanation of lesbianism which was not pathologising. The group was still looking for theories about lesbianism from outside the experience, from outside of the community. We were looking to the watchtower for a description of ourselves. The other co-founder and I left the group at this point. Instead of being counter-productive, the group was becoming normative-reproductive.*

The profession of psychotherapy has a history of creating ideas about others and imposing these ideas as if fixed and legislated by a separate invisible authority which we cannot easily challenge. This legacy can still affect us as a systemic community.

> *Harlene Anderson told a story at a workshop in Harrogate about a dilemma some supervisees had about whether to take up an invitation to dinner from clients with whom they had just finished*

working. She had discussed with them their concerns about how to manage boundaries and the upshot of the supervisory consultation was that the therapists decided that the most respectful response was to take up the invitation to dinner at the clients' house.

A member of the workshop audience expressed a concern as to whether some boundaries from the profession should be beyond challenge. Harlene replied: "Where do our rules and policies come from? They have been developed by our profession. If they don't fit the circumstance then it is our responsibility to challenge them, to undo them. Taking a questioning or sceptical stance will help us avoid being oppressed by our own body of knowledge." (Anderson 2007)

A supervisee later told me how shocked she had been on hearing this. And went on to say how shocked she was that she was so shocked.

By owning our profession, we have a right to re-write the rules and our most deeply held assumptions about what is right, what is normal, what is done and how the power is shared. John Burnham gave a nice example when he handed the remote control in a video review session to the trainee therapist and then invited that trainee therapist to supervise him supervising the trainee supervisor – and, in so doing, inverted the power structure in the team (Burnham 2007). Supervisors take a key role in the redrawing of these tenets.

> To engage in dialogue is one of the simplest ways we can begin as teachers, scholars, and critical thinkers to cross boundaries, and challenge the barriers that may or may not be erected by race, gender, class, professional standing and host of other differences.
>
> (hooks 1994, p.130)

Crossing boundaries in systemic supervision could mean connecting with the experiences of others, making new rules, building an enquiring culture which is valuing of diversity and continuing to resist pathologising and individualising discourses. At The Pink Practice, we have found it useful to make connections between sexuality, sexual orientation, gender and life choices with other marginalised life experiences and peoples. As a supervisor I feel committed to listening out for other ways of practising which may not be translatable into systemic-ese. It may be that not all cultural practices are reducible into a systemic account. There may be times when community culture, community theory is the highest context for understanding what is happening in the therapy. If so, how can we as supervisors participate in developing accounts of that? Questions which include others can build bridges of knowing and lived experience and can expose the tenuous influence of dominant narratives and practices.

- If this had not been a supervisory / therapeutic conversation you had had but one with a friend how would you have felt / behaved differently?"

- How would your language have changed if there had been no team with you?

- Or if the team was only made up of other lesbian therapists?

- What meaning do you think this black couple gave to the fact you as a black therapist are working with an all white supervisory team? And how might their story have affected you / us during the session? And affect you / us now in this post session discussion in how we are talking together as a team?

- How would it have been do you think, if you had asked your colleague what she thought other lesbians living in NW3 who work at this clinic would say regarding her dilemma about coming out at work?

- Can we imagine for a moment that your training course decided to always have a minimum of five black/ disabled / transgender/ lesbian or gay trainees in each intake? How would that be impacting on the choices you make for yourself in what you do

> here in the clinic? How would that impact on the kinds of accounts you as a team come up with for your practice? How do you think we might be behaving differently – if at all?

A primary concern for me as a supervisor is to find ways of encouraging supervisees to relax into being in relation to the people with whom they are working, find common cultural ground and live in a language which both parties recognise; to get them beyond a preoccupation with the dominant culture of the agency or course.

> *In one instance, a black supervisee felt he connected with a black client in a manner of talking which worked for them. With a change of manager he felt this way of communicating was frowned on and not seen as sufficiently systemic. As his supervisor, we had to find ways of developing bridging accounts between therapeutic connections made with people out of an ethics driven with-ness approach and a method driven "about-ness approach"* (Shotter 2006).

A tense supervisee, supervisor or manager may become more method driven, approval seeking and have lost the connection with their own cultural backgrounds or that of their clients and be preoccupied with the dominant language of systemic therapy or the host institution. Practitioners in training are even more vulnerable. They are practising ways of working in a therapy which privileges the immediacy of the therapeutic relationship yet they have to be simultaneously in relation to the well known concepts of distant printed others.

> *One supervisee, a young Asian women, a trainee, spent her first year of clinical practice trying to re-produce techniques and practices imported from systemic texts. With a change of job where she worked alongside more "out" black and Asian workers - and maybe with time - she started to relax into a style of working which allowed both for a culturally useable and relevant form of conversation as well using systemic opportunities for talk. She became increasingly pleased with the quality of connection she made with the families and with their feedback to her.*

Systemic training courses and allied registering bodies necessarily require that people are sufficiently connected to systemic ideas and that they pass for systemic. This might also involve passing *or being passed by others* for culturally straight, for demonstrating cultural ways from the dominant host culture and so on.

I find the concept of *being OUT* is useful in not only meaning proud and confident, but also in finding the courage to *add to* the language and practices of the dominant culture, to cha(lle)nge society, to *cha(lle)nge* professional practices and stories compared to fitting in, imperceptibly, changing only the statistics and not the practices.

I'm talking here of the individual – perhaps the most common unit for supervision outside of courses – but we do need to remember the *co-construction of self* and try to work with teams to create a space for La Différance (Derrida 1968) – not as a guest but as an ongoing, uncensored influence upon us all.

Transgression: The New Inversion

So what do we do with transgressive thoughts and practices? Do we keep them to ourselves, remain impassive while thinking ill-fitting things? Do we turn our back on the supervisor so they don't see what we are thinking or doing? Do we try to join these odd thoughts or practices up with a systemic discourse, a cultural discourse? Do we leave them in a parallel world?

How do we create the conditions for conversations about our practice if we don't see ourselves as writers, as authors of the rules?

A supervisee recently wondered aloud "But how would I know if I had gone too far, if I was behaving unethically?". We found ourselves discussing the context in which her behaviour had arisen, the strong commitment in systemic practice to examine what we are doing and with what consequences, to hold ethical practice at the forefront of our relationships, to practice reflexivity about all the major and minor choices we are making inside and outside of the conversations. Most importantly, we would ask ourselves either in the moment or retrospectively, "When and why am I being transgressive and what is it about the context that has invited this response?". By contextualising decisions about and within practice, we are beginning *"to comprehend the idea of rules as being socially constructed and start to develop our own style of choosing how to participate in the construction of rules in various contexts"* (Markovic 1993, p.237).

One of the most exciting uses of my authority as a supervisor is when trainees want further clarification when theory does not fit a situation. I say "*You* are inheriting systemic therapy. How are *you* going to develop it?" I am always struck by the stillness that follows, the surprise, the sense of seriousness, of deep reflection, realising the shift in the story of themselves from absorbent learner or challenging trainee to critical thinkers, creators of theory, contributors to the field.

In offering a pragmatic attempt to invert hierarchy, the World Upside Down movements connect with systemic practice reflexivity. It is a form of grassroots activism in which less powerful community groups promote a critical bottom up approach to social policy, work to decentralise power and challenge restraints imposed by dominant theories and practices of power. There seems to be many examples in Latin America, perhaps influenced by the work of Paolo Freire and others. Our commitment to live with changing values, practices and theories is a strength in systemic practice as demonstrated by John Burnham (above) and in his critique of hierarchically organised levels of context (Burnham 1993).

In Bakhtin's notion of carnival, there is "a reversal of the hierarchy of top and bottom" (Bakhtin 1968, p.81) in which the linguistic rules and grammatical order of the dominant classes are transgressed to create counter-meaning (Bakhtin 1968). But systemic practitioners are not invested in merely a *temporary* display of challenging power as might be found at carnival where those with power allow only a time-limited and event-based contestation of the rules (Balandier 1972; Eagleton 1981). Rather our commitment is to a *continual* and *persistent* undoing and reviewing practices of power (Amundson 1993, Anderson 1992, Krause 2002, Simon 1998, White 1991), achieving *"positive delinquency as a position from which the practitioner becomes interested in the processes that organise rule creation, rule adherence and rule questioning"* (Markovic 1993, p.243).

****

How would it be if we found ways of ensuring that therapeutic stories were influenced *by talk outside of therapy*, by a range of social stories *from within our different communities*? Perhaps we would be encouraging a critical and appreciative elaboration of theory and practice in a transgressive climate and minimise the risk of unfriendly self surveillance.

Psychotherapeutic training institutions and organisations can only take on this challenge if they are committed to deconstructing their own ideology. The diagram (fig. 1) illustrates the direction of influence of professional and social stories as it is and as it could be – the downward arrows lead to modernist 'knowledge' about 'others' and the upward arrows indicate the potential for an unfettered, critical elaboration and ownership of psychotherapeutic theory by all sections of the population.

What differences would it make to have service users, trainees 'running the asylum', really influencing the discursive and practical foundations of the institution? Or would institutions fear losing control of their identity and more?

Overcoming the problems of surveillance and self surveillance is not a matter of rolling out a welcome mat in 140 different languages. We live in a culture which is perfecting superficial inclusion practices. Many of our colleagues in their workplaces and training courses, will feel split between their two worlds, between acting with a conformative, normative self and feeling other parts of themselves are experienced as too different, too transgressive. Supervisors and consultants are well equipped within an ethics led, responsive and irreverent culture of systemic practice to enter into transgressive partnerships with the people whose work they are consulting. It is tempting, as I have noticed in my own practice, to think of systemic therapy's commitment to challenging unhelpful practices of power and irreverence as enough of a response but it can lead to self delusion and lost opportunities.

Fig. 1

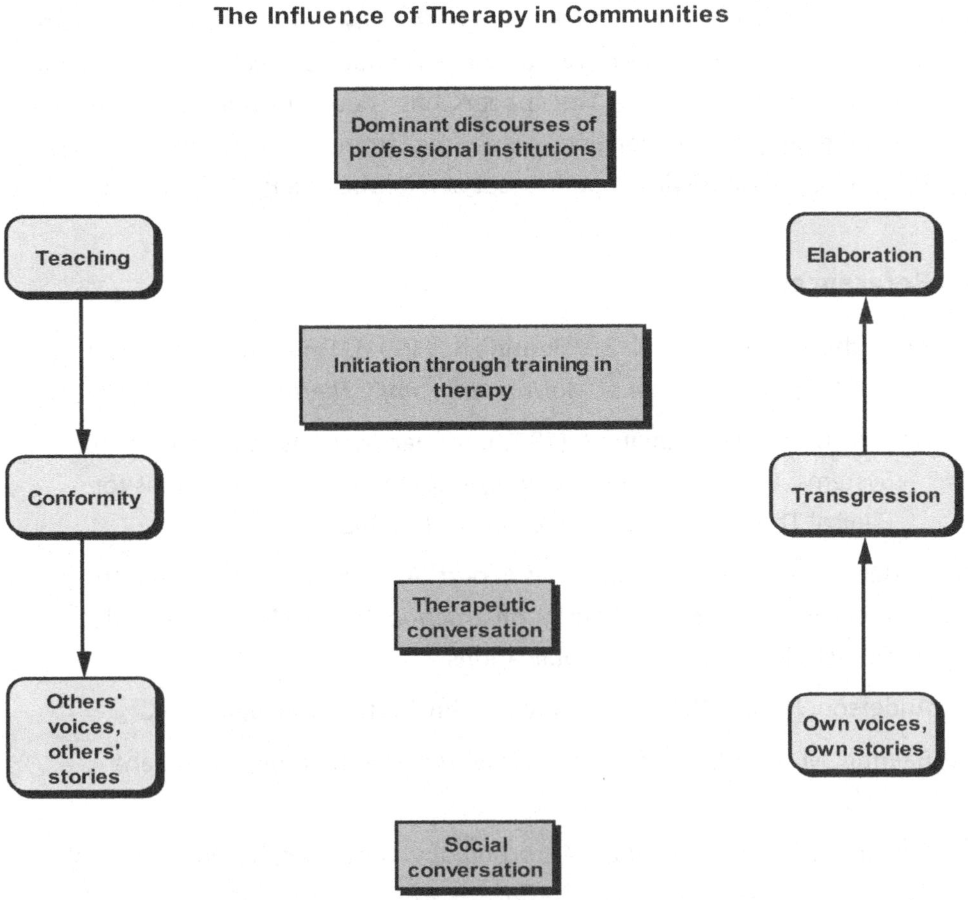

Systemic ideas can lead us to be seduced by our position on the margin (or meta – position), making us vulnerable to what I sometimes call "systemic arrogance". By privileging our critical ability to question, deconstruct, take risks and encompass multiple context levels, we can put ourselves above it all and ironically become blind to the limitations of our practice. Being systemic does not protect us from being compliant to the very practices we purport to combat....

(Markovic 2008)

Acknowledgements

Thanks to all the people with whom I have conversation about their work or my work and to Britt Krause for the invitation to speak at the Systemic Supervision Conference. The paper has been further enriched by encouraging and challenging responses from Desa Markovic, Gwyn Whitfield, Gill Goodwillie, Sue Jones, Lisen Kebbe and Rachel Purchase.

References

Amundson, J., Stewart, K. & Valentine, L. (1993). Temptations of Power and Certainty. *Journal of Marital and Family Therapy*, 9, 2, 111-123.

Anderson, H. & Goolishian, H. (1987). Human Systems as Linguistic Systems: Preliminary and Evolving Ideas about the Implications for Clinical Theory. *Family Process,* 27, 4, 371-393.

Anderson, H. (1992). The Client as Expert: A not knowing approach to therapy. In *Therapy as Social Construction*. Eds. McNamee, S. and Gergen, K. London: Sage Publications.

Anderson, H. (2007). Workshop with John Shotter. Harrogate, UK.

Bakhtin, M. (1968). *Rabelais and his world.* Bloomington, IN: Indiana University Press.

Balandier, G. (1972). *Political Anthropology*. New York, NY: Vintage Books.

Bateson, G. (2000). *Steps to an Ecology of Mind.* University Chicago Press.

Burnham, J. (1992). Approach, method, technique: making distinctions and creating connections. *Human Systems: Journal of Systemic Consultation and Management,* 3, 1, 3–26.

Burnham, J. (1993). Systemic supervision: the evolution of reflexivity in the context of the supervisory relationship. *Human Systems: Journal of Systemic Consultation and Management,* 4, 3-4, 349–381.

Burnham, J. (2007). *Presentation at Systemic Supervision Conference*, IFT and Tavistock Clinic. London.

Cecchin, G. (1987). Hypothesizing, circularity & neutrality revisited: an invitation to curiosity. *Family Process*. 26, 4, 405-414.

Cecchin, G., Ray, W. & Lane, G. (1993). *Irreverence: A Strategy for Therapists' Survival*. London: Karnac.

Derrida, J. (1968). *La Différance*. Bulletin de la Société Française de Philosophie, LXII.

Eagleton, T. (1981). *Walter Benjamin: Towards a Revolutionary Criticism*. London: Verso.

Foucault, M. (1981). Friendship as Lifestyle: An Interview. *Gay Information,* 7, 4, Spring 1981.

Foucault, M. (1972). *The Archaeology of Knowledge and the Discourse on Language.* London: Tavistock Publications.

Foucault, M. (1991 edition). *Discipline and Punish: The birth of prison.* Harmondsworth: Penguin.

Freire, P. (1972). *Pedagogy of the Oppressed.* London: Sheed and Ward.

Gross, V. (2007). Comment made in plenary at original presentation of these ideas, Systemic Supervision Conference, Tavistock Clinic, London.

hooks, b. (1994). *Teaching to Transgress: Education as the Practice of Freedom.* New York: Routledge.

Koskela, H. (2003). 'Cam-Era' – the contemporary urban Panopticon. *Surveillance and Society*, 1, 3, 292-313.

Krause, B. (2002). *Culture and System in Family Therapy*. Karnac Books.

Leppington, R. (1991). From Constructivism to Social Constructionism and Doing Critical Therapy. *Human Systems Journal of Systemic Consultation and Management.* 2, 2, 217-31.

Markovic, D. (1993). Knowing Systemic Rules. *Human Systems Journal of Systemic Consultation and Management,* 4, 3- 4, 235-258.

Markovic, D. (2008). Personal communication.

Shotter, J. (2006). *Getting It: With-ness Thinking and the Dialogical.... In Practice.* KCC Foundation Press.

Shotter, J. (2007). Personal communication.

Simon, G. (1996). Working with people in relationships. In Pink Therapy. Eds Davies, D. & Neal, C. Buckingham, UK: Open University Press.

Simon, G. (1998). Incitement to Riot? Individual Identity and Group Membership: Some Reflections on the Politics of a Post-Modernist Therapy in *Human Systems: Journal of Systemic Consultation and Management,* 9, 1, 33-49.

Stallybrass, P. & White, A. (1986). The Poetics and Politics of Transgression in *A Reader in the Anthropology of Religion*. Ed. Michael Lambek. London: Blackwell Publishing

Vazl, P. & Bruno, F. (2003). Types of Self-Surveillance: from abnormality to individuals "at risk". *Surveillance and Society*. 1, , 272-291.

White, M. (1991). Deconstruction and Therapy. *Dulwich Centre Newsletter*, 2, 21-40.

Zuboff, S. (1988). In *The Age Of The Smart Machine: The Future Of Work And Power*. New York, NY: Basic Books.

FIVE

Beyond the Spoken Word

Silence in therapy

Silence, as we may know from our own experiences, can be beautiful, welcoming, terrifying, confusing, grounding – so many things. But a therapist's reading of a silence may not tell us whether it is a desirable and friendly silence for people or whether people want help with talking in general or about something in particular.

My training in psychoanalytic therapy and my experience of having psychoanalytic therapy taught me about the uses of just sitting with people without feeling a responsibility to populate the space between us with a wordy attempt to understand and process through questions and answers and reflections. On the other hand, I think back with horror to other times in my therapeutic career, when I may have contributed to unnecessary discomfort for some people by not creating additional choices with them. The move in systemic therapy towards dialogical and collaborative relationships in therapy brings me great relief. A reflexive, appreciative and learning stance in therapy opens space for therapists and the clients to negotiate rewarding and creative ways of communicating together. This is a better ethical and practical fit for me. It opens up possibilities to get alongside people in their silence and find useful and fitting ways of being together.

The spoken word is not everyone's first or preferred language. In this chapter, I share some examples of how people coming to therapy and I have experimented and found ways of talking without being so dependent on talking aloud. And I show how I have tried to get over some of the insidious narratives in our profession which privilege aloud talk as the optimum medium for a successful therapeutic outcome and the use of therapeutic techniques over spontaneous responsiveness (Shotter & Katz, 1998; Vedeler, 2011) in therapeutic relationships.

In the following story, Susan and I work out how to coordinate in the silence. Despite what I said about being prepared for silences and not being in a rush to talk and understand, I can sometimes feel a discomfort which reflects my need to set a context for silences. If talking exchanges are not available in therapy, it creates a dilemma for the collaborative practitioner. How can I avoid imposing my agenda or my way of talking on people coming for therapy without them offering me guidance? The reflexive rescuer in me needs to know the extent of her responsibilities and establish that the 'call' button is working and that people know how to use it.

Susan and I try to work out how to talk

> *Months go by. We sit in silence most of the time. But it is a silence which is far from quiet. Susan's discomfort is apparent. She looks pained when I ask questions. And doesn't answer. Well, not in any way which I can make sense of. I just see-hear-feel her pain. There is an appearance of stillness in the room but I feel we are both busy. I try many things – including not trying things. I come up with all kinds of questions and suggestions. Perhaps just one or two each session. These attempts to open communication feel like I am making things more difficult. Which mean there are still long periods of silence. I have absolutely no idea how to navigate these meetings. I am not sure whose job it is to steer. I ask context setting questions and questions about talk.*
>
> *"Would you like me to ask you questions?"*
>
> *"Is this a comfortable silence or one you'd like us to get rid of?"*
>
> *"What makes you more comfortable when we are together? Is it for me to imagine quietly to myself what you might be thinking? Or for me to imagine aloud to you what you might be thinking and for you to give me signs if I am on the right track or not?"*

"Am I talking too much? Or too little?"

But I am in a bind. Susan cannot answer me. And I cannot interpret what signs there might be like blinks, her appearing more tense and so on. Sometimes I just try to sink into a mellow frame of mind and let the silence be kindly and exude an acceptance that this is part of the therapeutic process. Other times, I feel I am sitting opposite someone trapped by a lack of openings and that the therapy is torture to her. At these times I try to talk, reflect aloud, share my wonderings, share stories, ask about safe topics and immerse myself in the experience of one word answers. At other times, I allow myself to feel lost. And with her.

I am often struck by the effort she is making an effort to get to the appointments. There is the long journey, the fares, not being able to ask for a seat on the train if she feels unwell, the difficulty managing her feelings and the stuff in her head when she is here, and the challenge of communicating with me. I have the feeling she has invested a lot in coming to therapy. I just don't know what.

One of the turning points in our work together comes when I refocus from seeing Susan as stuck, as unable to speak and start to share with her my noticings about how much thinking she appears to be doing. I say to her that she seems to be doing a lot of talking with me and with herself in her head. Susan nods vigorously and then appears to collapse into the chair with what comes over to me as relief. She starts to breathe with her whole body. It is only now that I realise how much of her energy is going into holding something so tightly that her body has been rigid. Months later, Susan tells me "I was ready to explode with the thoughts I was having. In my mind, I was shouting. I needed you to know that I did have things to say. I would sit there imagining myself talking to you. I was telling you things. Lots of things. But you couldn't hear me."

I still catch myself at times positioning myself as a kindly facilitator, focused on helping Susan overcome her 'disabilities' and things quickly start to feel stuck. So I shift to noticing her determination, her courage, her pensiveness, and her sense of humour, her achievements throughout her childhood, her education, her relationships, and her career. When I reposition myself to foreground her abilities, communication becomes easier between us. I see and appreciate her attempts to communicate and we find ways of going forward.

Silence as response

My experience of working with people who use silence in therapy is that they have often experienced trauma which has, one way or another, impacted on voluntary and involuntary choices about speaking. Moshe Lang, in his paper on silence in therapy with holocaust survivors, gives some examples of what silence might mean and reasons people might have for maintaining silence about terrible experiences.

In psychotherapy, talking is cure; silence is usually associated with defensiveness, resistance, negativism and denial. The positive aspects of silence are often overlooked. The sufferer may experience silence as strength and courage. Silence can be a mark of respect. To remember, we stand together in silence; in silence we pray to honor the dead. As one survivor said, "When they walked into the gas chambers they were silent. Those who watched them watched in silence. The whole world remained silent. To talk about it now in order to gain personal relief is to desecrate their memory". Silent suffering and guilt is often a testimonial – a memorial to those who have perished. (Lang, 1995, p.22)

Living with silence is often a strategy for survival. What might this mean for how we can communicate in the therapeutic relationship?

Stepping into and out of binds

During the second year of our therapy together, Nona found ways of letting me know some of what had happened to her as a child. She didn't talk aloud about it. She had been instructed as a child not to tell anyone about the violence she experienced or something very bad would happen to her. She felt sure that her survival owed a good deal to her not speaking out about these events. She had developed skills at hiding her pain and masking her fear so others would not put her at risk by asking about her distress. When a teacher she liked did ask, she was too scared to answer truthfully. Nona was certain the abuser would be believed over her and that her life would be further at risk. The abuse continued for several more years.

Somehow I knew that my invitations to communicate had to be soft and tempered to communicate real choice. I did not want to inadvertently become allied with instructive abusive persons or with kindly noticing others who might unwittingly enhance risk. Any asking I did brought forth more evasion and more masking. But over time, somehow we made it safe enough for her to speak with looks and gestures. Any aloud talk I did in relation to this was unpredictable in consequence. Sometimes my aloud talk made her jump and seemed to create disturbance, not relief. At other times, she appeared very relieved. I tried to follow her communications but I had to do this without apparently acting on all my noticings. Her privacy was an important and necessary protection and to acknowledge everything or just anything she said or felt might have created an unbearable amount of exposure. We muddled along. Or perhaps we were attempting to coordinate like improvisational jazz musicians, following each other, elaborating but not overpowering each other's unique contribution, not staying too long in the domains of either complementarity or symmetry (Bateson, 1972). Even though more everyday kinds of outer talk were not easy for us, we interspersed the painful talk with talk about work and home life and this seemed to create a helpful sense of relief before we decided to pick up on a difficult refrain at another point.

Silence as a relational space

Silence in therapy is not something which one person does or which exists separate to the different participants in a conversation. It takes place in the relational space between therapist and client(s). It may also be taking place in relation to others who might or might not be present but who are significant to the stories informing the silence. Silence has a human and physical geography, and a temporal quality which are perhaps not immediately apparent or audible to a therapist. When in silence, one can forget time and it can 'fly by' if one gets lost in it, with or without a companion. Silence can prolong a sense of time. It can be exciting or excruciating if waiting for someone or something to happen. But in my experience, whatever the feelings that accompany silence between people, something still moves on and time does not stand still.

Sometimes I have a sense of ghostly presences, out of focus movements between people, indecipherable texts, muffled communications and the massive dimensionless silence which can follow an explosion. In this space, I am lost. It is not entirely my territory. I cannot see or hear what I have not been told. I may want to reach out to find something familiar to get my bearings - such as a way of talking. As a systemic therapist, it is not difficult for me to turn to questions, histories, family trees, life maps, hopes for the future. I might search for some 'facts', play with some tentative ideas, try to set a context with people in an attempt to recreate a familiar and reassuring geography of what it means to be a therapist and do therapy.

Rules of the game

At a workshop, a therapist wants to discuss a client who is not talking. It sounds familiar to me. It is a conversation I am hearing more and more - therapeutic concerns are becoming conflated with economic and productivity matters and therapeutic relational know-how is being diminished.

"My manager says I should close the case. She says the client is not yet ready for therapy."

"Do she turn up for appointments?" I ask.

> *"Oh yes, always," the therapist replies.*
>
> *"Does she come on time to the appointments?"*
>
> *"Oh yes. She's on time. But she doesn't really use the time."*
>
> *And we get into a conversation about what using the time therapeutically might look like.*

Several things are going on here. The first is that the subject of silence in mental health discourses leads us back into the modernist story of problems being located in an individual: "If *I* am willing and able to talk and the client doesn't talk, then they clearly have the problem". This thinking reflects the dominant discourse of individualised pathology as opposed to something being a social challenge for all participants in a relationship. I find it useful to nudge myself to get beyond restrictive and negating explanations for silence and use my empathic imagination to assume strength instead of weakness, to look for profundity in intent than confusion in action.

> *"If the woman you are thinking about could show you that she is getting some really important things from the time with you, how would it change how you felt when you were with her?"*
>
> *"If you could develop your own criteria for being helpful with this client based on some of your favourite texts, what do you think you might come up with?"*

Secondly, in the apparent silence and privacy of a therapeutic relationship, it turns out there are others present in the room: a watchful, monitoring voice, audible only to the therapist-employee. "How do you account for this time spent in silence as being part of an active therapeutic piece of work?" asks the watchful panopticist eye of the internalised institution. Government led definitions of which ways of talking count as therapy and the move towards prescribed and proscribed ways of psychotherapeutic working, influence what kind of talk is allowed by and within institutions (Whitfield, 2012). Gwyn Whitfield suggests that in becoming increasingly accountable to institutions over the profession of systemic therapy, the voices of practitioners become owned and shaped by the institution as we are encouraged to speak and perform in institutionally prescribed ways within therapeutic relationships. As practitioners, Whitfield adds, we become subject to the same kinds of threats as many people coming to therapy, so resulting in professional restriction and silence (Whitfield, 2012). So one could ask,

> *"If you weren't feeling the presence of a value-for-money watcher, what else might you be noticing about how she is engaged in the time with you?"*

> *"Suppose at some point in the future, this woman shows you how you were helpful to her and you write up what she says for commissioners. How would you want commissioners to learn from her experience? What kind of advocate would you want to be for people using therapy like she has done?"*

Thirdly, systemic therapists are likely to approach silence in therapy with a critical appreciation of power relations in the therapeutic relationship and therefore with a concern not to just take charge and do something method-led, formulaic. In employing self and relational reflexivity as part of an ethical and practical stance, systemic therapists will ask themselves, "What else could I be doing?" But institutional watchfulness coupled with nervous reflexivity that sitting in silence can provoke can lead to a use of systemic techniques and questions without a critique of power in therapeutic relationships which reminds me of earlier attempts in systemic practice to develop a reproducible method with associated techniques. Seikkula points out that "Therapists no longer attempt to control dialogue by their questions or interventions. Therapists must instead constantly adapt to the utterances of the clients in order for the dialogue to take on life, since the dialogue itself generates new meanings." (Seikkula, 2003, p.89)

"What kind of strengths and vulnerabilities do you need to work with people who invite you into an unfamiliar therapeutic space?"

"If you were to reposition her use of therapy as a way of doing therapy, what learning opportunities might there be for you and the rest of the systemic therapy community?"

Silence as dialogue

It was the activist and pioneer, Bertha Pappenheim, who coined the term 'the talking cure' as a description of psychoanalysis following her therapy with Breuer, a colleague of Sigmund Freud (Freud, 1895). Since this time, most of the psychotherapies have structured their way of working as being dependent on outer talk and it is common practice to regard therapeutic success is in part dependent on talking aloud about difficult matters.

The idea of 'silence' usually refers to outer silence in a shared physical space. Silence does not exist on its own. Bateson's idea about the difference that makes a difference (Bateson, 1972) makes me think that something called 'silence' only comes into being when contrasted to something else, for example, the sound of people talking. And that 'talking' only comes into the realm of language as a result of people wanting to name a difference between one thing and another.

Silence is often far from silent to the people involved in it. Silence stops being silent the moment one acknowledges it as silence and starts to listen to it. I am not sure how it would be possible to experience silence in inner dialogue. It is the conversation in inner dialogue which debates how to go on in outer talk. Silence in outer dialogue might not in itself cause any discomfort. The noisy inner dialogue about how to respond to silence in outer dialogue might create some strain for therapist and client(s). Some voices in inner dialogue and the narratives they are connecting with, might feel a bigger sense of entitlement than other voices to make themselves heard. They might attempt to push conversational participants towards a particular story of what good therapy requires in the way of outer talk. For example, in moments of anxiety during silences, with the voice of a worried referrer in mind or in response to a person's distress, I will act with manualised thinking and do something I have done before which has worked. And sometimes it works again. More often it doesn't. And then I have to manage my intolerance of discomfort or turn down the volume on the voice of the referrer's worried request for me to *do* something and, instead, do that other kind of something in which I surrender to the 'not knowing' and allow the map to unfold between us rather than follow prescribed ways of working.

It is a common assumption, that therapy takes place in 'the therapeutic relationship' of outer conversation. This positions both clients and therapists as conversational respondents belonging to the visible and audible arena of outer talk. But, of course, there are other relational therapeutic spaces. There are the worlds of inner dialogue for all parties which run parallel to the outer dialogue and which shape and are shaped in the movements between *and in* inner and outer dialogue. *Thinking* is popularly considered to be a silent activity – something which happens in the apparently soundproof enclosure *in one's own head*. Thinking is made up of thoughts. And, in this cognitive understanding of the relationship between speaking and thinking, thoughts inform the acts of speech. Some have described thought as monologue (Vygotsky, 1934) but I have come to think of monologue *not* as a thing in itself, as if existing outside of a relational context. I understand monologue less as a fixed thing so much as a relational response, subject to change through conversation. Systemic thinking has moved away from the cognitive notion of 'thought' as an isolated definable, fixed thing in the brain to Bateson's idea of mind as meaning making activities in the fluid social spaces between people and their environment. In post-positivist, relational constructionism (McNamee & Hosking, 2012), we can understand thinking in a relational way as inner conversation between different voices each with their own relationships with various narratives (Simon, 2013).

> "Silence, like talking, is interactive"
>
> (Lang, 1995)

The emphasis on outer expressions, on utterance (Bakhtin, 1986) distracts us from a parallel activity of *gutterance* (Whitfield & Simon 2008) which precedes the expression of any utterance. Gutterance refers to inner movements which precede, accompany and follow any outer talk. It is activated by the narratives living within the body which control whether talk stays 'inner' or makes it into outer talk. Gutteral responses from the bodies of conversational participants or witnesses to conversations make themselves heard before more recognisable inner dialogue kicks in and before any outer utterance. In my relational restorying of 'thought', I hear the inner dialogue discussing the body's message and deciding how to respond inwardly and outwardly. This conversation influences the shape of outer talk. Systemic therapist and supervisor Anne Hedvig Vedeler, develops the work of John Shotter and Mikhail Bakhtin in her detailed accounting of the relationship between embodied knowing, inner dialogue and joint outer movement with clients and supervisees (Vedeler, 2004, 2011).

I could easily slip into describing Susan (above) as *sitting in silence* or *'thinking' things to herself.* I could also say that she was experiencing, as I was at the same time, much *activity in inner dialogue*. From her later descriptions, these were not single isolated thoughts but a busy and noisy exchange of conversational responses to different voices each with its own suggestions and anticipation of possible consequences of these articulations – both inner and anticipated outer articulation.

While it is sometimes difficult to attribute these monological sounding voices and their narratives to a *particular* relationship or event, conversing with the concerns behind the narrative *as if it were a person with an opinion,* allows for conversation to develop and we find a way of going on in conversation. I hear more talk within systemic practice inviting reflexivity about the quality of the silence, about how to co-mission an appropriate response to silence. I have been considering all utterances (Bakhtin 1986) – inner and outer, audible and inaudible, understandable or not - as a form of dialogue but with different intentions based on a person's narratives about probable social consequences.

Reading and Writing as Therapeutic Dialogue

Sara Maitland in her A Book of Silence discusses the problems of the Oxford English Dictionary's definitions of silence and applies it to writing reading material and reading writing. "If you take the first OED definition and understand silence as an absence of *language* then simply there is and can be no silence on a printed page, because it is made up entirely of language. If, on the other hand, you take the second definition, that silence is an absence of sound, then written language is silent, because whatever else it does, a printed page of text does not make any sound." (Maitland, 2008, p.146). The page of writing 'in itself' makes no sound despite being full of language. It needs a reader to render the words into soundfulness and enter the writing into a relational arena in which words can be heard and experienced and meaning can come into being. The writer needs a reader for their writing to be heard and to have a chance of being understood, really heard with 'mind' and 'body'.

> *Somehow, despite minimal outer talk in our time together, Ben lets me know how painful it is to speak about the dislocation he feels in the UK. 'Home' no longer exists and, in any case, is loaded with unrepeatable memories. In the silences with Ben's pain I somehow know that any attempts on my part to attempt to understand or inquire could be too clumsy and dilute or fracture something rich and precious. This gutterance phase is followed by a lot of inner talk for me in which I hear some of the many reasons which are stopping me from speaking. Something important, both strong and vulnerable, has surfaced and it feels to me like we have something left exposed and out in the open. I ask Ben if I can read something. Well, read someone. And I invite in to our conversation the voice of another therapist, Maxwell Mudarikiri. I read aloud Maxwell's feelings on returning 'home' to Zimbabwe.*
>
>> *"In my reflections on my experiences, I realised how much I missed the people, relationships, practices and environment that I had grown up with in Zimbabwe. The*

> *different aspects of life that had gained special significance and meaning seemed less accessible living in London. At the same time the strife and trouble happening there created added pressure in how to be an enfranchised Zimbabwean in white Britain. All these are not always public conversations; they are private conversations (of course with an internal audience) which here I am calling, musings." (Mudarikiri, 2002, p.6)*

We hear some of these musings together. They speak volumes to my client about things I could never know about. Ben is very moved. So am I. After this, aloud talk comes into the conversation. Ben speaks about his sense of not feeling at home anywhere and grounds his experience in a community of dislocated others who know something of how he feels. I do not need to speak. Ben can see I have understood something. I have already used my voice to hear Maxwell in our conversation. Now it is my turn to be silent.

By my inviting the voice of Maxwell Mudarikiri into our conversational space, another conversation is foregrounded over the therapist-client relationship. I could have just given Ben the text to read on his own. But then we would probably not have had that experience of both being moved and seeing the other moved. We didn't talk about it. It just happened. And then other things happened. Our conversation progressed. It was as if Ben had told me those things himself.

With Susan, she writes and then passes me the notepad. Sometimes I read her words 'silently' but often aloud, and then I hand her back the notepad. On occasions, I share my thoughts on her writing with her and she goes on to write more. In the following episode, I write back on the notepad after a period of my reading her writing aloud.

Susan writes: "I guess I am just 'talking' about mum because she is on my mind."

Gail writes: "Why the quotes?" I draw an arrow pointing to 'talking'.

Susan writes: "Am I talking or writing – perhaps communicating, expressing myself and asking questions."

I look up and say: "I feel I hear your voice when I read aloud what you have written."

Susan nods vigorously and writes: "Sounds like me".

I have found it useful to borrow from Burnham's practice of 'lending someone his imagination' in thinking about lending someone your voice or, indeed, borrowing their voice with which to speak (Burnham, 2003).

Susan has taught me much about the use of writing as a first or preferred language in therapy but there are sometimes binds we create for and with each other.

After weeks of trying out different ways of being in mostly silent conversation with each other, I noticed her looking at my clipboard. She was looking at it very intently as if she was trying to tell me something. Eventually, I thought to ask her if she would like to write what she was thinking or feeling. Susan suddenly twitched violently. It looked like she was about to leap out the chair and grab the clipboard. But she stopped herself. I pushed the clipboard across the floor to her. "Use it if you want. Ignore it if you prefer." Again Susan started as if to pick it up, hesitated and then bent down and picked it up. For a moment she looked relieved but then the frozenness returned. She looked anxiously around. She did not have a pen but she could not ask for one. This was an example of the speechless bind in which she was living: a pen would have enabled her to ask for a pen. I got her one. And then Susan transformed in front of my eyes. I saw the tension fall away. She looked relieved, animated and ready to get going. Her demeanour showed confidence and

> *thoughtfulness. And so it came to pass that Susan brought writing to each session and my clipboard started to travel beyond my lap and between us. She wrote, handed it to me. I read and handed it back. She wrote some more. I don't think either of us could have imagined back then that one day Susan would arrive, take something from her bag and say "I've brought you a present." Susan can be quite ironic. It wasn't for me. It was a bright pink clipboard for other people coming to therapy to use. My facilitation was needed even less. Now Susan used her own clipboard.*

People who need or want to use an alternative language through which to communicate, need to speak in the dominant language to get to speak in their preferred language. For example, when I go to Norway, I avoid some confusion and feel it is respectful to start with the question "Snakker du engelsk?" (Do you speak English?) but the answer cannot be too complicated and I cannot carry on the conversation in Norwegian because I cannot speak that language. My foray into the host or dominant language is simply a way of opening up the possibility of continuing together in a common language. As it happens, most Norwegian people who I get to meet do speak English. And fortunately most therapists can both read and write. However, many therapists still question whether they should be accepting and reading written communications, poems, journal entries and so on from and by people with whom they are working. And I remember this from my own therapy when I handed things I had so carefully written to my therapist only to be asked to 'tell her about it' instead. This is a practice I still hear time and time again from therapists. They ask people to either read it aloud to them or tell them about it. I spoke with some of my doctoral colleagues about the problem of trying to describe in spontaneous spoken language things which were intricately crafted in and for written language over a much longer period of time than can hope for in swift conversation. A doctoral colleague said, "It took me so long to choose my words, to put them in this order or that – until it felt right, like that was what I intended it to say. But I didn't always know what I wanted to say until I started writing. And then things happened. And I couldn't hope to speak such complexity with any fluency. Or even accuracy. It is written for readers. Some things are not for casual conversation. When I try to say them, I become speechless."

> *"Writing in some respects requires more trust and openness than words – in writing the words can not be erased – they are in front of you and I feel sometimes have more meaning than the spoken word. Sometimes perhaps more feeling too – poetry – sometimes just reading poetry evokes as much or more meaning."*
>
> (Susan, in Simon, 2012)

"I wish I never had to speak again," said one rather tired colleague soon after getting her doctorate. "They should just call me Dr Silence. Dr Silence. That would be nice. Then I can just listen and I won't have to talk. People can just read my papers."

Summary

By inventing our own ways of communicating with those people with whom we are working, we can create opportunities for overcoming isolating and limiting effects of compulsory speech practices expected in mainstream psychotherapy. The professional expectation that people will feel able to tell a therapist what has been going on, how they have come to this point in their lives might inadvertently bring forth shame and a sense of inadequacy. It can echo a person's earlier experience of coercive and restrictive demands which could result in paralysis. By creating alternative approaches for articulating, sharing and responding to accounts of experiences, we open up the possibility for the production of witness-able, respond-able-to accounts (White & Denborough, 2005; Andersen, 1997; Anderson, 1997). I am reminded of John Shotter's idea that "if our ways of talking are constrained in any way - if, for instance, only certain ways of talking are considered legitimate and not others - then our understanding, and apparently our experience of ourselves, will be constrained also." (Shotter, 1989, p.141).

When Susan says, *"I was ready to explode with the thoughts I was having. In my mind, I was shouting. I needed you to know that I did have things to say. I would sit there imagining myself talking to you. I was telling you things. Lots of things. But you couldn't hear me"*, John Shotter can offer some support for Susan's experience. "I act not simply 'out of' my own plans and desires, unrestricted by the social circumstances of my performances, but in some sense also 'in to' the opportunities offered to me to act, or else my attempts to communicate will fail or be sanctioned in some way." (Shotter, 1989, p.144)

Language, in whatever form, has its limits. Attempts to use language which result in a feeling of inadequacy are opportunities for alternative ways of being in relation (Vedeler, 2004) and not for attributing stories of deficit and inadequacy to participants in the conversational process. However, feelings of inadequacy - for clients and therapists - might be an important part of a therapeutic process and wordlessness, feeling there is nothing one can do but be in a conversation somehow might reflect something more important than attempting a narration of events and feelings.

Ken Gergen has said "If you change the activities you change the language." (Gergen, 2007) There is a reflexive relationship between the two. One changes the other. Silence is never 'just silence'. Nor is it without sound or without language or even without speakers. Silence can be a busy, interactive, news-ful space. It is also a co-created space with potentially a range of relational possibilities. Systemic therapists, psychotherapists and counsellors working within other approaches face ethical and practical challenges in a changing resource-led landscape of mental health provision whose industry standards prescribe fixed ways of working with individual persons as the prescribed site for treatment. It seems that different media and different activities allow us to find new ways of going on in conversation, in relationship with each other. Negotiating changes in activities introduces a shift in the balance of power and in the means of negotiating what will count as useful and productive therapeutic practice. When I made the shift from thinking of Susan as someone who struggled with communication to seeing her as a writer, as someone who can communicate well, there is a transformation in our relationship. The movement in our activities creates the conditions for us to foreground *mutual abilities* over *individualised struggles.*

References

Andersen, T. (1997). Researching client-therapist relationships: a collaborative study for informing therapy. *Journal of Systemic Therapies,* 16, 2, 125-133.

Anderson, H. (1997). *Conversation, Language and Possibilities: A Postmodern Approach to Therapy.* New York, NY: Basic Books.

Bakhtin, M. (1986 [2007 reprint]). *Speech Genres and Other Late Essays.* Trans. V.W. McGee, Eds. Caryl Emerson & Michael Holquist. Austin, TX: University of Texas Press.

Bateson, G. (1972). *Steps to an Ecology of Mind.* London: Paladin.

Burnham, J. (2003). Systemic Questions. Workshop. Harrogate, UK.

Freud, S. and Breuer, J. (1895). [1980 reprint] *Studies in Hysteria.* Translated and edited by J. and A. Strachey. Harmondsworth: Penguin.

Gergen, K. J. & Gergen, M. (2007). *Positive Aging Workshop.* Kensington Consultation Centre, London.

Kebbe, L. (2012). Keep the Conversation Going: A study of conversational spaces in family business succession. Unpublished doctoral thesis. KCC & University of Bedfordshire.

Lang, M. (1995). Silence: Therapy with Holocaust Survivors and their Families. Draft from *Resilience: Stories of a Family Therapist.* Lang, M. & Lang, T. (Eds.). Melbourne: Reed Books.

Levi, P. (1988). *The Drowned and the Saved.* London: Penguin.

Maitland, S. (2008). *A Book of Silence.* London: Granta.

McNamee, S. & Hosking, D. M. (2012). Research and Social Change: A Relational Constructionist Approach. London: Routledge.

Mudarikiri, M. M. (2002). Spiritual Disgruntlement. *Human Systems: The Journal of Systemic Consultation and Management,* 13, 1, 5-14.

Seikkula, J. (2003). Dialogue is the Change: Understanding Psychotherapy as a Semiotic Process of Bakhtin, Voloshinov and Vygotsky. *Human Systems: The Journal of Systemic Consultation and Management,* 14, 2, 83-94.

Selvini Palazzoli, M., Boscolo, L., Cecchin, G. & Prata, G. (1980). Hypothesising - circularity - neutrality: Three guidelines for the conductor of the session. *Family Process*, 19, 1, 3-12.

Shotter, J. (1989). *Social accountability* and the social construction of '*you*'. In K. Gergen & J. *Shotter* (Eds.). *Texts of Identity*. London: Sage Publications.

Shotter, J. & Katz, A. (1998). 'Living moments' in dialogical exchanges. *Human Systems: Journal of Systemic Consultation and Management*, 9, 2, 81-93.

Shotter, J. (2009). *Movements of Feeling and Moments of Judgement: Towards an Ontological Social Constructionism.* Constructing Worlds Conference, Taos Institute and MacMann Berg, 20th- 23rd August 2009, Denmark.

Simon, G. (2011). *Writing (as) Systemic Practice.* Doctoral Dissertation, Institute of Applied Social Research, University of Bedfordshire, http://hdl.handle.net/10547/223012 [Date of access: 3rd March 2012].

Simon, G. (2012). Writing as Talk. *International Journal of Collaborative Practices*. Issue 3, 2012.

Simon, G. (2013). Relational Ethnography: Writing and Reading in and about Research Relationships. F*orum Qualitative Sozialforschung / Forum: Qualitative Social Research.*

Tomm, K. (1987). Interventive Interviewing: Part I. Strategizing as fourth guideline for the therapist. *Family Process*, 26, 1, 3-13.

Vedeler, A. H. (2004). *Do you hear me? About therapeutic listening creating space for voices to emerge and to be heard.* MSc Dissertation in Systemic Therapy. KCC International & University of Luton.

Vedeler, A. H. (2011). *Dialogical Practices: Diving in the Poetic Mo(ve)ment. Exploring 'supervision' and 'therapy'*. Doctoral Dissertation, Department of Applied Social Studies, University of Bedfordshire.

Vygotsky, L. S. (1934 [Reprint 1987]). *Thinking and speech. The collected works of L. S. Vygotsky (1).* New York, NY: Plenum.

White, C. & Denborough, D. (2005). *A Community of Ideas: Behind the Scenes.* Adelaide: Dulwich Centre Publications.

Whitfield, G. & Simon, G. (2008) Personal communication. 10th June 2008.

Whitfield, G. (2012). Personal communication. 1st March 2012.

SIX

Thinking Systems. 'Mind' as relational activity

Introduction

> All new knowledge comes from people on the margins and they tend not to be from within institutional/ised knowledge and resources.
>
> (Whitfield 2014, p.4)

In this chapter, I propose how as professionals, we need to shift our skills from diagnostic activities to relational curiosity and so develop collaborative ways of conversing with people who have Asperger Syndrome and others in their networks. Through immersing ourselves in dialogue with people and their social and professional networks, we can bring forth evidence of people with Asperger Syndrome having unique and useful expertise which can play a part in resolving concerns and improving communication between those in their networks. Not only is it socially productive but it is also ethical for professionals to shift their focus from an exploration of 'mind' as commonly believed to exist solely within an individual person and to the relational contexts so influential on what we are constructing with each other through talk and how that shapes what is able to be recognised and developed.

By foregrounding dialogue over diagnosis, we see how experimenting with user friendly talk can provide opportunities for symptoms and features of High Functioning Autism / Asperger Syndrome (Wing 1981; Gillberg 1991) to be understood as meaningful communications in which the 'disabled' person is experienced as able and enabling. The individualised account of the person having been diagnosed as having Asperger's Syndrome is exchanged for descriptions of an interactive social system. I will show how 'mind' is relocated from the cognitive brain to the social opportunistic space created between people.

Relational Opportunities

> *So, you take this case and I will make notes and we can discuss it afterwards. Okay?" The supervisor takes herself behind the one-way screen and the nervous trainee clinical psychologist goes to fetch the family to the consulting room. Once back in the room, the psychologist quickly gives up on conversation with the child suspected of having Asperger Syndrome who gives responses not apparently connected to her questions. Instead, she asks the parents questions about the child's physical, emotional and social history going back to birth. She fends off questions from the child which she feels are inappropriate and distracting and completes her information gathering exercise. After a break to discuss the case with her supervisor, she negotiates spending some time alone with the child and proceeds to conduct some tests one of which is the Sally-Anne test. At the end of the session, the trainee says to the parents that she will let them know the outcome of the assessment and says a nice goodbye to the child. The trainee and her supervisor agree that the child could be diagnosed as having Asperger Syndrome and they arrange for a diagnostic letter to go out to the parents and for the parents to be invited to a group for parents with children who have Asperger Syndrome.*
>
> (Extract from composite diagnostic interview)

So what did we hear from the parents in this diagnostic interview? We heard that meal-times and bedtimes are hell; that they are worried about neglecting other children in the family; that they are arguing with each other about how best to respond to the child in question; that they are concerned with how the school are responding to their child and what the neighbours must think. But what we end up with is a report focused on the child with parental information being lined up to re-inforce a story of an individual with cognitive and communication difficulties. The family is seen as a victim of unfortunate circumstances and offered information and advice to cope with their child. The professional system, with *its* limited cognitive framework, fails to see that the family is a *system* struggling with communication challenges and that it is resourceful, creative and open to collaborative approaches. There is no expectation that the family can teach the professionals anything. They provide supporting information for diagnostic purposes. The family is shuffled into a passive service 'user', advice-recipient position. There is no consideration that the family may be able and interested in sharing or creating knowledge with the professional system nor that they could be part of the knowledge innovation for resourcing the wider community.

The problems parents and children want help with occur almost exclusively in the context of relationships. Communication difficulties are the most common presenting concern in therapy. Parents want to talk about how to manage meal-times, changes of routine, about arguments between family members, co-parenting communications, dealing with the frequent fall-out from school and other "Now What?" episodes.

Areas of special interest as relational systems

Systemic lines of enquiry have been successful when treating the child's area of special interest as a resource (Simon 2004). For a start, it is the one thing that is likely to engage the young person with a diagnosis of Asperger Syndrome. "Their special interest is often their sole topic of conversation. Asperger individuals seem to love talking about their interest, regardless of whether one has heard it all before." (Frith 1991, p.11). Whether one has heard it all before is not simply to do with repetition by the person with the interest. It is matter of how others listen, understand and engage with the conversation. Obsessive behaviour of the symptom spotter – and here I am talking about the diagnostic clinician – results in lost opportunities to hear about relational functioning within an area of special interest. This can also transfer itself to parents emulating what the professionals consider to be good practice.

A person with an area of special interest is likely to have in-depth knowledge about complex relational activities which make up communicating systems. Talking about them creates and brings forth new ways of relational being and relational knowing.

Exploration of the area of special interest of the child diagnosed as having Asperger's Syndrome, might bring forth a description of a meaningful, communication system. By understanding the area of special interest as such a system, the therapist and family can be invited to communicate at times with each other through the metaphor of the area of special interest. This system might be useful in generating a language to describe the workings of that family which all family members can use. This may facilitate and help understand processes of communication, change and what makes a difference. Compare these two conversations.

Example 1

Parent: *The teachers tell him off because he charges across the playground and doesn't stop in time. Then he crashes into one of the younger children and hurts them. And he gets in trouble.*

Professional: *What game were you playing when you were running so fast?*

Will: *The Sir Nigel Gresley is an A4 Pacific locomotive 4468.*

Parent (to professional): *He's train mad.*

Parent (to child): *You can't be a train in the playground. You will crash into people like you did into that young child. And hurt them.*

Professional: *Did you see the other child cry?*

Will: *It broke the record in 1938. It went at 126 miles an hour.*

Professional: *When you crashed into the little girl, what did she do?*

Parent: *She cried, didn't she? Because you bumped into her.*

Will (in flat monotone voice): *She fell over.*

So what is happening here? The professional is asking about perception, noticing and trying to activate the child's cognition as though it can be awakened through noticing questions. The professional is in a bind. One the one hand, they are seeing evidence of fixed characteristics typical of Asperger Syndrome: lack of cooperation in difficult conversations, possible cognitive difficulties, apparent inability to imagine and empathise with another person and so on. On the other hand, the professional, like the parent, is trying to effect change with those same, apparently unmovable features. And nothing new emerges so reinforcing the story of fixed characteristics. What is fixed or repetitive is the pattern of communication between those in the room. Behind this pattern is the contradictory belief that the professional will be able to change the fixed problematic behaviours of the person with Asperger Syndrome.

Let's look at another excerpt in which the professional shifts their approach and becomes curious about the relational co-ordinations between parts of the system.

Example 2

Professional:	*So how does the Sir Nigel Gresley get to go that fast?*
Will:	*Its engine.*
Professional:	*Does is just go like that immediately or does it build up speed?*
Will:	*Builds up speed.*
Professional:	*How does it build up speed? Can you tell me how it all works? I am interested to know. I like steam trains but I don't know that much about them.*
Will:	*Well, it doesn't just start going at 128 mph.*
Professional:	*Okay.*
Will:	*It depends on how much coal goes into the furnace.*
Professional:	*What does the coal do in the furnace?*
Will:	*It heats the water to make steam which makes the engine*

	go faster.
Professional:	*How does the fireman know when to put coal into the furnace?*
Will:	*The driver tells him.*
Professional:	*And what happens when the driver wants the train to slow down?*
Will:	*The train has to reduce its steam and apply the brakes.*
Professional:	*How does the driver let the fireman know to put on less coal to make less steam?*
Will:	*He tells him.*
Professional:	*How come the fireman does as he is told?*
Will:	*He just does. Or the train would crash.*
Professional:	*Okay. So they don't want the train to crash. And who tells the driver how fast to go?*
Will:	*The signals.*
Professional:	*So who works the signals?*
Will:	*Outside York, there are seventeen signal boxes. We've got one near us.*
Professional:	*And how do the signalmen know when to switch the levers?*
Will:	*It depends. It could be to make sure the train goes in the correct direction at a junction or it may be to avoid a collision especially on single tracks where they need to use sidings for trains to pass each other safely.*
Professional:	*Yes, I see. Why does the train driver agree to follow the rules of the signals?*
Will:	*Well, they would derail if they didn't slow down and crash into another train.*
Professional:	*And if they derailed?*
Will:	*It takes four cranes to get one engine back onto the track. We saw it up in Shap.*
Professional:	*Do people sometimes get hurt?*

Will:	*Yes, if they are carrying passengers.*
Professional:	*And why do drivers sometimes hoot before a crossing?*
Will:	*To warn pedestrians and cars.*
Professional:	*Of what?*
Will:	*Of a train coming…*
Professional:	*So they don't go on the tracks?*
Professional:	*And what would happen if they didn't hoot?*
Will:	*There would be risk to life and limb.*
Professional:	*You know a lot about how things work, how train drivers and fireman and signalmen all work together to get places and keep people safe, don't you?*
Parent:	*I guess when you are charging about the playground, you have to be the driver, the fireman and the signalman all in one! It's great hearing you talk about trains in this way. You know so much.*

Several things appear to be going on here:

i) The child's answers start cautiously and appear to confirm non-sequitur responses typical of Asperger Syndrome but this behaviour changes when the professional changes their behaviour. The child starts to see there are other forms of talk on offer than being required to change or tested.

ii) In this excerpt, the professional re-positions herself as a learner. She listens and asks *as if for the first time*, without trying to create any evidence. The repositioning by the professional brings forth a story of the person with Asperger Syndrome as having knowledge and expertise.

iii) This knowledge and expertise is about the moving parts of a communicating, interactive system with a feedback loop. The narrative describes a relationally responsive system (train, driver, fireman, signalman, signals, pedestrians, passengers) in which all the component parts/people are cooperative and sensitive to communications. Conversational participants have to recalibrate their expectations and learn to leave their expectation of hearing repetitive, decontextualised facts so they can be receptive to noticing a narrative of a system at work in the area of special interest.

iv) The knowledge and expertise of the child is clearly not simply a list of decontextualized facts. The child demonstrates both contextualised knowledge and hypothesising abilities. A coherent narrative is made visible by having an interested enquirer.

v) The parent has an unusual experience of not feeling bored by the repetitive nature of the area of special interest and leaves with increased admiration for their child's abilities.

vi) The professional and parent are careful not to rush into advice giving and making connections to the playground activity which might well have alienated the child from collaborating in the conversation further. But they are now equipped with a meaningful metaphor which is of immediate interest to the young person and which they will be able to draw on further in future conversations.

Areas of special interest often contain a communicating system between the characters or component parts. These areas of special interest often seemed to be connected to a subject in which there is a system at work, such as trains, computers, and electricity. Within these cybernetic systems are feedback loops, mechanisms for managing cyclical or unusual events, rule-bound *and* rule-creating ways of being.

By foregrounding relational curiosity, the area of special interest ceases to be constructed as symptomatic of an embodied condition and instead becomes a social opportunity dependent on others becoming engaged in understanding and meaning making. The area of special interest might be used both by the person diagnosed as having Asperger's Syndrome and by others close to him as a means through which to connect, to communicate.

> I act not simply 'out of' my own plans and desires, unrestricted by the social circumstances of my performances, but in some sense also 'in to' the opportunities offered to me to act, or else my attempts to communicate will fail or be sanctioned in some way.
>
> Shotter 1989, p.144

When exploring a person's area of special interest in detail, it is common for friends and families to become totally engrossed – as if for the first time of hearing - and often elaborate with questions of their own. "Viewed in this way, as calling out from us possibly quite new, **first-time responsive movements, rather than as being about something in the world"** (Shotter 2015) we immerse ourselves within the area of special interest and take an alongside position with the other speakers. We approach the subject with openness and wonder. We surrender our preconceived knowing and with it, the inevitable about-ness position which sites us outside of the others' world so scuppering the possibilities of new ways of knowing how to go in the conversations.

Within a systemic social constructionist framework, the child's special area of interest could be thought of as a narrative or collection of connecting narratives, as a way of languaging and therefore, as a potential resource to the therapeutic process and to the family or other social relationships. An important contextualising factor in systemic therapy would involve understanding how family members interact with the child around their area of special interest, exploring the stories they bring to this feature and looking at the contexts in which these stories have arisen.

For example, it can be useful to ask about:

- roles of individuals or individual parts
- means of communication
- patterns of communication
- power relations between parts/people
- rule bound or rule creating systems

- patterns of change
- alliances
- decision making
- movements between parts/people

In creating a shared means of talking about relationships which had not previously existed for families and professionals, there emerges a useful resource which enables family and friends to access some of narratives about the workings of the world of the person diagnosed with Asperger Syndrome. Of course, this kind of conversation also feels more relevant to the person with the area of special interest and it can be a pleasure for them to experience genuine attention and interest of others in areas of their world which are important to them. They also have the experience of not being positioned in a mono-dimensional way as the problematic person or the identified patient but as an authority in an area which others in the room know only a little about and as someone with something useful to contribute.

Conceptualising 'Mind' as Relational Activity

When people first hear the expression 'Theory of Mind', they often believe that this refers to a broad philosophical debate on what counts as 'mind'; an understandable response. However, in the field of child psychology and child psychiatry, there is assumed to be only one 'Theory of Mind' and it dominates the field with a limited set of assumptions about what 'mind' is. This cluster of ideas plays a central part in explaining and diagnosing autistic spectrum conditions (Baron-Cohen *et al* 1985). 'Theory of mind' centres individual cognition at the heart of its hypothesis. This reflects a wider trend of de-contextualising human behaviour within contemporary mental health which dominates the field theoretically and therefore has implications for what forms of treatment are available. The problem is that the dominant approach focuses only on the individual. It relies on an idea that it is the individual who has the problem *in them*. This approach reflects an attachment to a deficit model of human beings and discourages a focus on people's relational world. This model does not foreground the exploration of relational possibilities and drawing out evidence of resourcefulness in people. Hickcok (2014) situates what are perceived as cognitive deficits in people with autism not so much as to do with individual cognition but reflecting limited opportunities for mirror neuron systems. McGuire and Michalko situate autism within a relational system. "Rather than conceiving autism as an individualising medical problem, we understand autism as a complex interactional process. We treat autism as belonging squarely in the realm of the social and not in the realm of the individual." (McGuire and Michalko 20011 p.164).

In the working fields of autism, professional theory has focused on the individual participants in the conversation. A family of three may be conceptualised as one plus one plus one, for example. Separate entities. The individual parts are separated from the whole. The prominence of an embodied self in the literature arises out of the early biological sciences which investigated the inner workings the human body to correct any perceived problems whether manifesting as physical or social. The physical body is still used as the metaphorical container and site for investigation and treatment of physical and 'mental' problems as is the case for professional activities with people who are diagnosed as being on the autistic spectrum. To speak about 'mental health' or 'learning disability' is a way of individualising experience and communications. It takes the person out of their social world and locates 'issues' within a notion of physical self made up of organic matter. The brain is frequently understood as the organic container and structural influence of something called the 'mind'. This model proposes that mind is damaged by atypical neurological differences which impact on the individual's social functioning.

Timimi, Gardner and McCabe are concerned about the production of knowledge associated with autism and how it is presented. "Perhaps more than any other child and adolescent psychiatry category, autism is viewed as the product of sound science with knowledge arising from ..... the 'positivistic' or technical approach" (Timimi *et al* 2011, p. 7). Brownlow and O'Dell (2009) critically review the literature on Theory of Mind and conclude that the research has been carried out by outsiders and makes fundamental assumptions about neurotypicailty which undermines new knowledge emerging about ability and the whole person. Autism research is almost exclusively dedicated to proving this connection and to finding a cure to prevent atypical neurology. It is a strategy which overlooks the cultural and relational contexts and which sidesteps any invitations to reflexivity which could be of use in considering what kinds of talk, for example, count and are valued and which are not. Leppington says that the constructivist concept of 'thought' is not proof of the individual mind but of the social world. The question is not so much "how does the individual rational consciousness account for the social world?" but "how, in a social world, to account for culturally specific notions of the individual?" (Leppington 1991, p.86). Nevertheless, the term 'Asperger's Syndrome' exists, to date, as a *description* of a 'state of mind' and of behaviours associated with that state of mind. Gergen and Gergen (2002, p.80) reflect that "we differ from the constructivists in that what is imported into the situation is not a 'state of mind' but an array of linguistic capacities. These capacities emerge primarily as we acquire the language of the culture".

A significant element in the diagnosis of Asperger's Syndrome and autism involves the Theory of Mind test (Baron-Cohen *et al* 1985) which assesses the ability to conceptualise beliefs and attribute them to another. The Sally - Anne test (Baron-Cohen *et al* 1985) can show that the child who has Asperger's Syndrome is not capable of a kind of third party thought (to empathise with another, imagine what another thinks etc.) and the learning that can arise from that. In the test, there are two dolls, Sally and Anne. Sally has a marble which she puts in her basket and then leaves the room. Anne has seen this and while Sally is out the room, Anne takes the marble and hides it in a box. When Sally comes back in the room, the tester asks the child "Where will Sally look for her marble?" The correct answer is Sally's basket. Children with Asperger's Syndrome are less likely to come to this conclusion, pointing instead to the box.

Gregory Bateson's ideas about the importance of situating actions within context are essential for understanding people. He says, "....'context' is linked to another undefined notion called 'meaning.' Without context, words and actions have no meaning at all. This is true not only of human communication in words but also of all communication whatsoever, of all mental process, of all mind, including that which tells the sea anemone how to grow and the amobea what he should do next." (Bateson 1973, p.15?). It would be interesting to experiment with this test across cultures, ages and with variations and see what "evidence" they produced. One of the problems here is that, while the test may be interesting, the conclusions drawn from it are attributed solely to the cognitive abilities of the individual child. Another problem is the acceptance of 'thought' as existing in isolation of human relationships. McGuire and Michalko critique the Sally-Anne exercise as de-contextualised and creating only a partial picture which has much undermining evidence about its reliability from other studies (McGuire and Michalko 20011. Unless we study play in other contexts, the apparent lack of creative play or ability to empathise might not be occurring across the board or may be a feature, for example, characteristic of family relationships. In the examples above and below, we see how people reorganising their expectations of communication open up new opportunities for self and other. "We do not treat 'Theory of Mind' as a 'thing-in-the-brain'. Instead, we understand intentionality, shared and otherwise, as a method whereby people, all people, attribute motives to one another as a way to make sense of human interaction." (McGuire and Michalko 2011, p.173).

Systemic theory and practice is interested is what counts as 'knowledge'. In the context of the social world, information is not seen as a free-floating and gatherable set of objective facts but as contextually produced and subjective narratives. Reflexive epistemological knowing is understood as a process rather than end product. Professionals often ask 'What can be observed and therefore known about X?" This is an ontological question to which modernist science expects answers that we will generate generalised conditions, syndromes and so on. The question "How do I observe and know about X?" is an epistemological question about methods of knowing. But to take a step further into "What are the contexts which are likely to be influencing what I think I know about X and how I am looking?" invites another level of critical reflexivity in which the enquirer takes responsibility for the inevitability of their bias. Further questions might also be useful, "Whose voices am I listening to in this enquiry?" and "How am I allowing my relationship with my hypothesis to open or restrict what we can together achieve?" These last two questions are important in that they invite ethical reflexivity about not only ontological knowing but about the methodological influences on one's interpretation and responses to data.

The child diagnosed as having Asperger Syndrome may set great value on knowing about their area of special interest, as do professionals on theirs. The question "Does the child diagnosed as having Asperger's Syndrome have the ability to move between what they know and how they know what they know?" is based on a particular notion of ability-deficit located in individual mind. Asking instead, "What do we need to do to create the dialogical conditions which bring forth co-creative conversation?" orientates the professional away from looking for evidence to experimenting with relational solutions.

Maturana suggests that every family member is a 'scientist' – in as much as people generate explanations for behaviour (Maturana 19891. He speaks of the *passion* in human beings to attempt to understand, relate parts of a system but points out that we can only generate explanations (descriptions) of workings *within the limits of our area of structural determinism* (Maturana 19891. One could then say that all the participants in collaborative action research (professionals, person diagnosed as having Asperger's Syndrome and other family members) are living systems and are part of other living systems which are determined by culturally generated linguistic structures such as going to the doctor if you have a worry and entering into a certain kind of individualised talk about the history and symptomology or that worry. Systemic social constructionists, as opposed to constructivists, might say that we act in to and out of the limits of the language and stories available to us and *opportunities to tell them.* (Shotter 1989).

According to Maturana, the only possible outcome of human interaction is that professionals and families are more likely to generate explanations and meanings coherent with the limits of their life experience as explained to themselves (Maturana 1991). From a systemic social constructionist understanding of human systems as linguistic systems, we not constrained by *experience* so much as by *conversational opportunities*.

Getting over determinism and diagnosis

This neurological story of connection creates a theory of inevitable causality. It determines that the individual is the site for treatment and draws on medical ideas to understand and to treat the problem which is firmly located in the individual. It does not allow for social, cultural and political influences. Nor does it allow for opportunities to a) make sense of behaviours and communications within relational contexts and b) to work with those relational contexts to create more opportunities for better communications between participants.

Following diagnosis, professional interventions encourage 'neurologically atypical' people to correct or adapt their communication styles to fit in with the dominant culture. Such interventions are based on behavioural correction with tailored cognitive learning.

Ideas about 'treatment' have been developed within a modernist scientific discourse in which it was assumed that it was possible for one person to acquire more knowledge on a subject than the people coming for 'treatment'. In a scientific model, there is an assumption that it is possible and desirable to achieve objective information by remaining impartial to the subject. This model does not allow for the ideological bias of the professional, nor of the familial, socio-cultural and economic influences on the information which is generated by examinations of the person to be assessed.

The information to diagnose a condition and inform a 'treatment' method is generated by a series of questions designed by professionals in relation to a hypothesis. This hypothesis is inevitably a product of the information available at the time and arises out of a hidden and therefore unquestionable ideology based on all manner of social, cultural, political, economic influences on methodological assumptions. Diagnostic questions trace the history and symptomatology of a condition and focus on the life of the condition and little on the circumstances in which people are or have been living.

Diagnostic formats restrict the imagination of professionals and families to be curious about what makes a difference to a person's lived experience and their relationships. Instead, there is the risk of enacting a rule-bound format of assessment. This is likely to produce a description of an individual which is limited and linear in development. Such an assessment pays no attention to family culture or school resources so there is no room for a circular analysis of how interpersonal behaviours are maintained or changed. It follows that what you ask influences what you find and, therefore, what you do - so medical model stories are likely to influence the methods of 'treatment' and result in a plan for managing the individual under scrutiny. Because diagnosis focuses on an individual's cognition, it entirely neglects the collaborative aspects of communication in which others are also responsible for how dialogue can take place and for what kind of talk counts. Instead of the meeting with professionals becoming an opportunity to experiment with what kind of talking and listening makes a difference, the process of diagnosis sets the professional and service users apart in different camps and reifies their positions.

Professionals engaged in diagnostic symptom spotting often appear to mirror monological ways of talking reminiscent of people talking about an area of special interest. This symmetrical form of communication results in the creation of misinformation because it is a one-way activity by the collector of information and precludes the possibility of dialogue. Dialogue is problematic in monological discourses such as modernist sciences as it requires an etiquette of being in relation with people and finding ways of going on in conversation without having a map or a set of instructions.

Instead, participants are required to work at coordinating with each other to get from a-b, to work out how to communicate in ways which are meaningful, appreciative and carry a sense of possibility in going forwards. Professionals need permission to not know in order to find new ways of communicating with people in ways that feel productive. Current prescribed diagnostic procedures are i) restricting professionals ways of speaking and being with families; ii) not enabling professionals to explore new ways of being and therefore learning with families what kinds of talk makes a positive difference; iii) very important opportunities are being missed by the emphasis on diagnosis over exploratory interventions.

It has been my experience that normally sparky and empathic professionals can fall into demonstrating a lack of imagination when acting in relation to their area of special interest - diagnostic criteria; and that they can fail to empathise sufficiently with the person in front of them to find out how they do think, how they are communicating and what their abilities are. The Clinic becomes the corridor for monological behaviours, single stories which sadly emphasise deficit and inability. Diagnostic procedures become restrictive to happening upon new ways of knowing and being.

Linguistic systems and relational know-how

A shift from a reverent demonstration of knowledge about the area of special interest to a shared world of imaginary play can result in a more ironic relationship with the area of special interest and more know-how in relationships.

The following example demonstrates my re-creating of a difficulty when I ask six year old James to pretend something to be something. I am struggling with competing narratives about how to be with James. One the one hand, I am looking for confirmation of evidence that James has Asperger Syndrome. On the other hand, I am trying to find ways of coordinating with James in the moment of play. In effect, I am in two systems simultaneously: the professional system of diagnostic linguistics and the *making it up as we go* system of being in spontaneous knowledge-creating relationships. The system in focus eventually becomes the relationships in the room between people and play objects.

The process of using questions with James is immediately problematic. He appears not to like being asked questions. In addition to conversation with James proving difficult, there does not seem to be an obvious interactive system in his area of special interest, dinosaurs.

Therapist -	*Can you pretend to be a dinosaur?*
James -	*I'm not a dinosaur.*
Therapist -	*Do like you're pretending*
James -	*I'm not a dinosaur*
James -	*I'm Godzilla*
Therapist -	*Okay, why don't you pretend to be Godzilla?*
James -	*I-don't-know (sing song, looking elsewhere)*

I don't think James had a problem with understanding the concept of "pretend play" as would be suggested by the criteria for diagnosing Asperger's Syndrome. I was asking him to act in isolation. I think he may well have pretended to be a dinosaur if I had asked the grandparents to join in, me too perhaps and we had all pranced around making noises and talking to each other as dinosaurs. In effect, I was asking James to give a solo performance – and in the context of the House of Tests (the clinic) where he had been initiated into diagnostic tests in the recent past. Shotter is intrigued by "our immediate *sensing* of the qualitative 'shape' of *how* the others around us are *responding* to us, *spontaneously*, and the influence of that on how safe and secure we feel in being who we are to them, and how the 'shape' of that *feeling* arouses anticipations within us as to what next might come from them – anticipations as to how they will treat us as being *this* or *that* kind of person in the world" (Shotter 2013, p.2)

In this following example from a subsequent play session, I had learned that I needed to enter into the play and be in the relational interactions, take leaps myself, and create both in and out positions.

Therapist –	*I wonder what a Gigantosaurus moves like? Okay.* *Here comes the Gigantosaurus.* *It's taking gigantic leaps.* (Makes leaping noises)

Therapist (as Gigantosaurus) - *Hello James! How are you today?*

Therapist –	*Look the Gigantosaurus spoke.*

James fetches the T-Rex and makes it roar at the Gigantosaurus.

Gigantosaurus –	*Oh, I'm frightened!*
T–Rex –	*Roars.*
Gigantosaurus –	*Eeek!*
James –	*It's a T-Rex!*
Therapist –	*It makes a big roar. The Gigantosaurus says "it makes a big roar".*
Gigantosaurus -	*Are you friendly?*
Therapist –	*Maybe the Gigantosaurus wants to be friends with the T-Rex. Do you think he wants to be friends or not?*
James –	*He wants to be friends.*
Therapist A –	*Does the T-Rex want to be friends?*
James –	*Yes, he is.*
Therapist A –	*Maybe that's his way of saying hello - doing a big roar.*

Playing didn't only enable James to extend his range of communication, it enabled me to extend mine. Playing in this way created an "us". I moved between different person-positions and so did James. My earlier questions to James constructed an 'I-you'. These early questions were influenced by my relationship with diagnostic criteria and created a discord in our attempts to communicate with each other. When I entered into and created a shared world with James, this made for a more collaborative and creative culture which seemed not only to make for connection but which brought forth evidence of non- Asperger Syndrome abilities.

The imaginary and interactive play going on here with both parties initiating contact and responding to each other. We are creating a new linguistic system in which we are talking about talking and reflecting on relationships. We both know that we are ourselves and yet pretending to be another creature. We have created a meaning making system and have moved away from the rule bound naming, describing and collecting relationship with dinosaurs.

> When one person acts 'into' a jointly constructed setting rather than 'out of' his or her own plans or desires, an outcome is produced which is independent of any of the individuals involved and 'belongs' only to the collectivity they constitute
>
> (Shotter 1989, p.147).

In shifting the focus from the child to communicating systems, James' family started to follow James's lead in any imaginary play, elaborated themselves and enjoyed the intimacy arising out of this play. But the family also found it hard to step out of the naming games, the question-answer ways of speaking that they had witnessed and felt was expected by professionals in the clinic. Just as I had done.

Human beings have no innate ability to make sense of complex interactions. They are very difficult to learn to interpret as we are not usually aware of the contexts people are acting out of or think they are acting into. We often feel nervous while we are still in the process of sense-making or when we have misunderstood the other. We have to learn to be patient while we wonder what is going on and we have to learn to act respectfully while we are trying to work this out. The world of human interaction is awash with uncertainties. "Instead of understanding autism simply as a puzzle, we treat it as an example of the fundamental human features of uncertainty, of the incompleteness and partiality of communication, of the constant risk presented by the potential undoing of the tie that makes you and I a 'we'." (McGuire and Michalko 2011, p.164).

From expert professional knowing to a learning culture of collaborative action research

Rather than rush to a position of expert knowing from without a relationship, the invitation here is for professionals to develop a new culture akin to collaborative action research. Professional knowledge becomes a process of collaborative learning. Learning happens from within the living moment of interaction *with* people and not through theorising without and about them. It is a pragmatic response which foregrounding strengths and abilities over the culturally specific products of evidence of disability and communications difficulties. It is also an ethical response to one of the persistent bastions of the psychiatric, psychological and psychotherapeutic professions: the belief that the professional expert has more relevant knowledge than the client and their social network.

A collaborative action research approach repositions the identified patient as someone with a contribution to make to therapeutic conversation. Their expertise and abilities can be recognised in contrast to how the knowledge of the patient has become de-centred and peripheral (Foucault 1980). Lather's concept of "catalytic validity" proposes turning a symptom of disorder into a resource for both an identified patient and their family (Lather 1991). Professional expertise has a facilitative and creative function in finding ways of incorporating the contribution of all family members and in encouraging the activities and attitudes needed to achieve new ways of seeing and being with each other. This form of dialogue brings forth and showcases the ability of the person with a diagnosis of Asperger Syndrome to explain and develop lineal and circular accounts of complex relational systems. Conversation is not understood as a means to collecting knowledge so much as a means of generating knowledge. The shift, both for the person diagnosed with Asperger Syndrome and for the professional, facilitates new ways of knowing how to go on in conversation with less repetitive, rule-bound ways of talking.

Summary

The invitation in this chapter is to understand diagnosis is often a monological activity by one person about another. Dialogue, on the other hand, leads to improved communication with people and to better coordination with them.

By entering into a collaborative inquiry with people with Asperger Syndrome and their families, professionals can extend repertoires of communicating with people described as having autistic spectrum conditions and their families and friends. If we resist being governed by compulsive diagnosing behaviours (~~CDB~~) and symptom spotting tendencies (~~SST~~), we can open ourselves up to new ways of being with people in therapeutic play and conversation. We can encourage a reflexive curiosity about what makes a difference in what we are doing with each other that opens or closes opportunities for meaningful and fruitful dialogue. The study of grammar in both professional and family systems might generate more descriptions of connectedness than would otherwise be available to family members.

For professionals to point to parts of the brain and insist the knowledge will emerge in the future about the cause of autism is not of much use to people who want to be appreciated and enter into easier communications. Such lineal causality reduces people with Asperger Syndrome or High Functioning Autism to people with something inherently wrong with them and by doing so, further isolates them from others. This results in entire research budgets being diverted to the task of locating a mythical organic cause followed by a cure. In the meantime, many possibilities are yet to be explored with people diagnosed as having Asperger Syndrome and their social networks as to how to improve everyday communications, and with that, their quality of life. Given how much families crave meaningful interaction with their child with Asperger Syndrome and improved harmony across their family, there is much to commend a relationally oriented systemic approach in which all participants are positioned as collaborative action researchers.

References

Baron-Cohen, S., Leslie, A. M. & Frith, U. (1985). Does the autistic child have a "theory of mind"? *Cognition* 21, 37-46.

Bateson, G. (1972). *Steps to an Ecology of Mind*. Chicago, IL: University of Chicago Press.

Brownlow, C. & O'Dell, L. (2009). Challenging understandings of 'Theory of Mind': A brief report. *Intellectual and Developmental Disabilities*, 47, 6, 473-478.

Foucault, M. (1980). In Colin Gordeon (Ed.). Power/Knowledge - Selected Interviews and Other Writings 1972-1977. Brighton: Harvester Press.

Frith, U. (Ed.) (1991). *Autism & Asperger Syndrome*. Cambridge: Cambridge University Press.

Gergen, K. J. & Gergen, M. (2002). Ethnography as relationship. In A. Bochner and C. Ellis (Eds.) *Ethnographically Speaking. Autoethnography, Literature, and Aesthetics.* Walnut Creek, CA: AltaMira Press.

Gillberg, C. (1991). Clinical and neurobiological aspects of Asperger Syndrome in six family studies. In U. Frith (Ed.) *Autism and Asperger Syndrome.* Cambridge: Cambridge University Press.

Hickok, G. (2014). We might have autism backwards: What "broken mirror" and "broken mentalizing" theories could have wrong: the dominant autism theories assuming a lack of or diminished social sensitivity need to be re-examined. In *The Myth of Mirror Neurons: The Real Neuroscience of Communication and Cognition.* London: W. W. Norton & Company.

Lather, P. (1991). *Getting Smart.* New York, NY: Routledge.

Leppington, R. (1991). From Constructivism to Social Constructionism and Doing Critical Therapy. *Human Systems: Journal of Systemic Consultation and Management*, 2, 2, 79-104.

Maturana, H. (1991). Science and daily life: The ontology of scientific explanations. In F. Steier (Ed.) *Research and Reflexivity.* London: Sage.

McGuire, A. E. & Michalko, R. (2011). Minds between us: Autism, mindblindness and the uncertainty of communication. *Educational Philosophy and Theory*, 43, 2, 162-177.

Shotter, J. (1989). Social accountability and the social construction of "you". In J. Shotter & K. Gergen (Eds.) *Texts of Identity.* London: Sage.

Shotter, J. (2015). Ontological risks and communication anxieties — on what and whom others will 'allow' us to be. *International Journal of Collaborative-Dialogic Practices,* 6.

Shotter, J. (2015). Toward a third revolution in psychology: From inner mental representations to dialogical social practices. First draft of chapter. In D. Bakhurst & S. Shanker (Eds.) *Culture, Language, Self: the Philosophical Psychology of Jerome Bruner.* London: Sage.

Simon, G. (2004). Systemic family therapy with families with a child who has a diagnosis of Asperger Syndrome. *Human Systems: The Journal of Systemic Consultation and Management* 15, 4, 257-274.

Timimi, S., Gardner, N., & McCabe, B. (2010). *The Myth of Autism: Medicalising Men's and Boys' Social and Emotional Competence.* Basingstoke: Palgrave Macmillan.

Wing, L. (1981). Asperger's syndrome: A clinical account. *Psychological Medicine,* 11, 1, 115–29.

Whitfield, G. & Simon, G. (2014). *Unpublished Pink Practice working paper.*

PART TWO

GOING FURTHER AGAIN

SEVEN

Dublin Description of my Doctorate

A Methodological Poem

It was year four. 2010. Lisen Kebbe and I went to Dublin to get some consultation from Imelda McCarthy on our dissertations. It was all quite heady: intellectually and physically. Imelda said reading my dissertation was like falling off a cliff – in terms of the methodology. We were not doing traditional doctorates. We were developing new dialogical methodologies to show systemic practice in action. Lisen and I spent half a day bent over our notepads on the train travelling along Dublin Bay in the pouring rain, working out each of our remaining time frames to final submission. That evening we went out for dinner with Imelda and Michael. When they dropped us later at the bus stop, we went to two, maybe three pubs and gate-crashed someone's wedding where we danced until the early hours. The next morning when I woke up, I sat upright in the hotel bed and wrote this story of my systemic practice doctorate at KCC.

****

By the beginning of the second year I realised

I couldn't hear myself any more.

John sent through another paper.

I started to read it and then,

I just stopped

dead in my tracks.

It hit me:

I couldn't read anything more

by men.

I couldn't hear myself.

I rang Shoshana in San Francisco

she teaches transformative studies

and she said

Oh! but you should be reading...

and she gave me all these women's names

Carolyn Ellis, Laurel Richardson,

you know, the autoethnography people,

qualitative inquiry people

and that was it

oh, god

It felt like coming home!

Peter had mentioned bell hooks

so I created a reading list for myself

of women

and I started using first names in my references to

stay alert to the gender balance in the theory

I was exposing myself to.

I felt so much better

and I felt so much more confident

now I was reading, reading with friends.

I could see how some of them spoke my language and lived

in the same world as me.

They were bothered

about similar things.

But there were other things that happened too

early on

in the research process

life and death stuff,

treatment for cancer

(time changed hugely in its appearance and feel);

my mum died...

well, these things created a hiatus

a break in the movement towards

what was probably going to be

a more recognisable form of

narrative action research.

The politics were more obvious

but somehow

I got more interested

in what was happening

in my practice

I heard the talk

the tone

the miracle of living conversation

spontaneous coordination between people

and my practice took the lead.

I had a startling experience with someone coming to me for therapy.

She had never been one for talking.

I encouraged her to write instead.

I felt good that I was facilitating her being able to communicate.

One day I wrote some reflections for myself about our conversation.

I read them back.

A voice was missing.

I had written down our talk as I remembered it

and I had written down

my thoughts at the time and since

as I remembered them

but her voice was missing

as a commentator

as a co-respondent

so I sent her the stuff

you know, all of it

and I asked her if she wanted to

write her thoughts from at the time

and what she thought now while

she was reading it

reading what I had written

And, she wrote back - some interesting things.

But the thing that stands out for me

that I'll never forget

is

that despite all my efforts

    to be transparent

    to share my thoughts with her in our meetings

she said she was surprised

by how much else I was thinking

that I didn't share with her

how much I noticed

which she didn't know about

that she liked hearing what else I was thinking.

In effect she invited me

to talk

more how I write.

I hadn't just facilitated her 'speaking'

through writing.

She was facilitating me

to extend my talk as well.

So to begin with I used writing as a reflexive activity,

Just for myself,

to amplify the sound of the talk I was living in

and slow it down

right down

- not to analyse from a distance

- not to crack it all up into piles of ushered fragments

but to hear my inner dialogue

capture that polyphonic chat

and I found

that separating out some of those voices

allowed me to converse with them more

openly

and see which voices had most influence

which felt they had more right and expose

  the contradictions

  the power relations

  the problem of choice

and listen for
which ones made it into outer talk.

I've been wondering
How can I work 'collaboratively' with someone
if I'm making so many
choices
about which ideas to privilege
over others?
I don't know.
Some people coming for therapy
don't want too much
uncertainty
they don't want me
spilling my guts
you can't share everything
it would need too much explanation,
context setting,
it would be never ending.
It would be dead boring.

Well, it became obvious to me
that I needed to make

some different choices.

I decided to spend the second year

doing experimental writing.

John and I had a fight.

He said it was undergrowth.

I said undergrowth was where it was happening.

I knew my feminist and postmodernist mates

got it

that they understood that

stories

are often

hidden

and that a lot of activity

goes on

out of sight

and is as much

the main event

as anything more visible.

What is one man's undergrowth is another woman's research.

But how to find a writing style

not just a style

an ethical way of writing which reflects

the ethics-led living practices in my working life
in my professional community
how do I write this living with ethics
into writing
and open an invitation
to new forms of joint action?

And then
there was the challenge in
how to engage with the literature
in a conversational manner.
Waves of relief
in finding textual friends,
theoretical allies
who lent their artistic skill
and ethical conviction
so rendering more malleable
the characters and scenarios
in my everyday working life.

My writings contextualise each other.
They are real stories
and

sounds-enough-like real stories;

a discussion of the literature

appears in several places:

using students' voices,

fictitious characters,

using my voices

and the resituated words of the writers

sometimes

spoken by them;

there's a lot of talk

about the relationship between reader and writer

and about the writer as reader.

Writing can be a transformative experience

– for the writer as a reader of their own work

And what else is there?

There is sound and texture

an Irish Sea crossing away from mere vocabulary.

The socioacoustics of

interactive responsivity

there is animation, intonation, inflection,

physicality, passion, emotion

and how do I 'capture' that, share that

in writing

and write for a listening reader?

This is more than dialogical writing

though it is that proudly too

It is performance

speaking with, to and for an audience.

This is not – as you are gathering –

a scientific treatise flat

on the page,

It is not a formulaic submission submitting to prescription

lying down on a page in paragraphic form.

Subversive voices from philosophy, literature, literary criticism, poetry

and from systemic therapy

have encouraged me

to listen

really listen

to what feels ethically coherent,

to other stories also present

but not yet told – or heard – or recognised – or brought into earshot;

by form and ethics and musicality.

Three lynchpin positions

pull in this writing:

aboutness, withness and within-ness

with perpetual movement between those positions,

a waltz which continues beyond the playing of any orchestra.

There is always movement.

Such movement.

So much activity.

A snow storm,

a rushing river

a long hike.

Imagine now

that same hike step by uphill step

slowed down

slowed right down

so the frames per second were

not rushed

    together

not blurred

    with motion

but each frame separated

each shift captured in a frame

(not the camera never lies)

- a story of my telling

I lie

in an attempt to tell the truth

so it can be heard and felt

and slowed down enough for the reader

to come with

jump into the picture Mary Poppins and Bert style.

One foot in,

lost for a while perhaps in other people's lives

one foot out,

an observer of the work,

of the text,

of oneself,

the speaker making their own leaps.

Gail Simon (2010). Writing (as) Systemic Practice. Doctoral Dissertation

EIGHT

Systemic Inquiry as a form of Qualitative Inquiry

Introduction

There are some striking 'family resemblances' between Systemic Inquiry and research methodologies gathering under the umbrella of Qualitative Inquiry (Denzin & Lincoln 2005, 2011). In this chapter I draw out areas of commonality in qualitative and systemic inquiry in practice research and propose Systemic Inquiry as a form of Qualitative Inquiry.

Common interests include:

- a reflexive and emergent shaping of methodology, focus and participation
- a relational emphasis
- a critique of power in the social world
- a social justice agenda
- ethics-led practice
- fluidity
- asking what counts as 'knowledge', with whose authority and with what consequences for others
- a concern with the politics of description and with the creation of narratives
- relationships in inner dialogue and outer talk
- social accountability: speaking from within the first person, transparency, showing context
- reflexivity
- a critical approach to 'professionalism' and 'methods'

- collaborative participation
- irreverence and respect
- practice as an art

In this opening chapter, I invite you to consider two main areas which I see as challenging to systemic practitioner researchers. Firstly, there is the debate of what counts as method in practice and in research. Postmodern systemic practitioner researchers have treated method as a fluid development in response to context. In other words, methodology evolves, inspired by a reflexive movement between emergent theory and practice. Secondly, in practitioner research, *relationality* is foregrounded. Ethics, know-how and reflexivity are not seen as stand- alone things. Instead we tend to speak of relational ethics, relational know-how, and relational reflexivity. After exploring connections between the postmodern movements of Qualitative Inquiry and Systemic Practice, I show how Systemic Inquiry is a form of Qualitative Inquiry in which methodology is treated as an emergent and ethical activity. This ethics-led, relational model of practice research incorporates room for spontaneous, emergent and collaborative responses to power and decision making in research practices.

The Evolution of Systemic Methodology

> ... there is always a kind of developmental continuity involved in the unfolding of all living activities.
>
> Shotter 2005, p.26

As a systemic practitioner researcher, I have been concerned to find ways of creating accounts of my practice which reflect and respect the collaborative, conversational relationships of systemic-social constructionist practice. Finding or developing a model and a language for research which can be woven into the careful co-ordinations of therapeutic, consultancy, supervisory and learning conversations is not just a practical decision but an ethical one too.

In this chapter, I invite systemic practitioner-researchers to approach the problem of choosing a research methodology with some degree of irreverence and with a social constructionist critique to ensure that we initiate an ethical and an ideological fit with our practice. Markovic has spoken of the rule creating culture of systemic practice and encouraged a stance of *positive delinquency* to our theoretical heritage in the interest of usefulness in practice relationships (Markovic, then Radovanovic 1993). Harlene Anderson invites practitioners to question the relevance of inherited rules created by our profession (Anderson 2007, cited in Simon 2010) and Betty St Pierre comments, "I'm tired of old research designs being repeated so many times that we think they are real – we forget we made them up!" (St Pierre 2010). Sheila McNamee extends Cecchin's concern with *irreverence* (Cecchin 1987) in showing how p*romiscuity* in systemic practice allows practitioners to treat theories as discursive options which open up or close down relational possibilities (McNamee 2004).

We are reminded that, like all theories, research methodologies are products of time, place and culture. Research methodologies are not items on a shelf which one takes down and uses as ready-made products. It can be more useful and in keeping with a systemic approach to think about research as a process of mutual shaping in which researchers and co-researchers are changed by each other and by the activities; in turn, the research methods and activities also evolve through the influence of researchers and co-researchers. By accepting the inevitable mutual shaping in practice and research relationships, by fostering space for new and unanticipated stories to emerge, we privilege the ethics of methodological openness and move away from a notion of *choosing a research method to engaging with and shaping a research process.*

> when someone acts, their activity cannot be accounted as wholly their own activity – for a person's acts are inevitably 'shaped' in the course of their performance partly by the acts of the others around them, i.e., each individual's action is a joint creation, not the product of a sole author – this is where all the seeming strangeness of the dialogical begins.
>
> Shotter 2011, p.32

The Development of Systemic Inquiry

Types and Uses of Questions

The early Milan School developed a method of inquiry as a response to a finding: they noticed that people did not maintain any improvements gained in psychiatric hospital when discharged to their family (Boscolo et al 1987). This observation formed a premise for their work and, inspired by the work of Gregory Bateson (1972, 1979), Maturana & Varela (1980, 1987, 1988) and others, they developed a theory of family systems which developed innovative questioning techniques to explore how a family system organised itself in response to actual or imagined change, and how information could be obtained and used by the therapy team. The international systems community soon realised that the Milan approach was not simply a matter of using questions to understand the workings of a particular human system and explore a hypothesis; they recognised that their questions also had an impact on parts of the family system and that the relational act of asking questions of people is inevitably an intervention on the system (Selvini Palazzoli et al. 1980; Tomm 1987a).

This inspired a blossoming of interest in inquiry and in theorising what inquiry does. Systemic questions were developed to create opportunities for new tellings of old stories, for imagining alternative futures and for reconfigurations in relationships between people, their narratives and actions. Karl Tomm developed a range of practical interventive questions in his collection of papers on interventive interviewing (Tomm 1987a, 1987b, 1987c). Peggy Penn emphasised a need for a temporal dimension by introducing future oriented questions (Penn 1985). Insoo Kim Berg and Steve de Shazer proposed questions within a brief solution focused model (de Shazer 1985, 1988). Later, through a postmodern lens, John Burnham introduced questions which invited self reflexivity and relational reflexivity (Burnham 1992, 1993, 2005). Michael White and David Epston developed questions to identify problematic dominant narratives and inquire into their influence. They showed how questions could uncover and strengthen alternative, preferred narratives which created opportunities for overturning an unhappy status quo (White 1988; White & Epston 1990).

The concern in systemic practice to re-evaluate power in therapeutic and management relationships and in the storying of management and therapeutic practices, led to questions which enquired into the clients' strengths, abilities, dreams and hopes (Combs & Freedman 1990; Flaskas et al 2007; O'Hanlon et al 1998; Cooperrider and Srivastva 1987). The recognition of wider systems in which people were living influenced the development of questions which reframed the individual as members of different community groups (for example, McCarthy & Byrne, 1988; Burnham & Harris 1996; Simon 1998). These power and culture sensitive questions reframed the professional relationship so that knowledge of the systemic practitioner shifted from 'conductor' (Selvini Palazzoli et al. 1980) or expert knower (Anderson & Goolishian 1992) to curious respondent which foregrounded the expertise of the people with whom they are working.

Theorising practices of inquiry and the influence of context

Vernon Cronen's and Barnett Pearce's Coordinated Management of Meaning theory (CMM) invited us to question how the different contexts we are acting out of and into influence the direction, content and shaping of meaning in the professional relationship (Pearce 1989; Oliver 1996). The model of CMM invites us to question the range of narratives, theories and practices which influence a person's or team's systemic practice through the centring of *reflexivity* as an ethical response. This continuous reflexive influence between theory and practice makes for a continual methodological evolution of and as systemic practice (Leppington 1991; Burnham 1992; Simon 2012).

The Milan team's advice not to marry one's hypothesis was further developed by Cecchin by encouraging curiosity and irreverence in systemic practice (Cecchin 1987). John Burnham demonstrated the art of irreverence despite and, perhaps, because of the constant movement between creativity and respectful co-ordination in his work (Burnham

1992, 1993, 2005). In mapping out the relationships between approach, method and techniques Burnham used the model of interlinked levels of context from CMM to upturn and re-contextualise stories of power and influence (Burnham 1992, 1993, 2011). He suggests practical ways in which ideas can influence and re-shape systemic practice.

In both Leppington's (1991) and Burnham's (1992) descriptions of reflexive practice cycles, practitioners are invited to question their ideological influences: their most deeply held beliefs, their most cherished assumptions, cultural stories operating at a less mindful level but having an impact on practice choices and findings. The shift in postmodern systemic practice away from a model based on a one-sided embodiment of professional expertise to a model of collaborative inquiry (Anderson & Goolishian 1992), a shared process of reflection (Andersen 1987) invited systemic practitioners into a reflexive process in which all theories, personal, professional, cultural beliefs etc. are open to review. To actively engage in critical reflexivity about practices and the theories supporting them, to be aware of one's preferences and how they can serve to turn away countering voices and alternative narratives (White & Epston 1990) opens up possibilities for ethical consideration of the relationships between theory, practice and ideology (Leppington 1991).

By including ideology within methodology, Leppington advocates for the socio-political-philosophical contextualising of method and theory. This requires us to transparently reveal and own the ideological influences at work in our choice of any one research 'method'. By asking not only *'What counts as data?'* but the ethics-led question of *'What can data count as?'* Leppington proposes that we allow ourselves to be changed by what we find – our methods, theories and most deeply held beliefs - and not simply impose our own meaning on material with the risk of reproducing existing values and power relations. For these reasons, I suggest the term *research methodology*, as opposed to research method, is more coherent with an ethics-led approach to systemic practice.

Systemic practice has gone through many significant theoretical shifts – some in the name of a scientific attempt to perfect an approach, others arising out of ethical concerns. Emphasis has turned away from how we can 'really' understand systems to how we generate useful stories about people and relationships (Hoffman 1993; White & Epston 1990). This move away from generalising theory to contextually specific knowing is a more ethically comfortable fit with relationships involved in collaborative inquiry (Anderson 1997). In recognising that theory almost never works as a one-size-fits-all without exclusionary and dangerous consequences (Lather 1994), systemic practice has gone on to encourage dialogue about the differences in knowledge and knowing and know- how (Andersen 1997; Anderson & Goolishian 1992; Seikkula 2002). This ethical shift invited systemic practitioners to consider how to work collaboratively with people (Anderson & Gerhart 2006). Anne Hedvig Vedeler builds on Cecchin's idea of curiosity (Cecchin 1987) preferring the term *benevolent curiosity* which she feels better reflects a respectful dialogical and collaborative approach in consultation, teaching, supervision and therapy. Vedeler reinterprets fellow Norwegian, Tom Andersen's reflecting team as Resonance Groups and frames them as a means of embodied dialogical inquiry (Vedeler 2010).

Systemic practice has foregrounded the place of *inquiry* in a number of ways. In addition to our vast and extraordinary library of questions, systemic inquiry can be understood as technique, as method, as ethical, reflexive and collaborative ways of being with people, as reflexive inner and outer dialogue, as reflexive writing in training contexts. So why, when we have developed such rich and sophisticated theory about the emergent and co-constructionist nature of inquiry, would we look to a positivist research model advocating a prescribed model with one person extracting information from another or interpreting material without involving our co-researchers?

Certainly, the trend in economy-led public and private services encourages practitioners to employ positivist ways of measuring decontextualised improvement and overlook relational consequences of change and the meaningfulness of professional interaction. Practitioners are often bullied into stepping into a different language to co-ordinate with positivist discourses at the expense of developing professional knowledge and know-how. Opportunities need to be created for inquiry which is coherent with, for example, the coordination with micro-movements at bodily and emotional and temporal levels in the improvisational practice of systemic dialogue, practices which do not necessarily lend themselves, nor should they, to any form of categorisation or results tables.

Systemic inquiry is not intended to be a reproducible solution so much as a stance of methodological irreverence which abandons any modernist attempt to achieve and impose a streamlined scientific method. Instead, it advocates a form of inquiry which emphasises a shift from knowledge to ethics (Leppington 1991), in which we have a loose attachment to precious, hard come by theories and practices and one which is powered by self and relational reflexivity. Systemic inquiry is a form of research and professional practice which will always evolve as a reflexive response to news of difference (Bateson 1979).

A short story from practice

After a conversation with a supervisee, I feel a residue of conflicting feelings: an attachment to an idea and some discomfort about the degree of that attachment. I use reflexive writing as a form of inquiry (Richardson 1994) to create opportunities for further stories to emerge from my inner dialogue about the conversation with the supervisee. After a while of writing, I feel I am missing the voice of the supervisee. I share my writings with the supervisee and in the spirit of collaboration, I invite her responses. At our next meeting, she brings a lengthy written response and reads it aloud to me. As I listen, I am shocked by my mis- understanding of something she has said. I hear her voice and what she is saying in quite a different way. I hear my own listening and talking differently too. How I listen and what I hear, have been changed by this experience. I listen with a broader range of conversing voices in my mind akin to bringing the reflecting team into the room (Andersen 1997) and with more attempts at resonance (Vedeler 2010). The talk between us changes and my listening starts to feel more alongside her than about her.

This story demonstrates how the constant acting on one's noticings in an attempt to co-ordinate with the interests of the other, describes a model of practice which is not working towards refining a theoretical model with a static, scientifically 'accurate' body of knowledge to compete in acquiring academic and professional status and a secure identity. Instead, it is characterised by an ethics-led agenda which decentres the practitioner / researcher (Lather 2007; Tootell 2004) and, in improvisational reflexive inquiry, weaves narratives and relational responses.

Our attempts to communicate are inevitably not only flawed but messy. We ask, and expect to be asked, questions which help us know how to go in conversation with writers, colleagues, clients, research participants and so on. As we leave a fixed way of talking behind, our communications spring from spontaneous responsiveness (Shotter & Katz 1998), improvisation (Burnham 1992; Keeney 1990) and emotional openness (Anderson & Jensen 2007) which, as often seen and heard through video reviews or through transcriptions, appear chaotic and unpredictable. The *apparently* disorderly passages of interaction between people or within our inner dialogue may not require or lend themselves to examination through a methodology with a repeatable, re-describable method – something you learn to roll out and find ways of teaching to others for them to perform. Research with people, as with most relationships, professional or otherwise, can be an unpredictable process generating what some describe as 'messy texts' (Clifford & Marcus 1986; Lather 2007; Law 2007; Marcus 2007). Most forms of text analysis (for example, grounded theory, Charmaz 2012; Interpretive Phenomenological Analysis, Smith et al 2009; conversational analysis, Woolfitt 2005; discourse analysis, Woolfitt 2005) exclude opportunities to enter into learning from within the hub of systemic activity and have not addressed the complex inner and outer workings of *relational processes* (and the relationship between inner and outer).

Additionally, there are ethical dilemmas for systemic researchers concerned with the practice of co-creating of meaning. Despite an increasing interest in relational ethics, such methods still position the researcher in an about-ness position (Shotter 2011) in relation to 'the material' as if it is a thing in itself apart from the relational processes. This attempt at objectivity counters the situated collaborative and reflexive inquiry at the heart of systemic practice and often promotes a confused assumption that objectivity coupled with a prescribed method is synonymous with rigour.

Accounting Practices and Legitimacy

Michael White encourages an exploration of relationships between stories, storytellers and audience and he situates narratives in the relational context of texts. He says the "text analogy introduces us to an intertextual world. In the first sense, it proposes that persons' lives are situated in texts within texts. In the second sense, every telling or retelling of a story, through its performance, is a new telling that encapsulates, and expands upon the previous telling" (White & Epston 1990, p.13). White's suggestion that there is no ultimate truth to be told corresponds with Barnett Pearce's advice that we should "treat all stories, your own as well as others, as incomplete, unfinished, biased and inconsistent." (Pearce 2004, p.50). Their ideas help us understand why systemic inquiry needs to challenge 'research' as an attempt to make objective, decontextualised knowledge claims and offer instead a relational and reflexive understanding of research as producing of narratives-in-progress. White (1992) invited us to be curious about which narratives dominate people, families and the communities in which they live, to understand the contexts in which these narratives have established their dominance and he invites practitioners to look at how other accounts or descriptions of people or events have been lost or silenced. White draws on Foucault's idea of subjugated knowledges "that survive only at the margins of society and are lowly ranked-considered insufficient and exiled from the legitimate domain of the formal knowledges and the accepted sciences" and goes on to quote Foucault as saying these knowledges are the "naïve knowledges, located low down on the hierarchy, beneath the required level of cognition or scientificity" (White & Epston 1990, p.26).

Denzin and Lincoln point to the political backdrop for this methodologically dilemmic era as a climate which is dominated by narrow ideas about what counts as 'evidence' and research projects struggling to influence policies driven by economics over social need. They describe this time as the "methodologically contested present" and how it is "a time of great tension, substantial conflict, methodological retrenchment in some quarters ... and the disciplining and regulation of inquiry practices to conform with conservative, neoliberal programs and regimes that make claims regarding Truth." (Lincoln & Denzin 2005, p.1116).

The Narrative of Method

If we understand social constructionism as treating all theories as stories, we can also recognise methods as narrative products and as producing of narratives. The narratives people bring to their workplace or social life are co-constructed, shaped between people and subject to interpretation (Anderson & Goolishian 1988; Burr 1995). Our theoretical narratives arise out of our ideological beliefs, values and most taken for granted deeply held assumptions. Methods and techniques sit more or less neatly on the back of these ideologically influenced narrative structures but can easily appear as stand-alone entities without prejudice, without social underpinnings.

The more dominant stories of professional practice and research about methods suggest a clearly signposted order of events to be carried out by a trained individual or team who 'knows' what they are doing. This 'knowing' mostly corresponds to a learned technique or process. Case examples from many recent leaders in narrative and systemic practice often perpetuate an idea of a clean, reproducible method in their writings or presentations with an emphasis on what was *said*. There is little attention in most professional texts to the times between the sparkling moments which is probably 99% of time. In amongst the gems are messy, clumsy attempts to co-ordinate, half-finished sentences and retracted questions, mm's and aha's and a range of physical responses such as nods, eyebrow movements, outer and inner twitches. I have noticed through my work as a systemic therapist and as a supervisor that when a practitioner isn't using a particular technique, she or he is trying to co-ordinate with the client(s). Is this time wasted or does it set a context for the moments identified as important by the practitioner or their conversational partners?

We are hoping our attempts to communicate and understand the communications of the other will count as something important to participants in the conversation. We know, for example, that just coming up with a miracle question (de Shazer 1988) at any moment will not have as much impact as if the client feels the practitioner has been paying attention to what they have been saying and responding empathically. The human element in the work may count for more than we realise and this is supported by much research (Sexton & Whiston 1994) and more is being written about the relational activities in the professional relationship (Anderson & Gehart 2007; Flaskas 2002; Flaskas et al 2004).

The shift in systemic practice towards the dialogical and the collaborative brings an expectation of improvisational coordination between participants. John Burnham (Burnham 1993) has embraced the inevitability of chaos and confusion arising in conversation and taken an approach to not-knowing (Anderson & Goolishian 1992) how to go on with people as part of the negotiation about how to go on. He has given many examples of his practice in which he demonstrates meaningfulness arising out of the random. He advocates a model of therapy, supervision or consultation in which any governing level of context can be upturned and reviewed at any moment in time (Burnham 1992, 1993, 2005). This approach is not led by some theory about the importance of the random (though random choices can be very generative of useful connections) so much as by an ethical concern to be client-led or supervisee-led and by a pragmatic approach to find a way forward. Burnham tries to co-ordinate with people in recognising any meaningful elements in exchanges however bizarre or unexpected they may be. This model of ethics-led systemic practice involves a negotiation with the people with whom one is working throughout the process otherwise the practitioner stance is that of imposing a method on others. In engaging in a practice-research process, it is often important and fruitful to mirror this commitment to spontaneous, relational co-ordination.

A Relational Focus

Social Justice: Inspiration for Practices of Inquiry

> Critical researchers start from an ethical principle and do research designed to emancipate people from patterns of social relations prejudged to be oppressive, to expose patterns of exploitation, or to subvert structures of power that allow some people to be dominated by others.
>
> Pearce and Walters 1996, p.10

An overarching link between Systemic Inquiry with Qualitative Inquiry is the commitment to open up space for a multiverse with polyvocal participation across all parts of a research process concerned with beneficial consequences for participants of research intervention (Denzin & Lincoln 2005, 2011; Lather 1994; Parker 2005; Pearce and Walters 1996; Tuhiwai Smith 2005; Visweswaran 1994; Reynolds 2010, 2013 and elsewhere in this book).

Social constructionist-systemic-collaborative-dialogical therapy has moved away from normative and pathologising discourses. Narrative therapy invites therapists and community workers to allow themselves to be moved to action by the stories they hear, become activists in trying to overturn injustices and experiment with creative, socially inclusive, relational practices. (White & Denborough 2005). Sheila McNamee shows the significance of women taking hold of research and responding in a way which privileges finding their own ways of researching (McNamee 1994). Tom Andersen encouraged practitioners to be moved by the circumstances of the people whose story one was hearing (Shotter 2007). Jaakko Seikkula suggests that if a person is drowning, one has to jump in the water too in order to try and save them even if that puts the practitioner in some degree of risk (Seikkula 2002). Reynolds speaks of the practitioner researcher as a "fluid, imperfect ally" in describing the importance of ethics led alliances in getting beyond the constraints of colonial professional positioning (Reynolds 2013).

We can frame the practice of systemic inquiry as caring, as involvement in the lives and communities of others, as an openness to be changed by the words and feelings of others, as a preparedness to be moved to action in and beyond the consulting room or classroom. Both Systemic Inquiry and Qualitative Inquiry encourage experimentation with useful and user-friendly ways of inquiring into the lives of people and communities. Qualitative Inquiry methodologies try to amplify the voices of research participants over those of researchers (for example, Lather & Smithies 1997) and position the researcher as a reflexive research participant (Etherington 2004). There are many echoes some of the understanding in postmodern systemic therapies about the reflexive positioning of the practitioner (Amundson et al 1993; Andersen 1987; Anderson and Goolishian 1988, 1992; Anderson 1997; Burnham 2011; Reynolds 2013; Rober 2005; Shotter & Katz 1998; Seikkula & Arnkil 2006).

Working the Prejudicial Turn

> Producing 'things' always involves value—what to produce, what to name the productions, and what the relationship between the producers and the named things will be. Writing 'things' is no exception. No textual staging is ever innocent (including this one). Styles of writing are neither fixed nor neutral but reflect the historically shifting domination of particular schools or paradigms.
>
> Richardson 1994, p.518

Systemic practitioners drawing on a postmodern critique recognise that it is impossible to be value free and that we work with our prejudice in a mindful manner through reflexive inner and outer dialogue. When it comes to *researching* our work, we may feel the pull of 'objectivity' to depict process and outcomes 'fairly'.

It is, in this moment, that the language of systemic practice is often assumed by systemic practitioners to be redundant. There is a strong story of expertise from other professional academic discourses which teach us to evaluate our work 'fairly' or 'accurately' and without prejudice. We are keen to be fair and rigorous but we are already trained in methods of inquiry. And we are prejudiced because we value the stories people tell us, we recognise their uniqueness, we want to be moved by people and perhaps show people how we are moved – and we want this movement between us to count as something. We hear stories which many people do not get to hear but which are worth hearing; stories which will have taken their time to choose a suitable platform to speak from and audience to speak with. We use selective hearing to influence our ways forward because we allow ourselves to be moved by our conversational partners. We work with people so they can hear what it is they want to say and find ways of saying it to themselves, to us and to others who matter. Systemic practitioners have dialogical, communicating abilities which help to create the circumstances for the performances of other selves, alternative narratives and we want to be supportive of those preferred stories or more useful ideas and life choices. We are far from neutral in our work and the intricacies of our co-ordinations do not lend themselves to a system of measurement.

> Value-neutrality elaborates the disinterested aspect of objectivity: the conviction that knowers have no vested interest in the objects of their knowledge; that they have no reasons other than the pursuit of 'pure' inquiry to seek knowledge. These ideals are best suited to regulate the knowledge making of people who believe in the possibility of achieving a 'view from nowhere' – of performing what Donna Haraway calls 'the god trick'.
>
> Code 1995, p.15

And then there is the question of whether just anyone or any systemic practitioner or researcher can ask and get the same answer. We know that not to be true. Why? Because the systemic community has reclaimed the importance of the working relationship and we have recognised how different relationships and contexts bring out different parts of us, different stories resulting in different tellings, hearings and meanings. Lorraine Code challenges the idea that:

> knowers are substitutable for one another in the sense that they can act as 'surrogate knowers' who can put themselves in anyone's place and know exactly what she or he would know.
>
> Code 1995, p.16

Cronen makes a suggestion for systemic inquiry:

> It would be better to say that in the process of inquiry we make determinations of what related elements need to be included for any purpose of inquiry and call that the 'situation-in-view'. Identifying the situation-in-view is a provisional judgment. Further inquiry may lead to including new elements and disregarding others. Situations-in-view must be understood to include the inquirer. The inquirer cannot be outside the system. **The only choice to make is what kind(s) of relationship(s) one chooses for the purposes of inquiry**.
>
> Cronen 2000 [my emboldening of last sentence]

Leppington emphasised the importance of relational know-how and provided a way of contextualising which stories and which voices had more prominence (Leppington 1991). In proposing a move away from a method-led model of systemic practice which advocated training therapists and consultants to learn the theory and the application of techniques, Leppington described systemic practice as 'discursive practice'. She emphasised a significant paradigmatic movement which she referred to as the shift *'from knowledge to ethics'*.

These methodological differences link qualitative inquiry with postmodern systemic practice in confronting the ethics of method-led versus client-led or research participant-led practice. In a systemic practice context, theory and ethics merge to suggest the word ***theorethical*** which may be useful in highlighting the integrated and reflexive relationship between theory and ethics.

Both systemic practice and qualitative inquiry have adopted social constructionism as a *theorethical* context of influence. My intention is to see theory and ethics as one in order to highlight the ethics-led choices we make about selecting which practices to employ and how.

Relational Ethics

Relational ethics has been at the heart of systemic practice since the linguistic turn in the late nineteen eighties (Anderson and Goolishian 1988; Andersen 1987; Goldner et al 1990; Lang et al 1990; McCarthy & Byrne 1988; White 1992).

It is not uncommon in quantitative research and positivist qualitative research for the area of ethics to constitute a task which is *additional* to the research. Applications to research ethics committees or research advisory boards are often experienced by researchers as an irritating but necessary authoritative hurdle to overcome in order for the real thing – the research activity - to commence. Like systemic practice, qualitative inquiry is an ethics led activity. The research design has participants in mind and involved in consultation from the start. 'Warming the context' activities (Burnham 2005) make it comfortable for people to participate in research but are not simply a prelude to the 'real' research so much as an opportunity to create a culture of collaborative inquiry, exploring and generating practices together.

Systemic practice is an ethics-led way of being and doing with others. Ethics is not an add-on: it is our guiding light, whatever the area of relational practice. As such, systemic inquiry is an ethics-led practice and can proudly offer this approach to the broader field of qualitative research.

A systemic approach to research brings something unique and useful to the qualitative inquiry movement. Our preoccupation with *relational ethics* requires us to address:

- how we coordinate fairly in conversation with each other
- how we critically approach, acknowledge or challenge power in the relationship or in broader socio-political contexts

- how we manage the relationship between the polyvocality of our inner dialogue with the polyvocality in our outer dialogue
- which of our many selves we use and how
- how we reflexively question our attachments with theories, hypotheses, methods and other taken-for-granted values
- how we offer transparent accounts to others as to which stories we privilege and which we discard
- how we re-view what we have done together, what it means for now and what else we might have done
- how we acknowledge the value of the exchange between us and co-researchers

The reflections of qualitative researchers Ellis (2008), Bochner (2000), Richardson (1994, 1997), Gergen & Gergen (2002) include criteria for qualitative inquiry which address relational ethics. Mary and Kenneth Gergen remind us of how modernist research has positioned researcher and researched: "the traditional treatment of research 'subjects' was inclined to be alienating, demeaning, exploitative...... We are now highly sensitized to the 'politics of representation', the ways in which we as researchers construct – for good or ill – those whose lives we attempt to illuminate. A new array of collaborative, polyvocal, and self-reflexive methodologies has thus been given birth (see, for example, Denzin and Lincoln 2005)." (Gergen & Gergen 2002, p.13).

In reviewing her work as an autoethnographer, Carolyn Ellis addresses relationships with research participants:

> Relational ethics recognizes and values mutual respect, dignity, and connectedness between researcher and researched, and between researchers and the communities in which they live and work focuses on the changing relationship between researcher and research participants.
>
> Ellis 2008, p.308

> Relational ethics draws attention to how our relationships with our research participants can change over time... How can we act in a humane, nonexploitative way while being mindful of our role as researchers?"
>
> Ellis 2008, p.308

> Relational ethics requires us as researchers to act from our hearts and minds, to acknowledge our interpersonal bonds to others, and to initiate and maintain conversations (Bergum, 1998; Slattery & Rapp, 2003). The concept of relational ethics is closely related to an ethics of care (Gilligan, 1982; Noddings, 1984), communication ethics (Arnett, 2002), feminist and feminist communitarian ethics (see Christians, 2000; Denzin, 1997, 2003; Dougherty & Atkinson, 2006; Olesen, 2000; Punch, 1994)
>
> Ellis 2008, p.308

The points Ellis raises and the questions she encourages researchers to ask themselves and discuss with their co-researchers and colleagues, bear a strong linguistic and ethical resemblance to the in-the-moment-of- the-relationship questions systemic practitioners might ask themselves.

There is also another research relationship to take into account with regard to ethics – the relationship between writer and reader. Researchers are expected to produce research in a format designed to be accessible to an audience, and more, meaningful. A challenge inherent in critical reflexive practice is to make transparent to the reader the range and extent of inner dialogue in either the application of method or in the apparently spontaneous responses between people. Bochner's vision of poetic social science and alternative ethnography requires that research should allow space for interpretation and use language in a way that allows readers (and writers) to extract meaning from experience, "rather than depict experience exactly as it was lived" (Bochner 2000, p.270).

Mary and Kenneth Gergen draw attention to the researcher-audience relationship:

> Yet, there is one relational domain that has received little attention to date, that is, the relationship between the rhetor and reader, researcher and audience. As deeply engaged social scientists, the way we represent the world to our colleagues and related audiences contributes to our ongoing relationships within these life worlds (see Shotter 1997). Our words constitute forms of action that invite others into certain forms of relationships as opposed to others. Thus our manner of writing and speaking contributes to life forms that may be extended throughout the educational sphere and into public modes of existence.
>
> Gergen & Gergen 2002, p.13

The Place of the Researcher in the Research: the Question of Transparency

> The writer has a theory about how the world works, and this theory is never far from the surface of the text.
>
> Denzin 2003, p.117

One of the main principles in qualitative inquiry is to render oneself visible as the researcher – both in the doing of research with participants and in the writing of the research for the reader - to make some sense of who is doing the inquiry and the reporting. In the same way that participants can decide how to participate in the research, readers can make choices about how to engage with the text.

This challenge has been taken up in different ways within qualitative inquiry where, to a large extent, the choices have been influenced by the researcher's story of the 'self': single, contextually varied, or polyvocal. Qualitative researchers are interested in establishing a 'real' relationship with co-researchers so they become relaxed and give fuller responses. A woman researcher hoped that using an interpreter in interviews would strengthen her understanding of what research participants were saying. However, she noticed that they were more engaged with the interpreter than with her. So she decided to stop using the interpreter and privilege connection over accuracy. This generated an unexpected richness which she had not been able to access using an interpreter (Quiros 2010).

I was struck by a story told by an African American man who was conducting research interviews with women who had had breast cancer in the southern states of the USA. He described how one research participant, an African American woman, told him that she was alienated by his professional veneer at a research interview. She advised him to act and sound like the southern African American man he was so that she and other women would find it easier to open up to him about quite personal experiences. He reflected that while he was trying to fade himself out to foreground the research questions and be a 'good' (meaning unobtrusive) researcher, he wasn't allowing for how others saw him (Gregg 2010).

> A crucial first step in developing an adequately sensitive feminist methodology is learning to see what is not there and hear what is not being said. Donna Haraway urges feminists to 'become answerable for what we learn how to see'. To be thus accountable, feminists have to see what is systematically and systemically screened from view by the most basic assumptions about how people know the world; and they have to understand the power structures that effect these erasures.
>
> Code 1995, p.19

In ethnography, sharing stories about their own experience is some- thing researchers are expected to be open to; to be themselves in the research as a context for the conversation so as to level the conversational playing field. In the case of autoethnography or performance ethnography, there is an expectation of extended openness to make space for any difficult, unlikely, taken for granted, unthinkable, normally unsayable things which are around in our lives and which could go unnoticed unless described against a backdrop which render them visible. This involves 'relational risk-taking' (Mason 2005) as part of an ethical attempt to connect with readers and audience as well as with research participants. In systemic practice, we have learned to become the kind of conversational partner who is not only emotionally present but also, where useful, with intentionally visible life experience (Roberts 2005).

Some things touch us more than others and it is perhaps rarely a coincidence that we choose to work with a particular client group or do research on a particular subject or find some theoretical ideas more attractive than others. In a traditional research context, there is little expectation of the researcher 'outing' themselves as having an investment in the subject under investigation. In qualitative inquiry, there is an ethics-led expectation that the researcher will express their interest - not to counter any idea of bias but to illuminate the inevitability of prejudice and minimise any power imbalance in *knowing* between researcher and research participant (Etherington 2004) and to lend weight to one's conviction that something is worthy of investigation and public sharing.

In systemic practice, we also recognise the impossibility of neutrality and objectivity. We own our prejudices and work with them. How we use our own experiences, how we share them and discuss them with people with whom we work, varies. We are careful not to burden people with whom we are working with what might be experienced as troublesome information, particularly vulnerable clients. On the other hand, perhaps we have something to learn from practitioners whose starting point can involve some personal disclosure to conversational partners, research participants. This would make an interesting area to research.

Relational Reflexivity in Relational Know-How

Visweswaran criticises the normative ethnographic approach that presumes an observer and a subject with stable identities. She contrasts this stance with deconstructive ethnography, where the observer refuses to presume a stable identity for self or other (Visweswaran 1994). Denzin suggests "Deconstructive reflexivity is post-modern, confessional, critical, and intertextual." (Denzin 2003, p.236). In the field of qualitative inquiry tends to treat reflexivity as a form of *self-reflexivity* for the researcher.

Through a social constructionist-systemic-collaborative-dialogical lens, reflexivity is an ethical processing in and of research or practice activities. Reflexivity is always relational in that there is polyphonic responsivity in both inner dialogue and outer dialogue, be it of a cognitive, emotional, neurological or environmental source (Simon 2013).

The actions arising out of continual relational reflexivity in our practice as consultants, leaders, therapists, supervisors, trainers, researchers and writers might be described as a dance which requires attention to certain themes: a sensibility to any externally imposed tempo and other environmental demands and influences; a sensibility to a relational tempo in which dancers respectfully share the directorship of pace, challenge and movement; a responsivity to the invitations of other(s) and a selectivity about the choices offered and taken up. Relational reflexivity is not only something which can be observed with the eye. To observe only visible movements would overlook the drama of the inner movements of self and partners in the dance: emotional, embodied, cognitive and theoretical responses, fluent and jerky. We negotiate context, agenda, roles, language and a moment to moment focus. We exercise reflexivity in our co-ordinations with the other; we ask, check levels of comfort, understanding and meaning.

Reflexivity is also a form of self-supervision driven by a desire to coordinate with others in an ethical manner:

- What choices I am making and with what possible consequences for me, for them, for others not present?
- What is informing those choices?
- What other choices am I overlooking?
- Where are those guiding values/prejudices coming from?

We find ways of creating space to recognise the less mindful processes at work: embodied, emotional, cognitive, normative discourses, desire, personal gain, for example. A significant offering from systemic practitioners to the field of qualitative inquiry is a sophisticated understanding and articulation of relationally reflexive activities in researching practice.

Emergent Collaborations

The social sciences have been engaging in a paradigm shift which is being hailed as *the relational turn.* It invites an interest into ethics-led co-ordinations of co-researchers and into the micro-detail of how those co-ordinations take place.

In discussing possible directions for qualitative inquiry, Betty St Pierre's reluctance "to accept the 'I' in Qualitative Inquiry" could be understood as a signpost indicating a need for more of a relational emphasis in research (St Pierre 2010). The field of qualitative research has embraced the concept of reflexivity with a significant contribution by practitioners within the field of counselling. The field of systemic practice has something to contribute to the place of *relationality* in research, research relationships, writing research for a readership and specifically on the subject of relational reflexivity. This is perhaps the area where systemic practice has most to bring to the field of qualitative research. Much has been written about Self and Other but there appears, to my systemic eye, to be some space in the research field to explore the dynamic elements in relationships between researcher and research participants. Descriptions of this relationship are either minimal, or sound as if participants are separate static entities. So whilst there is acknowledgement of social constructionism and the power of language and narratives, there is room for more understanding of co-creative activity in the development of those narratives.

Diane Gehart, Margarita Tarragona and Saliha Bava promote a model of research based on collaborative practices:

> Collaborative inquiry is a way of practising a philosophical stance of respect, curiosity, polyphony and social meaning making. More than the methods used, it is the intentions and the assumptions that inform the research process that constitute the collaborative nature of inquiries.
>
> Gehart et al 2007, p.385

Mary and Kenneth Gergen open an invitation to experiment with relational space:

> Alternative ethnographers break away from the conventions of social science inscription to experiment with polyvocality, poetry, pastiche, performance, and more. These experiments open new territories of expression; they also offer new spaces of relationship. They take different stances toward readers, describing them in new ways, calling into being alternative possibilities for going on together.
>
> Gergen & Gergen 2002, p.14

In this suggestion, Mary and Kenneth Gergen are suggesting a means of doing research more akin to the improvisational response to not- knowing (Anderson & Goolishian 1992; Anderson 1997) that we come up with in the doing of systemic practice. Shotter and Katz describe the interactions between participants involved in any human interaction, be it professional practice or research, as involving spontaneous attempts at responding and coordinating with another (Shotter & Katz 1998). This attention to improvisational and relational know-how casts ethical doubt on a stance of technological 'knowledge' and the rolling out of predictable practice or research method. All research constitutes an intervention in the lives of the researcher, the research participants and the audiences or witnesses to this research. Each act of inquiry invites, mindfully or otherwise, the possibility of an implicative force which changes lives.

Summary

In this opening chapter, I hope to have shown how much systemic practice research has in common with our cousins in qualitative inquiry. This familial culture provides an existing and sympathetic *theorethical* context for the systemic practice communities to develop ways of inquiring into our practice which are coherent with systemic values, ethics and theory. By engaging in a collaborative and reflexive process of inquiry with relational ethics to guide our movements in inner and outer conversation, we are inviting change for ourselves and others and creating new relational spaces and know-how through which we can inquire into the movements of practice/research relationships.

Qualitative inquiry has much to support a systemic model of practice research but systemic inquiry also has many useful offerings to bring to qualitative inquiry including:

- a rich seam of theories and stories about relational practice
- a critical history of diverse methods of inquiry and the place of the inquirer in a system
- a critique of power and culture in relationships
- in-depth studies of reflexivity in relationships
- access to many styles of inquiry
- attention to relational ethics

Systemic inquiry is already an integral part of social constructionist systemic practice in therapy, organisational consultancy, education, leadership and community work. It informs and shapes the activities of a reflexive research process which comfortably overlap with key features of qualitative inquiry. Systemic Inquiry finds an ethical, theoretical and practical home in the playing fields of Qualitative Inquiry.

References

Amundson, Jon; Stewart, Kenneth & Valentine, LaNae (1993). Temptations of Power and Certainty. *Journal of Marital & Family Therapy,* 19, 2, 111–123.

Andersen, Tom (1987). The Reflective team: dialogue and meta-dialogue in clinical work. *Family Process*, 26, 4, 415 – 427.

Anderson, Harlene (1997). *Conversation, Language and Possibilities: A Postmodern Approach to Therapy.* New York, NY: Basic Books.

Anderson, Harlene & Gehart, Diane (2007). *Collaborative Therapy: Relationships and Conversations that make A Difference.* London: Routledge.

Anderson, Harlene & Goolishian, Harold (1988). Human Systems as Linguistic Systems: Preliminary and evolving ideas about the implications for clinical theory. *Family Process,* 27, 4, 371-393.

Anderson, Harlene & Goolishian, Harold (1992). The client is the expert: a not- knowing approach to therapy. In Sheila McNamee & Kenneth Gergen (Eds.), *Therapy as Social Construction.* London: Sage.

Anderson, Harlene & Jensen, Per (2007). *Innovations in the Reflecting Process*. London: Karnac.

Bateson, Gregory (1972). *Steps to an Ecology of Mind.* London: Paladin.

Bateson, Gregory (1979). *Mind and Nature.* New York, NY: E.P. Dutton.

Bochner, Arthur P. (2000). Criteria Against Ourselves. *Qualitative Inquiry,* 6, 2, 266-272.

Boscolo, Luigi; Cecchin, Gianfranco; Hoffman, Lynn & Penn, Peggy (1987). *Milan Systemic Family Therapy: Conversations in Theory and Practice.* New York, NY: Basic Books.

Burnham, John (2011 [1992)]. Approach, Method, Technique: Making Distinctions and Creating Connections. *Human Systems: Journal of Systemic Consultation and Management,* 3, 1, 3-26.

Burnham, John (1993). Systemic Supervision: The evolution of reflexivity in the context of the supervisory relationship. *Human Systems Journal of Systemic Consultation and Management,* 4, 3-4,.349-381.

Burnham, John (2005). Relational reflexivity: a tool for socially constructing therapeutic relationships In Flaskas, C. et al. *The space between: experience, context and process in the therapeutic relationship.* London: Karnac

Burnham, John (2011). Developments in Social GRRAAACCEEESS: Visible and Invisible, Voiced and Unvoiced. In Britt Krause (ed.), *Mutual Perspectives: Culture & Reflexivity in Systemic Psychotherapy*. London: Karnac Books.

Burnham, John & Harris, Queenie (1996). Emerging Ethnicity: A Tale of Three Cultures. In *Meeting the Needs of Ethnic Minority Children. A Handbook for Professionals*. Ed. Dwivedi, Kedar N. London: Jessica Kingsley Publishers.

Burr, Vivien (1995). *An Introduction to Social Constructionism*. London:

Routledge.

Cecchin, Gianfranco (1987). Hypothesising, circularity and neutrality revisited: an invitation to curiosity. *Family Process,* 26, 4, 405-413.

Charmaz, Kathy (2008). *Constructing Grounded Theory.* Second Edition. London: Sage Publications.

Clifford, James & Marcus, George E. (Eds.) (1986). *Writing Culture: the poetics and politics of ethnography.* Berkley, CA: University of California Press.

Code, Lorraine (1995). Questions of method in feminist practice. In *Changing Methods: Feminists Transforming Practice.* Eds. Burt, S. & Code, L. Ontario: Broadview.

Combs, Gene & Freedman, Jill (1990). *Symbol, Story, and Ceremony: Using Metaphor in Individual and Family Therapy.* London: W. W. Norton.

Cooperrider, David L. & Srivastva, Suresh (1987). Appreciative Inquiry In Organizational Life. In W. Pasmore & R. Woodman (Eds.), *Research In Organization Change and Development* (Vol. 1, pp.129-169). Greenwich, CT: JAI Press.

Cronen, Vernon E. (2006). Practical Theory and a Naturalistic Account of Inquiry. *Communication Theory,* 11, 1, 14-35. https://doi.org/10.1111/j.1468-2885.2001.tb00231.x

Denzin, Norman K. (2003). *Performance Ethnography : critical pedagogy and the politics of culture.* London: Sage Publications.

Denzin, Norman K. & Lincoln, Yvonna S. (2005). *The SAGE Handbook of Qualitative Research.* 3rd Edition. London: Sage Publications.

Denzin, Norman K. & Lincoln, Yvonna S. (2011*). The SAGE Handbook of Qualitative Research*. 4th Edition. London: Sage Publications.

Ellis, Carolyn (2008). *Revision: Autoethnographic Reflections on Life and Work.* Walnut Creek, CA: Left Coast Press.

Etherington, Kim (2004). *Becoming a Reflexive Researcher: Using Our Selves in Research*. London: Jessica Kingsley Publishers.

Flaskas, Carmel (2002). *Family Therapy Beyond Postmodernism: Practice*

Challenges Theory. London: Routledge.

Flaskas, Carmel; Barry Mason & Perlesz, Amaryll (2004). *The Space Between: Experience, Context and the Process in the Therapeutic Relationship.* London: Karnac.

Flaskas, Carmel; McCarthy, Imelda & Sheehan, Jim (Eds.) (2007). *Hope and Despair in Narrative and Family Therapy: Adversity, Forgiveness and Reconciliation*. London: Routledge.

Foucault, Michel (1980). *language, counter-memory, practice*. Ed. D. Bouchard. Ithaca, NY: Cornell University Press.

Gehart, Diane; Tarragona, Margarita & Bava, Saliha (2007). A Collaborative Approach to Research and Inquiry. In Anderson, H. & Gehart, D. (Eds.), *Collaborative Therapy: Relationships and Conversations that make A Difference*. London: Routledge.

Gergen, Kenneth J. & Gergen, Mary (2002). Ethnography as Relationship. In Bochner, Art and Ellis, Carolyn Eds. (2002). *Ethnographically Speaking. Autoethnography, Literature, and Aesthetics*. Walnut Creek, CA: AltaMira Press.

Goldner, Virginia; Penn, Peggy; Scheinberg, Marcia & Walker, Gillian (1990). Love and Violence: Gender Paradoxes in Volatile Attachments. *Family Process*, 29, 4, 343–364.

Gregg, Godfrey (2010). *Keeping and crossing boundaries: Negotiating identities in qualitative research.* Paper presented on 29th May 2011 at 6th International Congress of Qualitative Inquiry 2011, University of Illinois.

Hoffman, Lynn (1993). *Exchanging Voices: Collaborative Approach to Family Therapy.* London: Karnac.

Keeney, Bradford P. (1990). Improvisational therapy: Evolving one's own clinical style. *Contemporary Family Therapy* 12, 4, 271-277.

Lang, Peter W., Little, Martin & Cronen, Vernon (1990). The systemic professional domains of action and the question of neutrality. *Human Systems: Journal of Systemic Consultation & Management*, 1, 1, 39-55.

Lather, Patti (1994). *Getting Smart: Feminist Research and Pedagogy within/ in the Postmodern*. London Routledge.

Lather, Patti (2007). *Getting Lost: Feminist Efforts Towards a Double(d). Science*. New York, NY: State University of New York Press.

Lather, Patti & Smithies, Christine S. (1997). *Troubling the Angels: Women Living with HIV/AIDS. New* York, NY: Perseus.

Law, John (2007). *After Method: Mess in Social Science Research.* Abingdon: Routledge.

Leppington, Rozanne (2011[1991]). *From Constructivism to Social Constructionism and Doing Critical Therapy. Human Systems: Journal of Systemic Consultation and Management.* 2, 2, 217-31.

Lincoln, Yvonna S. & Denzin, Norman K. (2005). The Eighth and Ninth Moments – Qualitative Research in/and the Fractured Future. In *SAGE Handbook of Qualitative Research*. 3rd Edition. London: Sage.

Marcus George E. (2007). Ethnography two decades after writing culture: from the experimental to the baroque. *Anthropological Quarterly*, 80, 4, 1127-1145.

Markovic (then Radovanovic), Desa (1993). Knowing Systemic Rules: From Stages of Disorder to Second Order Towards Positive Delinquency. *Human Systems: Journal of Systemic Consultation and Management,* 4, 3, 235- 258.

Mason, Barry (2005). Relational risk-taking and the therapeutic relationship. In: Flaskas, C. et al. (Eds.) *The space between: experience, context and process in the therapeutic relationship.* London: Karnac.

Maturana, Humberto & Varela, Francisco (1980), Autopoiesis and Cognition: The Realization of the Living, Boston. *Studies in the Philosophy of Science*, 42 (Dordrecht: D. Reidel).

Maturana, Humberto & Varela, Francisco (1987). *The tree of knowledge. Biological basis of human understanding.* London: Shambhala.

Maturana, Humberto (1988). Reality: The search for objectivity or the quest for a compelling argument. *The Irish Journal of Psychology,* 9, 1, 25-82.

McCarthy, Imelda Colgan & Byrne, Nollaig O'Reilly (1988). 'Mistaken-Love:

Conversations on the problem of incest in an Irish context'. *Family Process*, 27, 181–199.

McNamee, Sheila (1994). [Draft] Research as Relationally Situated Activity: Ethical Implications. *Journal of Feminist Family Therapy*, 6, 3, 69-83.

McNamee, Sheila (2004). Promiscuity in the practice of family therapy. *Journal of Family Therapy*, 26, 3, 224–244.

O'Hanlon, Bill and Bertolino, Bob (1998). *Even from a Broken Web: Brief, Respectful Solution-oriented Therapy for Sexual Abuse and Trauma.* Chichester: John Wiley.

Oliver, Christine (1996). Systemic Eloquence. *Human Systems: the Journal of Systemic Consultation and management*, 7, 247-264.

Parker, Ian (2005). *Qualitative Psychology: Introducing Radical Research.* Buckingham: Open University Press.

Pearce, W. Barnett (1989). *Communication and the human condition.* Carbondale, IL: Illinois University Press.

Pearce, W. Barnett & Walters, Kimberly A., (1996). *Research Methods: A Systemic Communications Approach.* Draft. Pearce Walters Inc. Pearce Associates.

Penn, Peggy (1985). Feed forward: future questions, future maps. *Family Process,* 24, 3, 299-310.

Quiros, Laura (2010). *Keeping and crossing boundaries: Negotiating identities in qualitative research.* Paper presented on 29th May 2011 at 6th International Congress of Qualitative Inquiry 2011. University of Illinois.

Reynolds, Vikki (2010). Doing Justice: A Witnessing Stance in Therapeutic Work Alongside Survivors of Torture and Political Violence , in J. Raskin, S. Bridges, & R. Neimeyer (Eds.), Studies in meaning 4: Constructivist perspectives on theory, practice, and social justice. New York, NY: Pace University Press.

Reynolds, Vikki (2013). "Leaning in" as imperfect allies in community work. Narrative and Conflict: Explorations in theory and practice, 1, 1,

53-75.

Richardson, Laurel (1994). Writing: A Method of Inquiry. In Denzin, Norman K. and Lincoln, Yvonna S. (Eds.),*The SAGE Handbook of Qualitative Research*. London: Sage Publications.

Richardson, Laurel (1997). *Fields of Play: Constructing an Academic Life.* New Brunswick: NJ: Rutgers University Press.

Rober, Peter (2005). The Therapist's Self in Dialogical Family Therapy: Some Ideas About Not-Knowing and the Therapist's Inner Conversation. *Family Process,* 44, 4, .477–495.

Roberts, Janine (2005). Transparency and Self-Disclosure in Family Therapy: Dangers and Possibilities. *Family Process*, 44, 1,.45–63.

St Pierre, Elizabeth (2010). Presentation. International Congress of Qualitative Inquiry, University of Illinois. May 2010.

Seikkula, Jaakko (2002). Monologue is the crisis - dialogue becomes the aim of therapy. *Journal of Marital and Family Therapy,* 28, 3, 283-284.

Seikkula, Jaakko & Arnkil, Tom Erik (2006). *Dialogical meetings in social networks.* London: Karnac.

Selvini Palazzoli, Mara; Boscolo, Luigi; Cecchin, Gianfranco & Prata, Giulianna (1980). Hypothesising – circularity – neutrality: Three guidelines for the conductor of the session. *Family Process,* 19, 1, 3-12.

Sexton, Thomas L. & Whiston, Susan C. (1994). The Status of the Counseling Relationship: An Empirical Review, Theoretical Implications, and Research Directions. *The Counseling Psychologist*, 22, 1, 6-78.

de Shazer, Steve (1985). *Keys to solution in brief therapy.* New York, NY: W.W. Norton.

de Shazer, Steve (1988). *Clues: Investigating Solutions in Brief Therapy.* New York: W.W. Norton.

Shotter, John (2005). *The Short Book of 'Withness'-Thinking.* London: KCCF Pre-Book.

Shotter, John (2007). Not to forget Tom Andersen's way of being Tom Andersen: the importance of what 'just happens' to us. *Human*

Systems: Journal of Systemic Consultation and Management, 18, 15-28.

Shotter, John (2011). *Getting It: With-ness Thinking and the Dialogical…. In Practice.* New York, NY: The Hampton Press Communication Series.

Shotter , John & Katz, Arlene (1998). 'Living moments' in dialogical exchanges. *Human Systems: Journal of Systemic Consultation and Management,* 9, 2, 81-93.

Simon, Gail (1998). Incitement to Riot? Individual Identity and Group Member- ship: Some Reflections on the Politics of a Post-Modernist Therapy. *Human Systems Journal of Systemic Consultation and Management,* 9, 1, 33-50.

Simon, Gail (2010). Self Supervision, Surveillance and Transgression. *Journal of Family Therapy*, 32, 3, 308–325.

Simon, Gail (2012). Praction Research: A Model of Systemic Inquiry. *Human Systems Journal of Systemic Consultation and Management.* 23, 1, 103-124.

Simon, Gail (2013). Relational Ethnography: Writing and Reading in and about Research Relationships. *Forum Qualitative Sozialforschung / Forum: Qualitative Social Research*, North America, 2012.

Smith, Jonathan; Flowers, Paul & Larkin, Michael (2009). *Interpretive Phenomenological Analysis.* London: Sage Publications.

Tomm, Karl (1987a). Interventive Interviewing: Part I. Strategizing as fourth guideline for the therapist. *Family Process*, 26, 1, 3-13.

Tomm, Karl (1987b). Interventive Interviewing: Part II. Reflexive Questioning as a Means to Enable Self Healing. *Family Process,* 26, 2, 153-183.

Tomm, Karl (1987c). Interventive Interviewing: Part III. Intending to Ask Lineal, Circular, Reflexive or Strategic Questions? *Family Process,* 27, 1, 1-15.

Tootell, Andrew (2004). Decentring research practice. *The International Journal of Narrative Therapy and Community Work,* No.3. Adelaide: Dulwich Centre Publications.

Vedeler, Anne Hedvig (2010). *Six Tales From My Practice on the Theme of*

Resonance. Paper presented at the Systemic Cafe, Farnhill, Yorkshire, UK, 25th June 2010.

Visweswaran, Kamala (1994). *Fictions of Feminist Ethnography.* University of Minnesota Press.

White, Cheryl & Denborough, David (2005). *A Community of Ideas: Behind the Scenes.* Adelaide: Dulwich Centre Publications.

White, Michael (1988). The process of questioning: A therapy of literary merit? *Dulwich Centre Newsletter*, Winter 1988, 8-14.

White, Michael & Epston, David (1990). *Narrative Means to Therapeutic Ends.* New York: Norton.

White, Michael (1992). *Deconstruction and therapy. In Experience, contradiction, narrative, & imagination: Selected papers of David Epston and Michael White, 1989-1991.* Adelaide, Australia: Dulwich Centre Publications.

Woolfitt, Robin (2005). *Conversation Analysis and Discourse Analysis. A Comparative and Critical Introduction.* London: Sage Publications.

NINE

Praction Research: A Model of Systemic Inquiry

> A sentence, a luminous argument, a compelling paper, a personal incident—any of these can create a breach between what we practised previously and what we can no longer practice, what we believed about the world and what we can no longer hold onto.
>
> Denzin & Lincoln, 2005, p.1116

Introduction

In teaching research to systemic practitioners, I have found there is a common assumption that they will need to sideline systemic theory and learn a new way of doing, being and speaking in order to conduct an inquiry. This can be deskilling for experienced practitioners and unnecessary given systemic therapy's strong relationship with reflexive inquiry. I have found it useful for my own research and for teaching purposes to develop a systemic description of a model of systemic practice and systemic inquiry which is coherent with collaborative-dialogical-social constructionist-systemic practice.

In this paper, I start by describing the interconnections in systemic methodology between ideological influences, theoretical propositions and the doing of systemic practice. I reorganise these levels of context and rename them *spheres of influence* and then I propose a model for therapy and research which reflects collaborative-dialogical-social constructionist-systemic practice. By drawing attention to *local reflexivity* and *global reflexivity,* the paper highlights the connections between practice activities and activism. The reflexive activities of listening out for and acting with the novel and the ethical take systemic practice into continual paradigmatic movement which make for transformation within and of the model. This has implications for the re-describability of systemic practice and systemic research.

This model lends itself to a form of action research for reflexive practice for which I have created the *portmanteau* term ***Praction Research***. If one thinks of Practice Research as reflection in, on and as *activity,* and Action Research, as it was originally intended (Freire 1972, Parker 2005), as a form of *activism*, then in the doing of therapy, supervision, training, writing *or research* I see both as having a part to play in systemic practitioner-research. The term ***Praction Research*** helps me stay mindful of the relationships between practice and research and between activity and activism. It invites critical, relational reflexivity to sustain respectful and irreverent movement across and between ideology, theory and practice. As a systemic practitioner working in the fields of teaching, research, writing, supervision and therapy, I look for a 'pink thread' which connects not only different areas of systemic practice but also the values and aspirations, the philosophical and the practical. I use the colour pink as it is a political colour for me. It helps me stay aware of the place and influence of power and injustice in a wider socio-political world, how this may influence what happens in systemic practice relationships and how systemic practice can play a part in challenging unjust practices of power 'out there'.

Reflexive Collaboration in Systemic Inquiry

I am thinking of systemic inquiry as an activity in which the practitioner and their conversational partners move between self and relational reflexivity in attempts to work out how to usefully go on in a process of inquiry (Burnham 1993, 2005). Contemporary systemic practice includes the relational activities of therapy, supervision, training, professional and organisational consultancy, coaching, leadership, writing and research which draw on the rich history of developing ways of inquiring into relationships between people, between people and their stories (Andersen 1987, Anderson and Goolishian 1987, 1992; Burnham 1992, 2011; Cecchin 1987; Selvini et al 1980; Penn 1985; de Shazer 1985, Tomm 1987, 1988; White & Epston 1990). Systemic inquiry has moved with a postmodern critique of professional narratives which objectify or generalise or which try to construct a static knowledge base. Instead, many systemic practitioners have found ethical coherence in embracing a reflexive and transparent acknowledgement of one's own prejudices. This has led to a stronger foregrounding of reflexivity and ethics-led practice which privileges the unique learning arising out of each piece of conversation rather than trying to create a scientifically sound method. The move to co-creating collaborative, dialogical relationships with our conversational partners is also characterised by the systemic practitioner's attention to the power of narratives and to narratives of power and how they may get played out in the working relationship and beyond.

Reflexive Practice and Reflexive Research

There has been some discussion as to whether all reflexive practice, all systemic inquiry is a form of research (Hosking & McNamee 2012, McNamee 2004, 2000, Oliver 2005, Steier 1991, Stronach 2007, Tootal 2004). Using the following example from my therapy practice, I offer a distinction between what I consider to be reflexive practice and reflexive research.

> *In a session with Susan, I read aloud what she has written and then we talk about it. Mostly she listens and thinks while I respond with wondering aloud. Then we reflect on my wonderings. This is the format she prefers. I am comfortable with that. It is something we have learned to do well together. But on this occasion I do something different. I find myself sharing some of my emerging thoughts about how I see Susan as a writer and suggest she might write an autobiography.*
>
> *After the session I write an account of our conversation for me to*

reflect on. After a while of writing with my inner dialogue, the exercise feels too solitary. I send Susan these reflections and ask for her thoughts about the conversations at the time and since. She writes back with her responses and tells me that she enjoys this written exchange and finds it useful. The next time we meet, Susan comments that she hasn't realised how much I notice and wonder about how she feels. She wants to hear more of what I notice and wonder about. So now I find ways of sharing my noticings and wonderings with her. I notice that our talking style is changing. We seem to be speaking more like we do when we write to each other.

At a later date, I discuss with Susan my hope that we might write about aspects of our work together for the benefit of other practitioners and the people with whom they work. Susan is keen for me to include and co-edit our conversations in a publishable paper and she writes something specially for it. She finds the writing we do together and separately interesting and it extends our therapeutic conversations which in turn add to the content of the paper for publication and so on.

We have created a full circle in the activities of our therapy conversation:

- she writes and hands me what she has written to read, to respond and reflect on
- now I hand her my writing and ask her to read it, to respond and reflect on

But there is a third reflexive movement which both embraces us and extends beyond us:

- we talk and write interchangeably *about* these exchanges and their *impact on* our conversations, on conversations with others and anticipate conversations with others we haven't yet had.

Am I describing the reflexive practice of systemic therapy? I think so: a collaborative way of being in relation to someone, an interest in the relationship between inner and outer dialogue, acting with a mindfulness about stories which open up possibilities, and stories which close them down and the use of reflexivity to learn and change in response to feedback from the other in working out how to go on with someone or something.

But is this practice research? I think of practice 'research' as a public sharing of private conversations. *It becomes practice research when introducing another level of relational context with the reader* in which the writer(s) develops a richly transparent, reflexive account of something with and for others, when the writer(s) enters into conversations with other writers, practitioners and readers. In this example, I am describing more than a technique and the consequences of its application. In the presentation of my reflexive writing in a paper for publication, I can render visible to the reader i) my own influence in the relational process, ii) the mutuality of influence between the client and myself, iii) how inner and outer conversations shape my learning and practice, iv) how I might share learning from practice with colleagues in a manner which is coherent with my practice. I am also treating writing research as an act of communication with another which requires an anticipatory appreciation of the reader. I draw on values and practices from collaborative, dialogical and reflexive thinking to guide me in how I might take the reader of this research into account in the writing of it (Ellis 2004, Gergen 2009). Reflexive research is then not only the act of being reflexively involved in practice relationships: it must also involve a reflexive and transparent approach to the selection and presentation of material, a reflexive commentary and a relational approach to the style of communicating about it - as opposed to reporting on it as if from a 'without' position (Shotter 2010).

Reflexivity as a Relational Activity

Much has been written about reflexivity and its uses in the area of qualitative research (Finlay & Gough 2003, Etherington 2004, Ellis 2004). The distinctions systemic therapists have made between self-reflexivity and relational reflexivity (Burnham 1992, 1993, 2005, 2011; Hedges 2010) have helped practitioners be sensitive to the influence of narratives in relationships and how we coordinate with others in ways which students, supervisees and people coming for therapy find useful.

The term 'self-reflexivity' can be confusing and misleading in a systemic world which acknowledges the presence of multiple, competing narratives or voices (Penn & Frankfurt 2004, White 1990), which pays attention to the polyvocality in inner dialogue (Bakhtin 1981, Pare 2006, Vygotsky 1986), which borrows from postmodern notions of many, fragmented, partial selves (Gergen 2008). I propose that *all reflexivity is relational.* The constructivist notion of 'a thought' isolates the thing from the interactivity which creates it. Social Constructionism reframes 'thought' as a product of an interactional relational context (Leppington 1991, 2011). Systemic Social Constructionism can appreciate that inner dialogue is not 'thought' so much as conversation between interacting voices. The term 'voice' draws attention to the connection between articulation and that which is articulated. Inner dialogue – an activity commonly described as 'thinking' - is not merely a biological or cognitive process. Bakhtin's idea of striving to 'find one's own voice' from within a polyvocal mix (Bakhtin 1986 p239) is quite an essentialist idea and could be extended to recognise a co-constructionist approach to contextually emergent 'selves'. I find it useful to treat inner dialogue as an exchange of views which are attached to voices with their own fixed (monological) or fluidly responsive (dialogical) character and as a series of relational responses between the voices influenced by the context they are acting in to and out of.

The difference in the tone accompanying an utterance could involve, for example, degrees of passion, a sense of danger, a certain sort of humour, impatience, fear, guesswork, conviction, knowledge of specialist language etc. It might sound like a chaotic interaction. But with a relational reflexive inquiry systemic practitioners work with the textual fabric of our lives. We have developed some kind of skills to manage the coordination of these voices and operate separate volume controls for each of the voices. Sometimes, when teaching, I notice people staring into space. For a moment I wonder if their concentration is drifting away from the subject. But it can *only* drift. Dialogical teaching invites the student into a reflexive space which requires much *listening* (Hibel & Polanco 2010, Penn 2009). In hearing a comment, they are reminded of something by another voice. By really listening – sometimes we call this concentrating – they are engaging with curiosity, rigour and reflexivity i) to witness how they are being moved by the different voices and why and with what possible consequences and ii) to listen out for what Michael White describes as other voices not yet heard but also present (White 1992).

Local and Global Reflexivity

Several things lead me to describe systemic research as a form of practice-based action research motivated by the desire to create political and social change or movement in communities:

i) the inevitability of sound and movement (and sound *as* relational movement) in human interaction
ii) the perpetual reflexivity in systemic practice or research driven by the preoccupation with ethics-led practice and an openness to being moved by the novel
iii) a transparently stated recognition that some discourses dominate, discredit and silence others
iv) a mindfulness that some voices carry more weight and meet the needs of the advantaged rather than the disadvantaged.

> Critical researchers start from an ethical principle and do research designed to emancipate people from patterns of social relations prejudged to be oppressive, to expose patterns of exploitation, or to subvert structures of power that allow some people to be dominated by others.
>
> Pearce and Walters 1996 p10

Freire always intended action research as a form of activism (Freire 1972). Parker suggests a model of Radical Action Research which, he says, "is not a method as such; rather it is *the transformation of research into a prefigurative political practice*" (Parker 2005 p123). Kenneth Gergen has said how important it is to state one's political aims clearly when doing research (Gergen 2007). Patti Lather cites the philosophy of Audrey Lorde's 1984 work "The Master's Tools Will Never Dismantle The Master's House." as an example of a need for research methodologies to use 'sub-altern ways of knowing' and which step outside of and challenge dominant stories of knowledge and ways of knowing (Lather 1994 p36). Narrative Therapy has made an explicit commitment to challenge oppressive discourses and practices and to recognise injustice from the past and in the present and has built practice methods to support this commitment (White 1988, 1990, 1992).

These ideas sit very comfortably with me as a systemic practitioner. I have always thought of systemic practice as an opportunity for people to cha(lle)nge the narratives and power structures in their lives (Simon 1998, 2010). So many of the people I have met through work at The Pink Practice, a systemic therapy service in London working with the lesbian, gay, bisexual and genderqueer communities, have arrived in therapy with narratives which have been influenced by populist, self-deprecating ideas about themselves and the communities they belong to. To treat this as 'internalised homophobia' further individualises a problem caused by prejudice on a wider socio-political scale. When speaking with individuals, couples and families in The Pink Practice, my colleagues and I have been aware that we are speaking with community members. 'Clients' and 'supervisees' are members of larger communities and they take the language of systemic practice back into those communities. This is another level of systemic intervention and one which I actively subscribe to if it encourages a reflexive curiosity from community members about which narratives they are subscribing to and for whom those narratives are working and what the alternatives might be.

I want to introduce the idea of *local reflexivity* and *global reflexivity* to systemic practice and practice research. Psycho-/socio-therapists, social workers, counsellors and educators might have a primary agenda which may turn on *local reflexivity* – meaning, the focus of their work may be on a localised problem - but their work is influenced by and influencing of a critique of the broader social and political environment in which the people they work with live. This adds a dimension of *global reflexivity*.

With *local reflexivity*, the practitioner is moving

- → between the voices of their inner dialogue
- → with their inner dialogue into outer dialogue
- → in response to others and the polyvocality in outer conversation
- → with emergent ideas and actions within the moment
- → in response to reflections on the moment in the moment
- → with a sensitivity to the context one is acting into and out of

With *global reflexivity*, movement occurs

- → in reflecting on the reflections on, in and after the moment
- → when we find something new to say about movement in practice
- → in finding ways of describing this movement to others
- → when using learning from practice to cha(lle)nge socio-economic power structures
- → when inquiring into what counts as professional practice
- → when addressing an audience with a mindfulness about relational communication choices and possible consequences of those choices for self and others
- → when there is a stretching of the boundary of what counts as knowledge or knowing

By making the connections between local and global reflexivity, we are staying alert to the limits, possibilities and responsibilities in co-creating activities which have repercussions for the people with whom we are immediately working and the various communities in which we all live.

The Quest for Ethics-led Practice and the use of the Novel

Collaborative-dialogical-social constructionist-systemic practice involves reflexive activities which encourage transformation at *every* level of context through its attention to the novel, to the specific needs in that moment. This has huge implications for learning, teaching and researching *practice.*

Kuhn observed that science appeared to progress through the *elimination* of significant anomalies and unsolved puzzles, that problem solving would lead to a scientific revolution - a paradigm shift (Kuhn 1962). This contrasts with the valuing and *utilisation* in systemic therapy of exceptions (De Shazer 1991), unique outcomes (White & Epston 1990), contradictions (Bateson 1972, Cecchin et al 1993, Oliver 1996, Pearce 1989, White & Epston 1992), differences (Burnham et al 2008, White & Epston 1992), the unexpected, the novel - things that Kuhn referred to as *anomalies.*

In a post-paradigmatic culture (Lather 1994), the emphasis is perhaps on *evolution* over revolution (Denzin 2000), on evolving structures, evolving discourses, evolving activities, going with ontological drift (Law 2007, Lather 2007). The 'anomaly' in systemic therapy is not so much connected with the matter of success or failure of the profession or professional discourse, as Kuhn might have suggested, so much as with aesthetics. I am using the term aesthetics here to encompass ethics. I understand aesthetic (Lang et al 1990), in a systemic context, as being less concerned with personal perception so much as the shared doing of a relationship in which power is negotiated, held in critical abeyance and where ways of seeing shift from second to second. Change is driven less by a need to *find out* anything but by a need for moral coherence, respect and a critique of power against a backdrop of political and social shifts.

By addressing 'novel' data during and as part of the process, by reflexively questioning one's ideological attachments and their influence on what is noticed and acted on, one is questioning each paradigm at every turn. In focusing on our attachment to unspoken, tacit assumptions, practices and how to go on with people over truth-out-there, systemic therapy becomes a *fast science* changing its model by the moment in the doing of the activities.

Kuhn's suggestion that an anomaly appears only against the background provided by its paradigm makes me wonder *how we notice the unexpected* against a backdrop of theory which is ordered so as to show up some things but not others. In effect, it is the expectation of order, the search for pattern which allows us to spot an exception, a variation. The normative production of order can provide a contrasting backdrop for the noticing of difference (Bateson 1978).

This noticing is not possible without a lively epistemological reflexivity: What am I / are we noticing? How do I (*or* we) know what I am (*or* we are) noticing? What else might I (*or* we) not be noticing? How is what I am (*or* we are) noticing affecting what we focus on and what gets brought forth? Which stories are having a more organising effect on our conversation? How do I or we demonstrate and live respect for the other(s) in this exchange while remaining critically in relation to my /our preferred ideas and beliefs? Perhaps we can also ask how we might extend our curiosity to ensure that in focusing on anomalies, we don't overlook possible useful aspects of stasis and other patterns.

Models of Systemic Practice - Descriptions in Theory for a Moving Practice

I have wondered how to talk about practice, relational practices, without panning out so far as to render the moving relationships between these moving parts meaningless? But I have also found it useful to have available descriptions of systemic practice which transcend and connect a range of different systemic practices.

So to start with, I want to revisit two important diagrammatic models of postmodern systemic practice from 1991 and 1992 and then propose a development on them which I suggest lends itself more to a contemporary model for dialogical systemic practice and systemic research.

All of these *models* (read 'descriptions') place Social Constructionism as the highest ideological level of context. By Social Constructionism, I mean that we live in languages which are much more than an attempt at representation. Language activities and the stories we generate with and for each other shape our realities, help or hinder meaningful connections with others and with our environment. Our awareness that language both reveals and conceals cultural narratives often surfaces through attempts to translate to another person from outside the culture.

Leppington (1991) offered a framework for identifying and critiquing the relationships which connect ideology with practice, exposing the hidden influences of deeply held beliefs, values and choices practitioners make when selecting a particular theoretical orientation and its treatment or teaching methods (Fig. 1). More modernist attempts at describing scientific process have left the highest level of context as Method or perhaps a Theoretical Proposition where the direction of influence is top down only - a form of monological accounting (Shotter 2011). But what has been important to systemic practice is how these models demonstrate reflexivity-in-action between all and any levels of context and constitutes more of a dialogical process.

The inclusion of ideology into a reframing of methodology in postmodern systemic therapy corresponds to a similar development in the social sciences, the arts, literary criticism all of which have engaged with a feminist and post-modern critique of subject-object relations (Butler 1990, Fuss 1991, Lather 1994, Etherington 2004).

I have found it particularly useful when teaching, to use the Leppington diagram to describe different schools of therapy. In revealing hidden ideologies, coherences and incoherences within a theoretical approach, trainees can make more discriminating choices about their relationship

Fig 1 Levels of Context in Systemic Practice

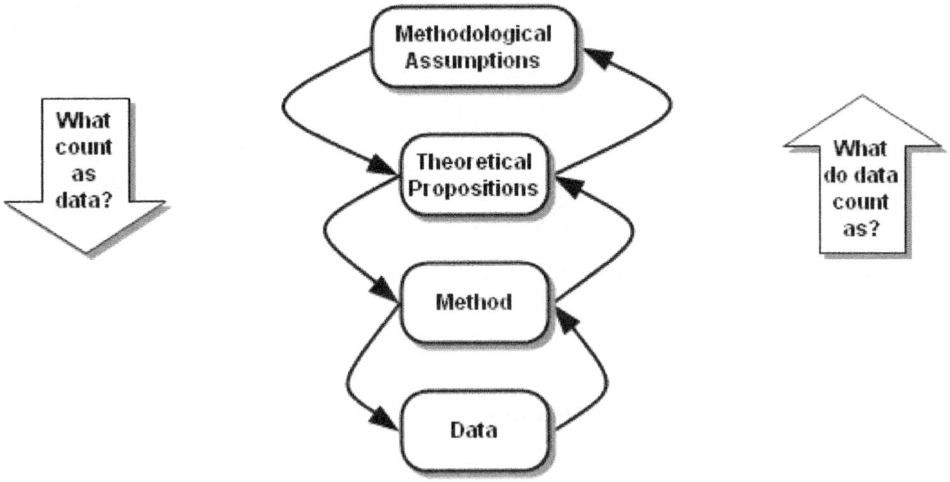

Leppington 1991

with theory, with the professional discourses embodied by institutions and how these play out in practice relationships. For example, therapies which teach normative ideas about sexuality may be influenced by traditional scientific or religious ideologies. Post-structuralist and postmodern writers have suggested that we cannot separate out what we *do* from what we 'find' (Gergen 2008, Leppington 1991, 2011). Whatever we do and how we do those things will ~~determine~~ influence what we *seem* to 'find'. There is no 'finding' outside of particular social, political, cultural contexts and know-how is reflexively constructed in the moment of 'finding'.

Like Leppington, Burnham's model of Approach – Method - Technique (Burnham 1992, 2011) borrows from Co-ordinated Management of Meaning theory (Cronen & Pearce 1985, Pearce 1989) in demonstrating ways of developing coherent accounts of different practices by exploring and linking levels of influencing contexts (Fig. 2). This is particularly useful in training and supervision when practitioners might be concerned with apparent incoherence between different levels of context.

Fig. 2 Approach Method Technique

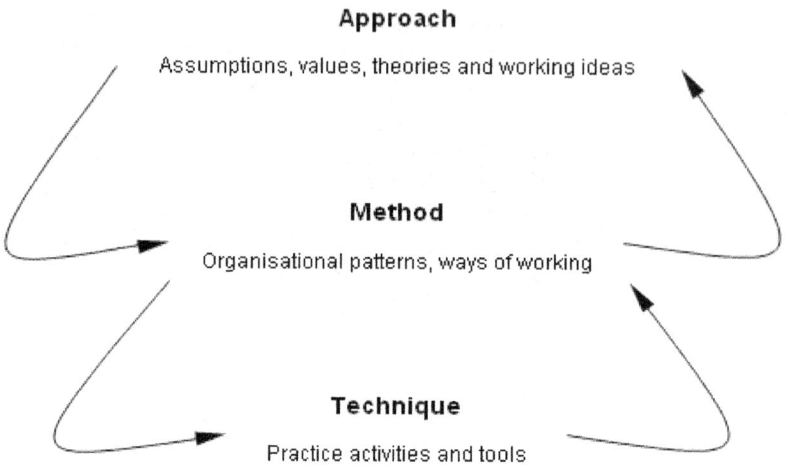

Burnham 1992

Burnham collapses ideology and theoretical propositions into a single level of context of *Approach*. Although the level of *Approach* includes the personal passions and prejudices of the therapist / person, I find this conflation obscures the influence of the therapist and other participants in relation to their leaning towards some theoretical stories over others. The systemic practitioner or researcher moves between these levels of context and has a significant shaping influence on which ideas predominate. On the other hand, Burnham's decision to separate out Method from Techniques can be helpful in generating opportunities to talk about a range of identifiable activities such as different kinds of questions, games or ways of talking which are characteristic of systemic practice.

When working with systemic trainees it has been useful to combine (Fig. 3) the Leppington and Burnham diagrams to utilise Leppington's important distinction between hidden ideology in the methodology and the theory arising out of those ideological assumptions while at the same time including the level of Technique which Leppington deliberately omits.

Fig. 3 Combination of Burnham and Leppington Diagrams

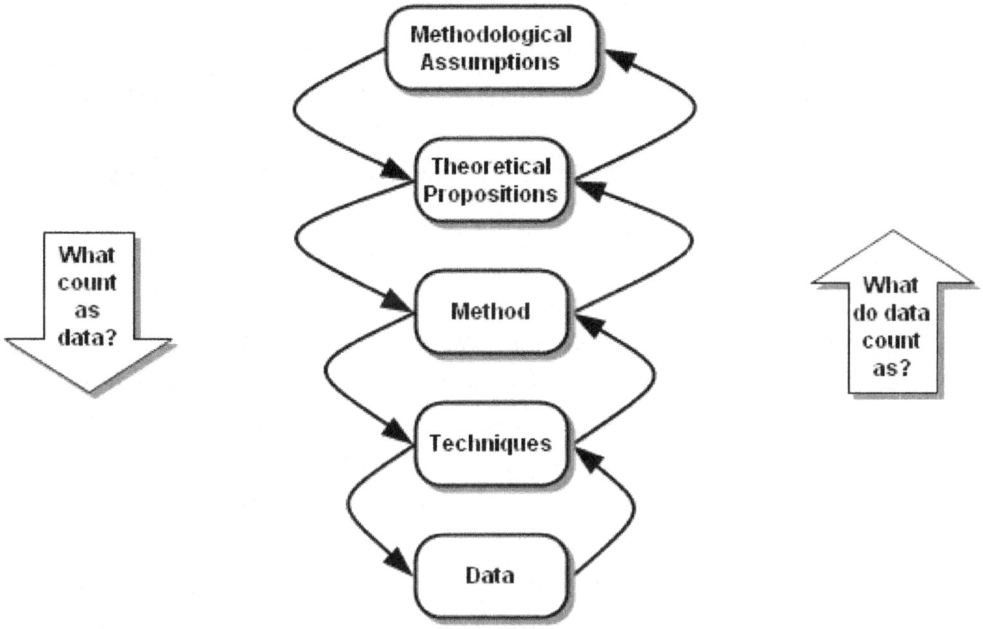

A Model for Practitioner Research

In drawing out a model of systemic inquiry, 'technique' is useful in drawing attention to the use of different systemic questions (Burnham 1992, 1993, 2005, 2011; McCarthy & Byrne 1988; Penn 1985; Selvini et al 1980; de Shazer 1985; Tomm 1987; White 1988). Leppington avoids the use of words like 'technique' because she says it sounds like the sort of thing an expert would use to work on something considered to be separate from him- or herself. Post-Milan systemic therapy situated the therapist as part of the system, not so much working on the system but *with* it and dialogical collaborative therapy has moved the therapist into a more *alongside* position (Andersen 1987, Anderson 1997, Seikkula 2002, Shotter 2011). Leppington suggests the notion of therapeutic tools is incoherent with a collaborative practice of inquiry and suggests we could think rather in terms of discursive practices. She proposes a shift *from knowledge to ethics*

(Leppington 1991, 2011) and foregrounds relational know-how over objective knowledge.

Similarly, I have noticed that the place of ethics in research often appears as an add-on, as a hurdle to be managed. Modernist research discourses encourage an awareness of *ethics in research* (Hudson 1992) but this is different to a more incorporative notion of *ethical research*. I suggest that *ethics in research* is an idea closer to *tools* and that *ethical research* is a *discursive practice*.

The ethics-led practice of collaborative-dialogic working in practice or research is not subject to shaping by a pre-existing method provided by one party in the relationship. Instead it involves continuous and mutual shaping and reshaping between any levels of context through discursive practices, through spontaneous responsivity (Anderson 2007, Shotter 2011).

This un-pre-scribed but attentive and attuned unfolding in relational activity can be connected to radical action research. "There is no method that can be applied in action research. The application of a 'method' in research is always fraught with difficulties, for it presupposes that you can fix what there is that will be of interest to you.... If you are really following through your decision to let your co-researchers determine the issues that are relevant to them, then the 'method' itself is likely to be something that will emerge in the course of the research." (Parker 2005 p125). John Burnham has amended the first line of Ian Parker's to "There is no *pre-scribed* method that can be applied in action research." (Burnham 2010). 'Method' may become apparent after the activity of research has taken place and while describing the research process.

The doing of collaborative- dialogical-social constructionist-systemic therapy, supervision, training or consultation in a *practice* action research model allows for the evolution of the research focus to come about in response to guidance from the participants including that of the practitioner-researchers and their consultants and, in so doing, takes on its own evolving or emergent shape and set of activities.

The absence of a level of 'data' in the Burnham diagram renders the movements and outcomes of the therapeutic relationship less visible than in the Leppington model which, through the inclusion of the level of 'data', shows the reflexive relationships between what we *find* (create with one another) and what we do, theorise and believe. While it may be important to include another sphere of influence (*level of context* in CMM terms) to acknowledge this set of relationships, 'data' is perhaps not such a useful term in co-constructionist systemic therapy. If, within a systemic and dialogic context, we take 'data' to stand for a range of relational activities based on discursive practices this sphere of activity describes 'joint action' (Shotter 2011).

The following model of systemic practice action research (Fig. 4), removes the levels of context representing 'Method', 'Techniques' and 'Data'. Instead they are replaced by a sphere of influence called 'Discursive Activities' which is made up of a systemic anthology of Discursive Practices.

This model maps a picture of reflexive practice and action research in practice. It includes reflexive movement between *spheres of influence* and within each sphere of influence. The meta-contexts of *Collaborative Inquiry* and *Reflexive Inner Dialogue* are an attempt to make present the dialogical self of the practitioner and the relationship between the people in conversation with each other. It is a way of describing dialogue between different voices, heard and not heard. But the major difference between this model and the previous models discussed above, is the removal of 'method' and 'data' in favour of descriptions which situate all discursive activities within an emergent and generative collaboration.

In the realm of 'Discursive Activities', all movements in the practice relationship or research relationship can be understood as discursive practices and as forms of spontaneous responsivity between people (Shotter 2011). This stands in contrast to a notion of static, pre-existing and *individualised* method-led know-how. The realm of Discursive Activities still allows for a systemic practitioner to use 'techniques' but my hope is that they are thought of and treated as discursive practices within a respectful

Fig. 4 Praction Research - A Model of Systemic Inquiry

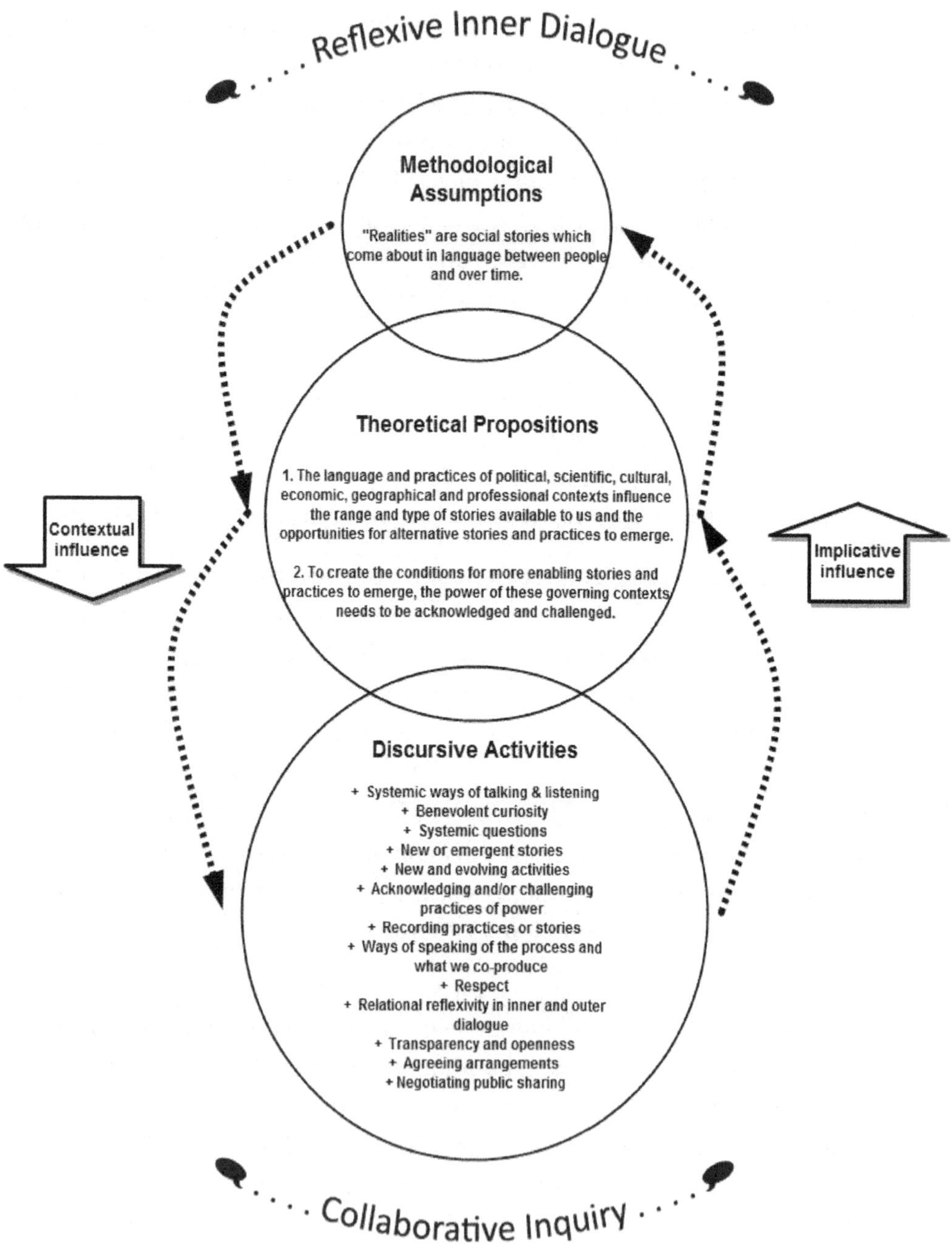

collaboration than as an isolated practice to perfect. But these activities do not 'exist' in this sphere alone. Movement from within these activities, no matter how apparently small or large, can and does act into and out of global and local networks of reflexive influences linking different spheres of influence in a hierarchical or non-hierarchical manner. The dotted lines of reflexive movement indicate ongoing movement between these spheres and, if one can imagine, within each sphere of influence.

Let's return to connect the example of reflexive systemic inquiry I gave at the beginning of this paper with this model of Praction Research.

Systemic Therapy: In my conversation with Susan, we extended the range of our discursive practices to include different reflexive writing processes, to move spontaneously, interchangeably between talk, writing and reflection on this process. And in so doing, we experienced what Shotter might call a "unique, never before encountered, 'first-time' event" (Shotter 2009). I noticed Susan's abilities as a writer, as someone who can communicate well instead of us being organised by a story of individualised difficulty. Ken Gergen (2007) has said "If you change the language you change the activities." The shift in the language created the conditions for us to foreground *abilities* over *struggles*. We found a way of moving our conversation into new forms of 'joint action' (Shotter 2010). By questioning a common therapeutic assumption (a theoretical proposition) that talking is the most useful means through which to communicate with adults in therapy, the 'we' in the dialogue start to invent the rules (meaning, rules-for-now) and so create further opportunities for articulating the forbidden, the silenced, the private into witness-able, respond-able-to accounts. There is a discussion about using this learning with others and writing for others.

Systemic Research: In moving from attempting to generate a retrospective account of what (really) happened in our conversation, I hold the pen at an angle to let the ink run with new and emergent thoughts, responses, knowings, questions. I move through different reflexive stages: i) writing for myself; ii) writing for and within the relationship being described; iii) deciding to share our experiences with others so those others can benefit from our experience; iv) writing for and within my professional community. All involve an honest reflecting process, a sharing of resonances with personal and professional narratives prompting further questions about what counts as ethical practice; stories of how I have been changed by practice relationships, by reading, by inquiry; how my practice relationships have changed in the course of these inquiries. It is this final reflexive stage of sharing stories from systemic practice relationships which transforms systemic practice into practitioner research. In reviewing the conversation and extending it to include others (members of the public, theorists, practitioners and so on), I generate a publicly sharable account which both tries to anticipate the reader and offers a transparent account of content, reflections, reflexive process and ultimately a review of practice and its reporting.

Summary

This model of systemic inquiry describes a reflexive, emergent process which reframes systemic practice and presents it as a framework for systemic research. The critique of power in postmodern systemic practice has led to an interest in a collaborative and dialogical way of being in relationship with people. Systemic practitioners are encouraged to review our subscriptions to hidden ideological influences, theories and values at every turn and how they play out in practice relationships. That can make for many more - sometimes dizzying - 'turns' than one might have found in a modernist methodology.

The shift from 'knowledge' to ethics invites us to shift the emphasis away from 'thoughts', 'tools' and 'ethics-as-add-on' to re-describe our practices as relational, textual activities, as discursive practices. With this in mind, I have found it useful to replace the levels of context representing method, techniques and data, as highlighted in previous models for systemic practice, with one inclusive and reflexive 'sphere of influence': *Discursive Activities*.

References

Andersen, T. (1987). The Reflective team: dialogue and meta-dialogue in clinical work. *Family Process,* 26, 4, 415 – 427.

Anderson, H. & Goolishian, H. (1988). Human Systems as Linguistic Systems: Preliminary and evolving ideas about the implications for clinical theory. *Family Process,* 27, 4, 371-393.

Anderson, H. & Goolishian, H. (1992). The client is the expert: a not-knowing approach to therapy. In S. McNamee and K. Gergen (Eds.) *Therapy as Social Construction.* London: Sage

Anderson, H. (1997). *Conversation, Language and Possibilities: A Postmodern Approach to Therapy.* New York: Basic Books.

Anderson, H. (2007). *Collaborative Therapy: Relationships and Conversations that make A Difference.* London: Routledge.

Bakhtin, M. (1981). *The Dialogic Imagination.* New edition (1982). Austin, TX: University of Texas Press.

Bakhtin, M. (1986). [2007 reprint] *Speech Genres and Other Late Essays.* Trans. V.W. McGee, Eds. C. Emerson & M. Holquist. Austin, TX: University of Texas Press.

Bateson, G. (1972). *Steps to an Ecology of Mind.* London: Paladin.

Bochner, A. & Ellis, C., (Eds.) (2002) *Ethnographically Speaking. Autoethnography, Literature, and Aesthetics.* Oxford: AltaMira Press.

Burnham, J. (1992). Approach, Method, Technique: Making Distinctions and Creating Connections. *Human Systems: Journal of Systemic Consultation and Management,* 3, 1, 3-26.

Burnham, J. (1993). Systemic Supervision: The evolution of reflexivity in the context of the supervisory relationship. *Human Systems: Journal of Systemic Consultation and Management,* 4, 3-4, 349-381.

Burnham, J. (2005). Relational reflexivity: a tool for socially constructing therapeutic relationships In Flaskas, C. et al. *The space between: experience, context and process in the therapeutic relationship.* London: Karnac.

Burnham, J.; Alvis Palma, D. & Whitehouse, L. (2008). Learning as a context for differences and differences as a context for learning. *Journal of Family Therapy*, 30, 4, 529–542.

Burnham, J. (2010). Personal communication.

Butler, J. (1990). *Gender Trouble: Feminism and the Subversion of Identity.* New York, NY: Routledge.

Cecchin, G.(1987). Hypothesising, circularity and neutrality revisited: an invitation to curiosity. *Family Process,* 26, 4, 405-413.

Cecchin, G.; Lane, G. & Ray, W. A. (1993). From strategising to nonintervention: toward irreverence in systemic practice. *Journal of Marital and Family Therapy,* 19, 2, 125-136.

Cronen, V., & Pearce, W. B. (1985). An explanation of how the Milan method works : an invitation to a systemic epistemology and the evolution of family systems. In D. Campbell & R. Draper (eds.) *Applications of systemic family therapy: the Milan approach.* London: Grune & Stratton.

Cronen, V. (2004). Something old, something new: CMM and mass communication. *Human Systems: The Journal of Systemic Consultation & Management.* 15, 3, 167-178.

Denzin, N. K. and Lincoln, Y. S. (2005). The Eighth and Ninth Moments—Qualitative Research in/and the Fractured Future in *The Sage Handbook of Qualitative Research*. London: Sage Publications.

Ellis, C. (2004). *The Ethnographic I: a methodological novel about autoethnography.* Walnut Creek, CA: Alta Mira Press

Ellis, C. (2008). *Revision: Autoethnographic Reflections on Life and Work.* Walnut Creek, CA: Left Coast Press.

Etherington, K. (2004). *Becoming a Reflexive Researcher: Using Our Selves in Research*. Jessica Kingsley Publishers.

Finlay, L. & Gough, B., (Eds.) (2003). *Reflexivity: A Practical Guide for Researchers in Health and Social Sciences.* Wiley-Blackwell.

Freire, P. (1972). *Pedagogy of the Oppressed.* Harmondsworth: Penguin.

Fuss, D. (1991). *Inside/Out: Lesbian Theories, Gay Theories.* London: Routledge.

Gergen, K. J. (2007). *Positive Aging Workshop* with Mary Gergen. Kensington Consultation Centre, London.

Gergen, K. J. & Gergen, M. (2001 ~). *Positive Aging Newsletter.*

Gergen, K. J. (2008). *Constructing Worlds Together: Interpersonal Communication as Relational Process.* Boston, MA: Allyn & Bacon. Penguin Academics.

Gergen, K. J. (2009). *Relational Being: Beyond Self and Community.* Oxford University Press.

Gergen, K. J. & Gergen, M. (2002). Ethnography as Relationship. In Bochner, A. and Ellis, C. Eds. (2002) *Ethnographically Speaking. Autoethnography, Literature, and Aesthetics.* Oxford: AltaMira Press.

Hibel, J. & Polanco, M. (2010). Tuning the Ear: Listening in Narrative Therapy. *Journal of Systemic Therapies,* 29, 1, 51–66.

Hosking, D. M. & McNamee, S. (2012). *Transforming Inquiry: A Relational Constructionist Approach.* London: Routledge.

Kuhn, T. (1962). *The Structure of Scientific Revolutions.* University of Chicago Press.

Lang, P. W., Little, M. & Cronen, V. (1990). The systemic professional domains of action. and the question of neutrality. *Human Systems Journal of Systemic Consultation and Management*, 1, 1, 39-55.

Lather, P. (1994). *Getting Smart: Feminist Research and Pedagogy within/in the Postmodern.* London: Routledge.

Lather, P. (2007). *Getting Lost: Feminist Efforts Towards a Double(d) Science.* State University of New York Press.

Law, J. (2007). *After Method: Mess in Social Science Research.* Abingdon: Routledge.

Leppington, R. (1991). From Constructivism to Social Constructionism and Doing Critical Therapy. *Human Systems Journal of Systemic Consultation and Management*, 2, 2 , 217-31.

Hudson, S. (1999). Ethics for Alternative Paradigms: An Exploration of Options. *Graduate Nursing Research,* October 1999.

McCarthy, I. C. & Byrne, N. O. (1988). 'Mistaken-Love: Conversations on the problem of incest in an Irish context'. *Family Process*, 27, 2, 181–199.

McNamee, S. (1994). Research as Relationally Situated Activity: Ethical Implications. *Journal of Feminist Family Therapy* 6, 3, 69-83.

McNamee, S. (2000). The Social Poetics of Relationally Engaged Research: Research as Conversation. In Deissler, K. & McNamee, S. (Eds.) *Philosophy in Therapy: The Social Poetics of Therapeutic Conversation.* (Phil und Sophie auf der couch: Die soziale poesie therapeutischer gesprache). Heidelberg: Carl-Auer-Systeme Verlag.

McNamee, S. (2004). Promiscuity in the practice of family therapy. *Journal of Family Therapy,* 26, 3, 224-244.

Oliver, C. (1996). Systemic Eloquence. *Human Systems: the Journal of Systemic Consultation and Management,* 7, 4, 247-264.

Oliver, C. (2005). *Reflexive Inquiry: A Framework for Consultancy Practice.* London: Karnac.

Paré, D. A. & Lysack, M. (2006). Exploring inner dialogue in counsellor education. *Canadian Journal of Counselling* 40, 3, 131- 144.

Parker, I. (2005). *Qualitative Psychology: Introducing Radical Research.* Buckingham: Open University Press.

Pearce, W. B. (1989). *Communication and the human condition.* Carbondale, IL: Illinois University Press.

Pearce, W. B. & Walters, K. A., (1996). *Research Methods: A Systemic Communications Approach.* Draft. Pearce Walters Inc.

Pearce Associates (1999, rev. 2004). *Using CMM.* http://www.pearceassociates.com/essays/cmm_seminar.pdf

Penn, P. (1985). Feed forward: future questions, future maps. *Family Process,* 24, 3, 299-310.

Penn, P. & Frankfurt, M. (2004). Creating a Participant Text: Writing,

Multiple Voices, Narrative Multiplicity. *Family Process*, 33, 3, 217–231.

Penn, P. (2009). *Joined Imaginations: Writing and Language in Therapy.* Chagrin Falls, OH: Taos Institute Publications.

Seikkula, J. (2002). Monologue is the crisis - dialogue becomes the aim of therapy. *Journal of Marital and Family Therapy,* 28, 3, 283-284.

Selvini Palazzoli, M., Boscolo, L., Cecchin, G. & Prata, G. (1980). Hypothesising - circularity - neutrality: Three guidelines for the conductor of the session. *Family Process* 19, 3-12.

de Shazer, S. (1985). *Keys to solution in brief therapy.* New York, NY: W.W. Norton.

Shotter, J. & Gergen, K. Eds. (1989). *Texts of Identity.* London: Sage.

Shotter, J. (2009). *Movements of Feeling and Moments of Judgement: Towards an Ontological Social Constructionism.* Constructing Worlds conference, Taos Institute and MacMann Berg, August 2009, Denmark.

Shotter, J. (2010). *Social Construction on the Edge: Withness-Thinking and Embodiment.* Chagrin Falls, OH: Taos Institute Publications.

Shotter, J. (2011). *Getting It: With-ness Thinking and the Dialogical…. In Practice.* New York, NY: Hampton Press Communication Series.

Simon, G. (1998). Incitement to Riot? Individual Identity and Group Membership: Some Reflections on the Politics of a Post-Modernist Therapy. *Human Systems: Journal of Systemic Consultation and Management,* 9, 1, 33 - 49.

Simon, G. (2010). Self Supervision, Surveillance and Transgression. *Journal of Family Therapy,* 32, 3, 308–325.

Steier, F. (1991). *Research and Reflexivity.* London: Sage Publications

Stronach, I., Garratt, D., Pearce, C. and Piper, H. (2007). Reflexivity, The Picturing of Selves, The Forging of Method. *Qualitative Inquiry,* 13, 2, 179-203.

Tomm, K. (1987). Interventive Interviewing: Part I. Strategizing as fourth guideline for the therapist. *Family Process,* 26, 1, 3-13.

Tomm, K. (1987). Interventive Interviewing: Part II. Reflexive questioning as a means to enable self-healing. *Family Process*. 26, 2, 167-183.

Tomm, K. (1988). Interventive Interviewing: Part III. Intending to ask lineal, circular, strategic or reflexive questions? *Family Process*, 27, 1, 1-15.

Tootell, A. (2004). Decentring research practice. *The International Journal of Narrative Therapy and Community Work,* 2004, No. 3, Dulwich Centre Publications.

Vygotsky, L. (1986). *Thought and Language*. 2nd Revised edition. Cambridge, MA: MIT Press.

White, M. (1988). The process of questioning: A therapy of literary merit? *Dulwich Centre Newsletter,* 1988, Winter, 8-14.

White, M. (1990). Story, Knowledge and Power in *Narrative Means to Therapeutic Ends*. White, M. and Epston, D. (Eds.), London: W. W. Norton

White, Michael (1992). Deconstruction and therapy. In *Experience, contradiction, narrative, & imagination: Selected papers of David Epston and Michael White, 1989-1991.* Adelaide, Australia: Dulwich Centre Publications.

White, M. & Epston, D. (1990). *Narrative Means to Therapeutic Ends*. New York, NY: Norton.

White, M. & Epston, D. (1992). *Experience, Contradiction, Narrative & Imagination.* Adelaide, Australia: Dulwich Centre Publications.

TEN

Relational Ethnography

Writing and Reading in Research Relationships

This article introduces relational ethnography as a form of inquiry which emphasizes reflexive dialogical aspects of research relationships. I have found the use of autoethnography inspiring in speaking from within my practice as a therapist and teacher however it has limited my focus on areas of relationality in research relationships. In developing a relational ethnography, I have been able to show how all areas of ethnographic research involve relationality. I draw on systemic and social constructionist theory in understanding relational activities. I offer illustrations of reflexive, dialogical relationships between the voices of inner dialogue, the voices of outer dialogue—and between the two. By making available description of reflexive inner dialogue to readers and participants in research relationships, we increase opportunities for transparent communication and collaboration in those relationships.

First, I write about the relationships between researcher and texts reframing reading as dialogical activity. Afterwards, I explore the emergent relationship between writers and readers as they enter into an anticipatory-responsive dialogue with each other. Finally, I discuss how reflexivity is always relational and informs a relational ethics, and offer some ideas for an ethics of care and for an aesthetics of care as guiding principles for relational ethnography. I have found that teaching relational ethnography has improved students' reflexivity in their research and has enhanced the relational and aesthetic quality of their research writing.

Becoming a Dialogical Reader

Since I started experimenting with how to write in ways which take relationality into account, I have become a different kind of reader. I find I am easily estranged from papers describing dialogical practices which write with a monological tone. I have developed expectations of the writer. I want them to talk to me, with me. I don't want them to talk *at* me or tell me the right way to do something. I want them to invite me into a conversation with them or spark some reflexive movement in my inner dialogue. I have come to expect a coherence between that which the writer is describing and how they are involving me in the presentation of those ideas. I am less driven to work at finding meaning in a paper. I used to think that there are some writings which I need to study more deeply to get to the usefulness of the content but now I am experiencing an ethical discomfort when meeting a contradiction between form and content. The writings which engage me the most are ones where the writer renders her- or himself visible and invites me into their tussle with ideas and practices. In such instances, I start to feel alongside the writer quite quickly.

Writing From Within Inner Dialogue and Outer Talk

As a member of several societal groups who have had professional texts written *about* them by outsiders, I have witnessed how about-ness writing can become concretized into oppressive theory and dominate over a century of psychotherapeutic, psychiatric and legislative practice. I connect this style of writing to relations of power played out in language. John Shotter (1999, 2011) encourages a critique of *about-ness writing* which he refers to as a *monological-retrospective-objective style of writing*. He suggests that writers can write instead from within relationships and alongside the people with whom they are working. He calls this *withness-writing* and describes it as a *dialogical-prospective-relational style of writing* and invites practitioner-writers to get inside the living moment and write into and out of the micro-detail of *spontaneous responsiveness* (Shotter & Katz, 1998).

I have found that writing into and out of intense or even casual conversation has required me to get into a kind of meditative state in which I hear, see, remember and notice all manner of things which I must have noticed at the time but moved on from—until I started to write. In this meditative state, I start to re-feel the atmosphere, hear other voices which I moved away from quickly in order to privilege another. I remember ethical dilemmas I had about my choices or about how I was managing my choice of responses. As I started to experiment with capturing reflexivity (Burnham, 1992, 2005; Etherington, 2004; Hedges, 2010) in inner and outer dialogue, I started to wonder how was I going to capture all the inner talk? Was I going to describe it as conversation or separate strands of thought? How could I lay my inner dialogue—often more cacophony than polyphony—on the page in a way which engaged the reader and did not bore or overwhelm them?

An example from practice

At the end of a supervision group with therapists, I noticed something in my intonation that made me uncomfortable. It kept coming to mind. The next day I tried to write about the episode to see what I could learn.

> *I glance at the clock—last couple of minutes. Jane is looking tired. I wonder, if as a group, we have focused too much on suggesting there may be other things she can do with a couple who are behaving disrespectfully towards her. I wonder if she wants to find a way of ending the work with them. Her wince, when I ask about this, seems to say "I am torn." Perhaps our discussion has been too respectful to the clients and not enough to the therapist. Our time to talk is running out. Perhaps a quick example from my own work life might create another option. I tell the group how I have, on a couple of occasions, spoken directly to couples where I have felt I can no longer tolerate their rudeness. As I repeat what I might have said to the couple at the time, I am surprised and a little alarmed by the sound of real irritation in my voice—as if I am back in the moment of*

directness with the couple. I wonder if the group is hearing this too. I have a flash-over of inner reactions.

......"Did I intend to sound that irritated? I don't think so. So how did that happen?"

......"Maybe I am tired. I thought I felt fine. Am I making good judgments now?"

......"I want to discuss this with someone. When is my next supervision?"

......"It's not an event that is worthy of major worry."

......"Nevertheless, how are the supervisees reacting to how I have just spoken? Is their apparent lack of visual response an indication of their sophistication or disinterest or am I unable to notice them at this very minute while I feel taken aback?"

......"Do I need to do anything else at this ending point in the group?"

I try to qualify what I have just said in a more reflective tone. It has the intention of casting a stitch to end a row neatly but I wonder how I became a little unraveled in that moment.

There is a time sequence and then, at a moment of crisis, many voices spoke in me at once in a timeless, polyphonic moment. As an ethics led practitioner and as an ethics led researcher, I am committed to a reflexive exploration of this inner dialogue and the connections with the outer dialogue. Writing slows things down and renders audible strains of voices I am not otherwise able to hear for long enough in order to make a relationship with. And as I write and listen, I hear further voices still and those vying for the position of moderator. I explore which voices have had most influence on this situation and with whose authority? I am awash in a sea of conversation, of voices and ideas, values and power dynamics. I could just get out the water and put my fingers in my ears, turn towards a modernist monological sounding voice and allow it the most volume. But that wouldn't be ethical. And yet I have to draw the line somewhere and move on—as happened in this episode when the outside structures of time required a response to conclude the session.

Peggy Penn built on Bakhtin's work (2007 [1986]) in making some distinctions between monologue and dialogue. "Unlike the monologue, dialogical conversation is many-voiced. It listens to others and is open, inviting, relative, and endless because it is future-oriented. It awaits an answer" (Penn, 2009, p.33). In this sense, monologue and dialogue are commonly understood as part of a dualism.

I have come to think of monologue *not* as a thing in itself, as if outside of a relational context. It is often difficult to attribute *monological sounding* voices and their narratives to a particular relationship or event but by entering into conversation with the concerns behind the narrative *as if it were a person with an opinion, can* allow for conversation to develop and we find a way of going on in inner or outer conversation Paré and Lysack (2004) use the term "self-enclosed monologues" as if there is a lack of a broader conversational context. I have been considering all utterances as a form of dialogue but with different intentions based on narratives about probable social consequences. I am treating a monologue less as a fixed thing and more as a relational response, subject to change through conversational opportunities.

Anticipating a Dialogical Reader

As part of my attempt to write dialogically, with readers in mind, I started to write "Dear Reader" at the top of each page. In script. In red. I wrote with an increased awareness of readers. But when I added "How're you doing?" I felt more of an inquiring writer who was not only in relation to her subject but to her reader. Sometimes it has worked quite well. But, on one occasion, when I tried to write a more traditional theory paper, I became quite distracted by the listening ear of the imagined academy. My draft readers pointed out that these texts had lost the very thing I wanted to highlight in my research into dialogical practice writing: relationality in writing, live-ness in tone, the sound of talk on the page. Gergen says that "writing is fundamentally an action within a relationship; it is within relationship that writing gains its meaning and significance, and our manner of writing simultaneously invites certain forms of relationship while discouraging or suppressing others" (2008, p.1).

This challenge of writing for readers, feels to me as if it involves more than a matter of technique or form. Social constructionism understands language as the means through which we construct narratives about each other and how relationships work in the world which then influence stories and practices of rights and responsibilities (Burr, 1995). With my ethical Geiger counter, I can feel my levels of comfort and discomfort point me towards writing practices which speak with my readers in a manner which more or less listens out for their responses, imagined and actual. In her critique of colonial research writers, Visweswaran (1994) warns that the subject as reader eventually writes back.

Speaking With Other Writers

Montuori (2005) encourages ways of engaging with literature reviews as a form of live conversation. Literature reviews pose an interesting challenge because they usually form a chapter or a specific section in a book or paper dedicated to a systematic review of an area of practice or research and they have a preordained place—for example, within a regular dissertation structure. Despite, often being quite a dry read, such literary gatherings can be very useful as a place to go for a round-up of connections.

For the writer to share some of his/her reflexive inner dialogue can offer the reader a range of voices - voices attached to particular narratives. Or perhaps narratives to which certain voices are attached? I have extended this dialogical expectation to the literature as well, meaning, I am not simply reporting what other writers say. I have tried to talk with other writers, responding as if in dialogue. Sometimes I have found it useful to introduce other characters in my texts through which I discuss the work of other writers.

For example, I wrote a four act play in which the two characters debated many ethical and technical matters about writing about others and quoted actual writers at each other. I worked at characterization, the sound of talk and pacing to bring it together as one coherent piece. It served as an alternative literature review. Here they are talking about some pros and cons of sharing their inner dialogue with readers.

Excerpt from the play "The Other in the Text"

> *Voice of God:* So what opportunities might you offer me to reveal more of my inner dialogue to others?
>
> *Fellow Writer:* Well, if someone offered you the opportunity to write a book on the story behind the writing of the history of the world, what sort of things would you say? Could it really just remain a chronological, monological narrative or would you share some of the tussles between your different inner voices and the artistic and strategic choices they made?
>
> *Voice of God:* No, no, no—it would ruin the effect for the reader. One God, one story. I might otherwise be tempted to reveal more than I wished.
>
> *Fellow Writer:* How come? Why would you be tempted?
>
> *Voice of God:* Well, suppose it was you reading it, I might be tempted to tell you how I did arrive at my decisions. Because we could talk about it then. So if I was writing with you in mind ...
>
> *Fellow Writer:* "It is not so much how 'I' can use language in itself that matters, as the way in which I *must* take 'you' into account in my use of it." —I'm quoting John Shotter[1]. So there is some fluidity between what inner speech one chooses to keep "for oneself" and the opportunities for actual and imagined audiences. I don't agree with Vygotsky's[2] distinction between talking to oneself and talking to others when he says, "Written speech and inner speech are monologic speech forms. Oral speech is generally dialogic."

Voice of God: Speech, as a word, does have monological associations. I hate listening to speeches. One feels so spoken at and often not particularly entertained.

Fellow Writer: I am trying to write written speech and inner speech in ways which render it dialogical—in that, I know and I say, "I am sharing this with you, dear reader."

Voice of God: But are they interested? I know my readers wouldn't care a jot to hear my inner dialogue about whether to call the Red Sea plain "red" as opposed to Pillarbox Red or Crimson Lake[3] —both of which could have been quite confusing for different reasons.

Fellow Writer: You have to kind of guess your reader, anticipate the other ...

Voice of God: Are we each other's other?

Fellow Writer: Well, yes. For now.

Voice of God: There are no others before us?

Fellow Writer: John Shotter says, "We have to let the others and othernesses around us 'teach' us how to relate to them; we have to let the otherness of the other enter us and make us other than we already are."

In another example of alternative literature review, I wrote a script of a radio panel with some of qualitative inquiry's more influential writers who spoke their own original words to each other along with some additional speech I added for them. I included references in ways so as not to upset the textual flow for the reader. Elaborating on people's speech, blurring distinctions between "real" and "not real" wording, flexible referencing all make for a creative but traditionally invalid text. Its validity comes from the meaning of using those words in that context, to situate extracted quotes from other texts as relationally situated speech acts.

---

1. Shotter 1989, p.141.
2. Vygotsky 1986, p.271
3. Pillarbox Red is so-called after the color of English mailboxes and Crimson Lake is also known as Carmine.

My experience of conversation in psychotherapy, teaching or research is that, like everyday talk, it can be quite chaotic. Conversations can move like a butterfly flitting from bush to bush and, as a therapist, supervisor, educator or researcher, I have to both follow the conversation and moderate my own butterfly-ness to take into account coordinating potential with the other person/s in a conversation. I find theory and other stories "come to mind" in response to the narrative movement in the conversation. The challenge for me is how to weave theory and practice/research writing in ways which are contextually relevant, live and interesting to the reader.

Text as Social Construction

In his book "After Method: Mess in Social Science Research", John Law asks

> What difference would it make if we were instead to apply the criteria that we usually apply to novels (or even more to poetry) to academic writing? ... if we had to write our academic pieces as if they were poems, as if every word counted, how would we write differently?
>
> Law, 2007, p.11

An answer from Barnett Pearce might have been to "[t]reat all stories, your own as well as others, as incomplete, unfinished, biased and inconsistent" (Pearce Associates Seminar, 2004 [1999], p.50).

I have been inspired by the bold and clear writing of Laurel Richardson. She counters the dualistic true/false split of modernism with an inclusive both/and position. Richardson's assertion that "a postmodernist position does allow us to know 'some-thing' without claiming to know everything. Having a partial, local, historical knowledge is still knowing" (1994, p.518) alleviates some of my dilemmas about the speaking rights from within the segregated knowing across my many selves and invites conversation between or despite them. And Richardson goes on to ask, "[h]ow do we put ourselves in our own texts, and with what consequences? How do we nurture our own individuality and at the same time lay claim to 'knowing' something?" (p.518).

I *could* say that the texts I have been producing are *my* stories—in that the bias must be owned by me and the descriptions of events are grounded in my lived experiences colored by gender, culture, ethnicity and those other aspects of life gathering under the expandable mnemonic of *The Social GGRRAAACCCEEEESSS*. [The Social GGRRAAACCCEEEESSS is a mnemonic developed jointly by Alison Roper-Hall (1998) and John Burnham (1992, 1993, 2011) to help therapists become more alert to inequalities and differences in lived experiences, is an expandable acronym for Gender, Geography, Race, Religion, Age, Ability, Appearance, Class, Culture, Conformity, Education, Ethnicity, Employment, Economics, Sexuality, Sexual orientation, Spirituality.] Lorraine Code (1995) points out, it is not possible for anyone to be a "surrogate knower" or writer and tell the same tale. Almost everything I write these days involves differing levels of collaboration or conversation with people who are both inside and outside of the texts: the people I speak with in research conversations, in therapy sessions, learning or supervision groups. They contribute not only with their words spoken in the context of practice or research conversations but collaborate or respond in the shaping of written texts. In this sense "my" writings could be seen as a further form of what Penn and Frankfurt (1994) have called *participant texts* (see also Penn, 2009).

I could think of the participants in the texts as a cast of characters whose voices and opinions (often monological-sounding but in the context of dialogue) are involved in some creative conversation. Most characters I invite into texts are "real" people but they are, nevertheless, portrayed through me and, as such, can only bear a resemblance to the richness of the "whole" person they are across a range of contexts. In other pieces of writing, characters are more deliberately fictionalized to allow for some things to be told, shared and shown which might not otherwise be possible. For example, I would not want anyone to be humiliated or upset by a portrayal which valued certain opinions over others. In these writings, I aim for descriptions of exchanges which *sound enough like* what I feel or recall having taken place. I think of this as a form of *pragmatic truth* (McNamee,

1994). In encouraging a more subjective relationship with writing, Richardson encourages a listening for one's own voice: "We feel its 'truth'—its moral, intellectual, aesthetic, emotional, intuitive, embodied, playful pull ... which should lead to writing that is more diverse, more author centered, less boring, and humbler" (1994, p.524).

Some readers may wonder if they are going to get the "full" picture where I have used composite characters and a fictionalized telling of real events. My answer to this is that I have, like many researchers and writers of practice, made decisions without too much consultation about which events to paint pictures of and how to paint those pictures and with whom. On the one hand, I am not attempting realism but I want the pictures to capture enough detail for readers to recognize themselves, others, scenarios, dilemmas and narratives in the stories I tell. I am using the word "stories" as I am thinking of all practice and research tellings as fabrications. I could have provided transcriptions for readers of teaching days or therapy sessions. They would have provided some additional factual detail of what was said but transcriptions are often hard to read and, in any case, I want to show people what happened with a wider range of senses—similar to the ones I use when I am in those situations. A transcription tells a reader very little about body language, bodily responses, movement in inner dialogue, dilemmas, choices, tone and time. I want to tell stories from within my practice so readers can hear and see the characters, so they "get" what is going on in the room, so they feel they are, to some degree, there. To try to create the conditions for readers to hear the voices of other participants is not simply a literary ploy, it's an ethical choice to find ways of turning up the volume on people's concerns and abilities, struggles and achievements.

Having created some literary license to have a range of responses, the reader is offered an invitation to position his- or herself in relation to the differing opinions and experiences. "Polyvocal writing stands as a critique of the criterion itself", says Ken Gergen,

> [i]n these writings clarity and certainty of the traditional variety give way to ambiguity and ambivalence; in reaching for

> a full relationship through writing there is no 'comprehensive account' for space must always remain for the added voice of the reader
>
> Gergen, 2008, p.8

The Sound of Talk

A further project for me arising out of the need to *speak* with the reader, has been to capture the sound of talk—talk between the writer and the reader, talk within my inner dialogue, and talk between other speakers in the texts. Bazerman (1988, p.21) suggests that when one accepts "language as a structured social creation, this position claims that the significant social and creative action occurs in the living moment of spoken language instead of on the dead written page." And Richardson asks, "[h]ow do we create texts that are vital? That are attended to? That make a difference?" (1994, p.517).

I have in my mind's ear, the voice of the writer Toni Morrison:

> When I do a first draft, it's usually very bad because my tendency is to write in the language of everyday speech, which is the language of business, the media, the language we use to get through the day. If you have friends you can speak to in your own language, you keep the vocabulary alive, the nuances, the complexity, the places where language had its original power, but in order to get there, I have to rewrite, discard, and remove the print-quality of language to put back the oral quality, where intonation, volume, gesture are all there
>
> Morrison in Yagoda, 2004, p.40

This reflection from Toni Morrison along with Laurel Richardson's (1994) assertion that no-one speaks in prose have been guiding voices for me in creating the conditions to hear and decipher the muddle in the concentrated time of inner dialogue.

My hearing has changed too so that the words in my ears now arrange themselves in stanza form to echo the pace, intonation, emphasis, emotion of their speaker. I had been hearing, no, rushing together lines of talk, forcing it into prose as I am doing now.

> An experiencing person is a person in a body. Poetry can re-create embodied speech in a way that standard sociological prose does not because poetry consciously employs such devices as line length, meter, cadence, speed, alliteration, assonance, connotation, rhyme and off-rhyme, variation, and repetition to elicit bodily response in readers/listeners
>
> Richardson, 1997, p.143

Of course, writers are readers too. And listeners. There is a relationship between reader and writer when a reader reads aloud the writer's writing. Writers can hear a range of inner, and perhaps outer, responses to how someone else is performing their text. I have been experimenting with a *bricolage* of voices, pieces of writing, designed to be heard by the reader as people speaking, as a performance piece which can and has been read aloud for others. This lifts the activity of talk, of conversational practice, back into its relational first language.

Beyond Autoethnography

I chose autoethnography as a methodological starting point for researching writing from within practice relationships because it encourages in-depth description of personal experience with a pronounced weaving of reflexivity throughout the process and content of writing (Ellis, Adams & Bochner, 2010). As a practitioner researching and reporting on my own practice, I was also concerned to act with transparency and find ways of sharing the range of responses in my inner and outer dialogue with the reader. Writing autoethnographically has offered me ways of "laying them bare" for all to see, to invite others into a privileged and otherwise unexposed view of the inner and outer workings in the life of a practitioner. Without detailed descriptions of inner and outer dialogue, there is no way of showing reflexivity in action. I can speak about it, from outside of those moments, but autoethnography allows me to speak from within the moment of the doing and try to capture the swirl of responses I have alongside the practical and ethical choices I am making. I am "outing" the hidden inner world of the therapist, supervisor, educator or researcher by situating my responses in the moment of interactions with others with whom I am working. To "out" these activities is an ethical stance as the writer is then offering readers an opportunity to witness happenings at different levels and reflexively listen out for their own responses to the events in the dialogue.

Laurel Richardson speaks of narratives of the *self*:

> Narratives of the self do not read like traditional ethnography because they use the writing techniques of fiction. They are specific stories of particular events. Accuracy is not the issue; rather, narratives of the self seek to meet literary criteria of coherence, verisimilitude, and interest
>
> Richardson, 1994, p.521

Carolyn Ellis, in one of my favorite books, "The Ethnographic 'I': A Methodological Novel" (2004), shares with the reader many examples of her inner turmoil about how best to proceed in response to her students. She writes inner dialogue as a shifting and responsive conversation in which she knows she must make a choice about how to go on in outer talk. ELLIS considers and sometimes worries about what she notices about her students. She anticipates how they might react to something. She rolls out a stream of detailed and connected thoughts for the reader to "really" see what can go on for a teacher of autoethnography. And she does this through an autoethnographic approach. It is an inspired and creative way of producing useful research for others, like me, to learn both about teaching, about teaching autoethnography and about the producing of autoethnography. This approach to research has offered additional support to my professional understanding of the value of listening to my inner talk and to see this as part of my working tools—messy, yes, but invaluable to the process of doing any reflexive activity. It is an area of professional activity which has received little attention until the advent of autoethnography which has opened the field to the showing of experience from within the moment of living it.

Yet I have a discomfort with the term *autoethnography.* The prefix *auto* doesn't sit very well for me. The pervasiveness of relationality on so many levels in research relationships and in writing-reading relationships moves me towards a more inclusive description of my research.

Relational Ethnography

I feel more at home as a relationally oriented practitioner and researcher to think in terms of *relational ethnography*. Like autoethnography, relational ethnography, is more of an approach to research, a form of inquiry, than a fixed method to be performed "properly". It is a philosophical and ethical stance which embraces reflexivity, responsivity, transparency of the researcher(s), relational awareness and dialogical coherence between that which is being researched and how research material is shared with others. It encourages an attitude to knowing based on a postmodern concern with what counts as knowledge; how, with and for whom "knowledge" is produced and with what social consequences. It invites the researcher to work with a literary eye and ear in anticipation of reader-respondents. It is one of "a new array of collaborative, polyvocal, and self-reflexive methodologies" (Gergen & Gergen, 2002, p.13) which constitutes a form of inquiry in its own right and can act as an influencing context alongside other research methods. I have found that teaching relational ethnography has significantly improved students' reflexivity in their research and practice and has enhanced the relational and aesthetic quality of their research writing.

I use the term *relational ethnography* for speaking reflexively and dialogically about *and from within* relationships—whether, for example, from within the different voices of the researcher's inner dialogue, between the researcher(s) and other texts, between the researcher and others in outer dialogue, between writers and readers of research writing. Relationality exists in every part of the research process (McNamee &

Hosking, 2011). Writing research is a relational activity in which the writer attempts to anticipate 1. the needs of readers and 2. a responsive dialogical readership which includes people who appear in the research writing, colleagues, members of the public and so on. Relational ethnography includes degrees of collaboration, co-creation and discussion with others in producing research into relational activities. This is supported by a social constructionist understanding of co-creating meaning, narratives and accounts.

As I have already explained, I am not telling "my" tale in isolation from others. Even when I am researching "my own" practice relationships from within living moments, the shaping of my research endeavor and its telling will be influenced by many others, directly and indirectly involved with it. We are always responding to people and narratives, actually present or remotely present, which act as authorizing or prohibiting voices—from culture, family, life experience, the academy, the arts, legal, professional or social policies and so on. I am researching the "we", the relational. It is not a study by "me" of "them". "They" do not exist except as a participant in the "we". I am researching how we go on together in conversation with ideas and feelings, emotional and embodied responses. As researchers involved in research relationships, it might be neither possible nor desirable to attempt to explore our own behavior in isolation from other research participants, and theirs from ours.

> How is it possible to situate ourselves as participant-observers in the lives of others and not affect them? The social skills we use to do ethnographies attach us to real human beings. They connect us to people in deeply human ways.
>
> Richardson, 1997, p.115

In particular, relational ethnography emphasizes 1. *reflexivity in research as a relational practice* and 2. *research as a relationally responsive ethics led practice*.

Relational reflexivity

While reflexivity has become part of good practice in qualitative research, it often appears to mean "self-reflection" or aims to offer the reader some transparency about researcher bias or their relationship with the research focus. Relational ethnography adopts a *relational reflexivity* (Burnham, 1993; Hedges, 2010; Simon, 2012) and *extends the idea of reflexivity beyond that of individual experience and into a relational context.* Relational reflexivity invites an increased sensitivity to the relationship between the voices in one's inner dialogue, in outer dialogue and a preparedness to find ways of connecting inner and outer dialogue. It encourages the writer to anticipate the needs of others involved in or affected by the research and write dialogically with readers in mind.

Relational reflexivity involves a commitment to pro-active and inquiring inner talk about one's understandings, one's responses, one's use of spoken language and body language. It invites mindfulness of one's relationship with "knowing", not-knowing (Anderson, 1997) and un-knowing (McCarthy, 2012) stances. It invites irreverence (Cecchin, Lane & Ray, 1993) about one's attachments to stories of what counts as good research practice so as to encourage a fresh, in-the-moment responsiveness to the research, participants, theory and so on. It is the opposite of a comfortable, "lazy" thinking which assumes, for example, that one is acting without cultural bias, with gender sensitivity, that one understands what the other person is saying, that one's theory or methodology is right—whatever the feedback might be from others.

Relational ethnography veers away from the monological towards the dialogical. It brings together interactivity in inner dialogue and a link with outer dialogue. It connects monologue and dialogue to voice, and voice to a narrative performance in time and place. And it encourages researchers to situate all of these within wider discourses and practices of power.

In keeping with qualitative inquiry's commitment to social and political justice, I am proposing that relational ethnographers move between *local reflexivity* and *global reflexivity* (Simon, 2012). By this, I mean that the researcher reflexivity and research writing move, as if on a piece of ethical elastic, to pan out, zoom in and make links between the detail of the immediate (local) dialogue and happenings with broader socio-political (global) contexts and discourses. Relational ethnography can act a means of extending conversation about important topics which is transformative for participants, for a community, for the research and its outcomes.

Relational ethics

Relational ethnography is ethics-led as opposed to method-led. This means the methodology emerges in response to and from within the relational activities under investigation as opposed to being pre-scribed by the researcher. Doing, writing and reading research are all dialogical activities with ethical responsibilities to not only visible participants in the text but also to the emergent relationships between writers and their readers, between readers and the writers whose work they are reading.

I identified two areas of relational ethics which offer guidance for the practice of relational ethnography: an *ethics of care* and an *aesthetics of care*.

An ethics of care

Exercising an *ethics of care* towards others in reflexive practice (McCarthy & Byrne, 2007) is perhaps my main motivation in developing this research approach. I offer some questions for attending to relational ethics in research:

- How can we bring relational awareness to all stages of research planning, process and presenting and in all activities?
- How are we to speak from within research relationships, alongside people rather than about them as if from "outside"?
- How are we to know if are writing with care, respect and concern in presenting people, characters and views?

- How can we listen to our inner dialogue, outer dialogue, texts and performance with reflexive curiosity and with an awareness of prejudicial, dominant and subjugated voices?
- How can we use transparency and reflexive, dialogical writing to show detail inner and outer dialogue, behaviors in research relationships which show dilemmas, prejudice, reactions etc?
- How can we collaborate with people and take their voices into account in our generating and presenting of research?
- How can we be reflexive about the relational consequences of choices and influencing contexts at all stages in the research process?
- Whose lives will this research change/improve and how?
- How can we commit to acting with reflexivity about one's bias, the limits of one's understanding, and ask "What might I be missing or assuming?"
- How might we act with care and awareness about the impact researchers and research participants can have on each other and on others?
- How can we write with anticipation of a dialogical and listening reader?
- How can we act with structural and theoretical irreverence to find ways of doing and presenting research which support or challenge the context for the research?
- How can we resist the pull to separate talking, writing and reading from the collaborative processes of meaning-making between conversational participants?
- How can we critically and appreciatively review what researchers and participants have done together, what it means for each of us, for others, for now and what else we might have done?

An aesthetics of care

Many qualitative researchers have attended to the aesthetic aspects of presenting qualitative research out of a need to speak well from within lived experience and with an audience in mind (Bochner, 2000; Denzin, 2003; Ellis, 2000, 2009; Richardson, 2000a, 2000b; Tracy, 2010). Here are some questions for holding the aesthetic challenges in mind:

- How can we "dress" the research and present it in ways which do justice to the work and which research participants recognize and are encouraged by?
- How can we present the research in ways which add to the quality of the experience for the reader and which render the research material accessible and useful?
- How do we find or create forms of presentation which fit the content and the context for the research and its intended audiences?
- How can we write dialogically and with respect for participants in the text and for the reader?
- How can we write in ways which offer readers opportunities to engage with texts and create their own connections rather than be taught something fixed?
- How can we produce research writing which is subjective, evocative and heart-felt as opposed to cognitive, "objective" and distant?
- What needs to happen to generate a text which reads easily and is written with a sensibility and sensitivity to research participants, textual others and others in the different areas of one's life?
- What permissions do we need to respond to the research focus, research design and participants with creativity, theoretical and structural freedom?

- What permissions can we create or borrow and which discourses need challenging to allow us to draw on and develop literary, artistic and creative ways of communicating with the research and non-research participants? How might these contribute to ethical research?

A Reader Writes Back

Weeks pass. It is time to write a concluding paragraph for this article. The final paragraph means you send it off—to reviewers, to readers, to a wider public, the world. As I start to write, I am unaware of the voices surrounding me, peeping over my shoulder, frowning and shaking their heads. When I read back what I have written, it feels as if someone has managed to wring every last drop of living conversation out of the text. The sound of an imagined academic authority seems to be winning. I stare into space and eventually turn to some feedback from friend and colleague, Ann Jinks. She has gone carefully through a draft of my paper and left her responses in handwritten notes alongside my typed draft. In green ink. As I read her handwriting, I start to hear her voice. She is thinking aloud on the page, telling me her reactions to this and that. And because she isn't anticipating being written or read by others, she feels free to just speak with me. I hear a tunefulness in her voice, in her writing and I start to hear the sound of talk again, of conversation. I move back to the keyboard and hear the strains of another conversation, a writer's bind in anticipating readers ...

"Take off the paper bag," she says.

"You sound muffled. What are you wanting to say?"

"I am shy," says the head-in-the-bag.

"Writing like this

is like a coming out party.

You don't know who is out there,

Who wants to come,

How they will react."

"Take off the paper bag," she says again.

"If you don't, you'll suffocate."

"You're not hearing me."

"No-one can hear you like that.

Take off the paper bag."

Acknowledgements

I would like to express my thanks to Ann Jinks, Anne Hedvig Vedeler, Lisen Kebbe, Gill Goodwillie, Imelda McCarthy and the FQS reviewers who helped me with this article and to Sheila McNamee whose words encouraged me to get this published.

References

Anderson, Harlene (1997). *Conversation, language and possibilities: A postmodern approach to therapy*. New York: Basic Books.

Bakhtin, Mikhail (2007 [1986]). *Speech genres and other late essays* (transl. by V.W. McGee, ed. by C. Emerson & M. Holquist). Austin, TX: University of Texas Press.

Bazerman, Charles (1988). *Shaping written knowledge: The genre and activity of the experimental article in science*. Madison: University of Wisconsin Press.

Bochner Arthur P. (2000). Criteria against ourselves. *Qualitative Inquiry*, 6, 2, 266-272.

Burnham, John (1992). Approach, Method, Technique: Making distinctions and creating connections. *Human Systems: Journal of Systemic Consultation and Management*, 3, 1, 3-26.

Burnham, John (1993). Systemic supervision: The evolution of reflexivity in the context of the supervisory relationship. *Human Systems: Journal of Systemic Consultation and Management*, *4*, 3&4, 349-381.

Burnham, John (2005). Relational reflexivity: A tool for socially constructing therapeutic relationships. In Carmel Flaskas, Barry Mason & Amaryll Perlesz (Eds.), *The space between: Experience, context and process in the therapeutic relationship* (pp.1-19). London: Karnac.

Burnham, John (2011). Developments in Social GRRAAACCEEESS: Visible and invisible, voiced and unvoiced. In Britt Krause (Ed.), *Mutual perspectives: Culture & reflexivity in systemic psychotherapy* (pp.139-162). London: Karnac Books.

Burr, Vivien (1995). *An introduction to social constructionism*. London: Routledge.

Cecchin, Gianfranco Lane, Gerry & Ray, Wendel A. (1993). From strategising to nonintervention: Toward irreverence in systemic practice. *Journal of Marital and Family Therapy*, 19, 2, 125-136.

Code, Lorraine (1995). Questions of method in feminist practice. In Sandra Burt & Lorraine Code (Eds.), *Changing methods: Feminists transforming practice* (pp.13-44). Ontario: Broadview.

Denzin, Norman K. (2003). *Performance ethnography: Critical pedagogy and the politics of culture*. London: Sage.

Ellis, Carolyn (2000). Creating criteria: An ethnographic short story. *Qualitative Inquiry*, 6, 2, 273-277.

Ellis, Carolyn (2004). *The ethnographic I: A methodological novel about autoethnography.* Walnut Creek, CA: Alta Mira Press.

Ellis, Carolyn (2009). *Revision: Autoethnographic reflections on life and work*. Walnut Creek, CA: Left Coast Press.

Ellis, Carolyn; Adams, Tony E. & Bochner, Arthur P. (2010). Autoethnography: An overview. *Forum Qualitative Sozialforschung / Forum: Qualitative Social Research*, 12, 1, 10.

Etherington, Kim (2004). *Becoming a reflexive researcher: Using our selves in research*. London: Jessica Kingsley Publishers.

Gergen, Kenneth J. (2000). *Writing as relationship*. Unpublished paper.

Gergen, Kenneth J. & Gergen, Mary (2002). Ethnography as relationship. In Art Bochner & Carolyn Ellis (Eds.), *Ethnographically speaking. Autoethnography, literature, and aesthetics* (pp.11-33). Walnut Creek, CA: Alta Mira Press.

Hedges, Fran (2010). *Reflexivity in therapeutic practice.* London: Palgrave Macmillan.

Jinks, Ann (2010). *Personal communication,* 17th June 2010.

Law, John (2007). *After method: Mess in social science research.* Abingdon: Routledge.

McCarthy, Imelda Colgan (2012). *Personal communication.*

McCarthy, Imelda Colgan & Byrne, Nollaig, O'Reilly (2007). A Fifth Province approach to intra-cultural issues in an Irish context: Marginal illuminations. In Monica McGoldrick & Ken Hardy (Eds.), *Revisioning family therapy: Race, class, culture, and gender in clinical practice* (2nd ed., pp. 387-403). New York, NY: Guilford Press.

McNamee, Sheila (1994). Research as relationally situated activity: Ethical implications. *Journal of Feminist Family Therapy,* 6, 3, 69-83.

McNamee, Sheila & Hosking, Dian Marie (2011). *Research and social change: A relational constructionist approach.* New York: Routledge.

Montuori, Alfonso (2005). Literature review as creative inquiry: Reframing scholarship as creative process. *Journal of Transformative Education*, 3, 4, 374-393.

Paré, David & Lysack, Mishka (2004). The willow and the oak: From monologue to dialogue in the scaffolding of therapeutic conversations. *Journal of Systemic Therapies*, 23, 1, 6-20.

Pearce Associates (2004 [1999]). *Using CMM,* http://www.pearceassociates.com/essays/cmm_seminar.pdf

Penn, Peggy (2009). *Joined imaginations: Writing and language in therapy.* Chagrin Falls, OH: Taos Institute Publications.

Penn, Peggy & Frankfurt, Marilyn (1994). Creating a participant text: Writing, multiple voices, narrative multiplicity. *Family Process*, 33, 3, 217-231.

Richardson, Laurel (1994). Writing: A method of inquiry. In Norman K. Denzin & Yvonna S. Lincoln (Eds.), *The SAGE handbook of qualitative research* (pp.516-529). London: Sage.

Richardson, Laurel (1997). *Fields of play: Constructing an academic life*. New Brunswick, NJ: Rutgers University Press.

Richardson, Laurel (2000a). Introduction—Assessing alternative modes of qualitative and ethnographic research: How do we judge? Who judges? *Qualitative Inquiry*, 6, 2, 251-252.

Richardson, Laurel (2000b). Evaluating ethnography. *Qualitative Inquiry,* 6, 2, 253-255.

Roper-Hall, Alison (1998). Working systemically with older people and their families who have "come to grief". In Pauline Sutcliffe, Guinevere Tufnell & Ursula Cornish (Eds.), *Working with the dying and bereaved: Systemic approaches to therapeutic work* (pp.177-208). London: Palgrave MacMillan.

Shotter, John (1989). *Social accountability* and the social construction of "you". In Kenneth Gergen & John *Shotter* (Eds.), *Texts of identity* (pp.133-151). London: Sage.

Shotter, John (1999). *Writing from within "living moments": "Withness-writing" rather than "aboutness-writing".* Fourth National Writing Across the Curriculum Conference: Multiple Intelligences, Cornell University, June 3-5, 1999.

Shotter, John (2011). *Getting it: With-ness thinking and the dialogical ... in practice.* New York, NY: The Hampton Press Communication Series.

Shotter, John & Katz, Arlene (1998). "Living moments" in dialogical exchanges. *Human Systems: Journal of Systemic Consultation and Management, 9*, 2, 81-93.

Simon, Gail (2011). Writing (as) systemic practice, *Doctoral Dissertation, Institute of Applied Social Research, University of Bedfordshire,* http://hdl.handle.net/10547/223012 [Date of access: May 5, 2012].

Simon, Gail (2012). Praction research: A model for systemic inquiry. *Human Systems: The Journal of Therapy, Consultation & Training*, 23, 1, 103-124

Tracy, Sarah J. (2010). Qualitative quality: Eight "big tent" criteria for excellent qualitative research. *Qualitative Inquiry*, 16, 10, 837-851.

Visweswaran, Kamala (1994). *Fictions of feminist ethnography.* Minneapolis, MN: University of Minnesota Press.

Vygotsky, Lev S. (1986). *Thought and language* (2nd rev. ed.). Cambridge, MA: MIT Press.

Yagoda, Ben (2004). *The sound on the page: Style and voice in writing.* New York, NY: Harper Collins.

ELEVEN

Ventriloquation and ghost writing as responses to oppression in therapy

> How can I make my writing matter? How can I write to help speed into this world a democratic project of social justice?
>
> Richardson & St Pierre, 2005, p.967

About-ness and with-ness writing

Nona came to therapy but she didn't talk. I could see she wanted to communicate and, in effect, she was communicating. She appeared to be having all kinds of feelings and thoughts and urges to share something. I sat in silence. I offered paper. We discussed sport. Sometimes I shared my imaginings of her inner thoughts, shared my reading of the atmosphere we were in, and I offered my wonderings to her in a loosely held kind of way so as to be careful not to mishandle her story.

My supervisor at the time, John Burnham, once asked her whether she experienced me more like a biographer or as a ghost-writer. What's a ghost-writer? asked Nona. A ghost-writer, said John, helps people who are not professional writers tell their story in their own voice and in their own words so it gets out there and is heard. Whereas, he continued, a biographer can tell stories about a person's life without that person being so involved. I held my breath. Here was a distinction I hadn't made. The first one, ghost-writer, she said. And I listened and learned what the difference was for her between potential misappropriation of her story and a rendering of it which lent it – and her - credibility and respect. In that moment both of our strengths were recognised and I felt more confident about how to understand ethical positioning in my work with people who want to tell their story but are not able to do so in taken-for-granted ways.

Later, I found another punctuation of the position I had been attempting to take. John Shotter exposes the credibility of scientific writing as being dependent on a position of about-ness writing, presenting the writer as distant from the subject resulting in an othering and objectifying relationship, and untrue stories. He contrasts this with what he calls with-ness writing: writing from within the living moments of mutually responsive, meaning-making conversations (Shotter, 1999, 2011). To write or speak from, what I call, an alongside stance was an attempt by me to witness the untellable but which the speaker wanted told, heard and witnessed despite not being able to articulate it on her own (Simon, 2013).

Professional expectations can become oppressive to people if they impose a way of speaking on people and do not take into account the power of other voices, of other experiences that have shaped their styles of communicating. If therapists or researchers interpret these speaking styles in terms of inability in the other, as opposed to behaviour based on wisdom arising out of complex and challenging experiences, they could invoke and re-enact oppressive power relations.

Irish Fifth Province practitioners, Imelda McCarthy and Nollaig Byrne, encourage ways of creating dialogical spaces in therapy that open up opportunities for hearing stories which might have remained untold and unwitnessed. McCarthy and Byrne draw on the concept of the mythical Fifth Province in Ireland as

> a province of possibilities in language and imagination it also becomes a province or domain of ethics. If those from marginalised groups are to be able to tell the stories of their lived experiences in a context where normative compliances are expected then we must also recognise that there is a

> danger of subjecting them to silence and co-option. [.........] We would hold that imposing normative expectations on marginalised clients without reference to their contexts of adversity constitutes a colonial therapeutic stance which distances us from the subjugated 'other'.
>
> McCarthy & Byrne, 2007, p.330

In the next section, I share a story which speaks to the problem of writing truth, the collapse of genuineness. It shows how professionals can also be subject to censorship of which stories can be told, and how, in what kind of voice, and with what addressee in mind.

From monologue to dialogue and back again

My research nearly killed somebody. I know that might sound a crazy thing to say and even when I explain, you may still feel it's a statement which is unreasonable. But it felt like this to me. What am I talking about? I am talking about being asked to write a report for the Immigration Courts after I was called as an expert witness to offer 'evidence', (deep breath)... evidence that my client, Yuma, was really a lesbian. Really, really, really... a lesbian.

The thing is, after such a long period of my experimenting with practice writing which critiqued authority implicit in authorship, I had forgotten how to write in a de-personalised way - with facts and an objectifying tone to construct a particular rendition of a professional relationship: i.e., expert therapist and 'needy' client. After the extended immersion in my doctoral research on writing as a relational practice and my devotion to developing ways of writing reflexively, transparently, collaboratively, with public sharing of inner dialogue (like this), I struggled to remember how to write a court report. I had to re-member the young social worker I used to be who had been proud to join in a language of professional expertise with my colleagues of the court. Trying to remember that way of being, that way of speaking, of writing, simply exposed the great gaps between what I believed to be good practice then - appearing 'professional' by writing about clients - and what I believe to be good practice now – collaborating reflexively on texts with people-coming-for-therapy.

I felt desperate. A life almost certainly depended on my conveying the truth in a believable style. I believed Yuma would kill herself rather than face deportation to life imprisonment and further systematic torture, abuse and possibly murder. So once I had written my report, I had to put it through the washing machine many times to wring every last drop of humane voice out of the text. The washing machine was a small select group of friends and neighbours who worked in the court system. This team effort dragged my writing back into the mainstream of cold and clinical, supposedly neutral and objective about-ness writing.

I was called as an expert witness because I was not only Yuma's therapist but her lesbian therapist. Lesbian. In the court's eyes, my expertise lay, I would say, about 10% with the therapist identity, 15% with the lesbian element and 75% with the combination term: lesbian-therapist. However, in becoming an expert witness, I also ceased to be a lesbian - a real lesbian! I had to play by different 'professional' rules and write all my statements in the first language of the racist, homophobic institution. And I worked hard to erase the familiar, the sounds-like-me-talking and do the opposite of what Black American novelist, Toni Morrison, says she has to do which is to write many versions to erase the sound of the mainstream authorities and dominant culture. I had to put back the mainstream. I had to be a nice, not too nice, non-threatening (improbable) lesbian and not look like I was suppressing subversive thoughts. I had to look like a therapist who was a certain kind of lesbian - not sure what kind. I couldn't be a sister. I must suspend what being a lesbian means to me. I must suspend all personal beliefs about race, class, gender and privilege. I must not question anyone else's thinking. I must speak and write from an about-ness position (Shotter, 1999). I must answer questions in the court about my 'professional' opinion of "my client's" sexual orientation and sound certain without sounding opinionated.

And I must be impassive as I participate in further objectifying her life experience. She has had her story told, retold, misquoted, interrogated, framed as untruths – in effect, trampled on by the authorities. The 'facts' of her life have been paraded in public courts, evidence photocopied in colour, challenged and ripped to shreds. Her lived experience ripped to shreds! Her life is at stake because she cannot produce officially witnessed transcripts from her former life, abuse hurled from a passing car, serious assaults, threats to her life and that of her partner.

At times, I fantasised that presenting the everyday inner dialogue of Yuma to the life-granting authorities would be more successful than the decontextualised parading of a catastrophic catalogue of events always referred to as 'alleged'. But, they would say I 'made it up' - so it wouldn't count for anything.

Perhaps we were all in a bind: to be believed her story had to be sufficiently evidenced and moving. Without sufficient evidence, a moving story is discounted. The subtle, subjective and complex ways of practitioner knowing (Scott et al, 2004) are not considered sufficiently scientific, and are therefore, not professionally robust for monological spaces such as immigration courts where knowledge must be evidenced in certain kinds of ways. This is especially the case concerning lesbian, gay or transgender asylum seekers as there is a chasm in comprehension in the statutory systems (see Bennett & Thomas, 2013; Gray & McDowell, 2013; Jordan & Morrissey, 2013).

> By positioning ourselves neither inside or outside but both and somewhere else which is always shifting, we describe the experience of being in relation to something or someone. There is no thing apart to be described but an interactive, mutually changing relationship between people or things.
>
> Bakhtin, in Shotter, 2011

In the piece of writing below, where I imagine Yuma sitting in the park, I am exercising an attempt at understanding but I am not presuming to present this as a truth of how it is for her. This writing of my imagining what Yuma would say, notice, feel, is based on hours and hours of conversation, sitting with Yuma, being in conversation not just about or with facts but with an emotional presence. But if I am going to speak about my own experience and about Yuma's or someone else's life, how do I do that without stealing their voices or exploiting their stories, without being sensationalist but honest, without becoming another colonising appropriator of lived experience?

I have used ghostwriting as an opportunity for reflexive collaborative inquiry with Yuma. It has helped me to imagine and understand the complexity in her everyday life, in her inner and outer dialogue. And readers may position themselves as critically informed participants. Texts, such as the one which follows, in which I imagine Yuma, are not intended as single, comprehensive or objective attempts at depiction. They are a human response to something complex and unspeakable in everyday talk and for which there is often no audience.

> In using the notion of representation in research, it is therefore important to problematize the relationship between representation and reality and to examine how texts can be seen both to represent something other than themselves (i.e., the experiences of research participants) as well as presenting themselves as texts.
>
> Rhodes, 2000, p.514

Risking writing 'as if'

> In exploring alternative forms of writing, so do we open the door to new modes of relationship. Thus to hammer out forms of relational representation may bring into being new forms of action.
>
> Gergen, 2009

In the writing *(Gail imagining) Yuma*, I felt, still feel, a huge sense of responsibility. In the context of her and my relationship and many aspects of the wider world, I am a person with privilege: I am white, English speaking, professional, have some financial stability, have UK citizenship; I have an education under my belt; I have a home, a partner and a different history in relation to safety. On the other hand, I wear chips on my shoulder with a Lesbian Feminist, European Jewish, Socialist Pride. These are cuts which speak to my metal, those of my sisters and brothers and act as a reminder of my responsibilities to those whose lives and life stories are at risk of erasure. They inform my commitment to creating opportunities for the telling of stories even if the reading or hearing of the story invites discomfort. I try to set out stories to invite reflexivity from the readership. I write from inside and outside of my 'own' experience with the responsibilities of care of what Vikki Reynolds calls a 'fluid and imperfect ally' (Reynolds, 2010).

Lorraine Code raises the problem of claiming to understand the other:

> Often we do not understand even "our own" experiences as well as that seemingly sacrosanct expression of ownership implies; and only rarely can we presume to understand exactly how it is for someone else even of our own class, race, sexual orientation and social group.
>
> Code, 1995, p.27

I am writing 'as if' from within the inner dialogue of another person, Yuma. Harlene Anderson (2005) has invited practitioners to imagine someone with whom they work by speaking their imagined thoughts and feelings 'as if' from within the first person of the other and from within the present tense. Imagining the lives of others allows us to peek into a person's environment, show interpersonal intimacies with others, identify areas of their lives where relational contexts influence personal choice and human rights.

The 'as if' exercise, like this form of ghostwriting, does more than simply portray imagined inner workings, content and narrative. It creates an invitation to intimacy between the 'as if' speaker and the person whom they are imagining. It extends their relationship. The reader is also entering into an intimate relationship with the speaker. They are getting to know this person.

(Gail imagining) Yuma. A May day in Bloomsbury Square, London

It is a cold day. But not as cold as I have known these last few years. I slept through that winter in Manchester. On the streets. That was cold! The blossom in the trees around me is calming. Pink, white, purple against a blue sky. I sit up straight with focus, with optimism and then inwardly sink back with a silent knowing and sigh slowly. Don't go there. It's not safe to feel safe. I wait to hear the word 'yet' on the end of my sentence but it doesn't come. 'Yet' too is an unsafe word in my desperation to stay calm while I await my fate.

Do the people who will decide my fate sit in offices like those surrounding this beautiful London square? Who are the people who work in such old and upright buildings? I wonder how they got a job there? Perhaps I too will one day work in such a building. I will walk with confidence in my salaried step. With security in a world as small as a list of things to do at work and a plan for lunch. And what I am going to watch on tv that night. Yes, I would have a tv, and a tv licence and I would cook for my friends, instead of them feeding me. I wonder whose house I can go to watch football this weekend? The sun makes for nice thoughts. A brace myself again. I cannot afford to relax. I am not a member of this society. No! I cannot say 'yet'! I cannot say that word. It is not in my power. It does not belong to me. I do not decide. I sag further into the park bench and feel the heaviest of nothings.

I think some time has passed because it has clouded over and someone is sitting eating their lunch on the other end of the bench. I am hungry. I wonder if Gail will have a hot chocolate waiting for me. I feel my spirit go up a degree but I also feel a twist inside, a tiredness at being seen as someone who has no money. I am so tired of that. When I was working as an administrator, I had my own money. I paid for myself. I am trying to keep that feeling of pride. That's why I get angry sometimes with those people who do not listen, who do not read, who do not believe me or the lawyers or the doctors. I feel anger rising in me and I hear myself grunt. The person on the end of the bench looks round. I want to say "I am as good as you!" They are folding up half of their sandwich to throw in the bin. Why have they spent money on food they are not going to eat? I want to tell them "You don't know how lucky you are!" but I don't say anything and neither of us is sure if we have been noticed by the other.

I do not like being a charity case. I still give money to charity. Once a month. When I get my money through. To that homeless man at the tube station. I have my pride and I know they have theirs. And that we are all deserving, worthy of a chance and the right to be respected. I like to think Gail giving me hot chocolate is a way of her showing me respect. She knows I like chocolate. But sometimes, I see her look awkward. She tries to play down what she is doing and I too play it down. That's what we have to do. That's alright. It's okay...

I am so tired again today. My nights are filled by scenes of me being picked up again, thrown into a van, taken to the removal centre. I try to get away but they always capture me. It is dark. They are raping me again... They say this is what lesbians deserve. Sleep is torture. I long for it but when it comes...

I can feel my body going very still again. My face is wet. I am in this between space. In a few moments I will talk about my week, how things are going and what is on my mind. It is sometimes too much to hear myself speak about anything so we sit and don't talk. Or just about practical things. I feel better afterwards but churned up.

I hope I am not going anywhere fast. To still be here at three o' clock on a Monday, is the high point of my week. My hour of relief. I am outside, I am free. They have not asked me suspicious questions, they have not taken me into another room, left me waiting, confiscated my mobile phone and packed me into the dark van to hell, the removal centre. They have let me go. Or did I escape? Does that mean I am free? I am not sure. My body tells me I am not free. Day or night, awake or asleep, I expect to be abducted and abused. Why do they have this law, this law which invites lesbians and gay men to apply for asylum on grounds of being persecuted for their sexual orientation – and then not believe them! Why does the British government not believe us? My own government does! The people in my country do. No-one has any idea what it is like to walk in the streets there. I try to tell people here but they cannot know. I will tell Gail. But she forgets. She asks me things and I tell her again. I did not go out there. I did not even go to the markets. They would call you things, push you. My father took me everywhere. It was not safe for me...

I am free here, yes, no-one will call me names. Even last night Maxine said why don't you marry someone? and I said "No!" I will not. I will not pretend to be something I am not. And what about all the people back there who are not here?

The anger lifts me. I get up and walk towards the park gate. I am a little stiff and unsteady. I have not eaten today. I needed to spend my last five pounds on phone credit before I went to report in case, in case ...

A big red bus is coming close to the kerb. I pull back. A part of me wants to keep going but I hear a sensible voice saying stand back from the kerb and mind the gap. Perhaps it is my father's voice, perhaps my mother's, perhaps Maxine's, perhaps Gail's, perhaps mine. For now, I try to cross the road carefully. I must stay alive in case... but I cannot dare to hope.

A form of inquiry

Imagining the other is likely to bring forth new information to the 'as if' speaker but potentially also to the person being described. 'As if' writings and speech acts need to be understood and treated as a form of collaborative inquiry in which there is room for the person whose life is being described to edit the descriptions. A responsibility of the imagining person is to hold their imaginings lightly and not become convinced that one's own imagining is the correct or only version of events. In principle, space should be made for the added voice of the other to establish that this attempt at description is accurate enough. The power of speech (especially with an audience) or print is seductive. Writing with an eraser is a moral stance but not to be confused with censorship. The ethical requirement is to make it clear to the reader what the context is for the writing. Who is speaking? How clearly has the writer set a clear and transparent context for the reader? And to consider what consequences there may be for the 'as if' writer and the person imagined in the text.

Rhodes also understands ghostwriting as a form of inquiry.

> the textual practice of research as a form of ghostwriting can provide useful avenues for understanding the relationship between the researcher and the researched and for accounting for reflexivity...... In this sense, ghostwriting is used to refer to a practice where a researcher engages with a research participant and, as a result, creates a new text that both tells a story of that participant and implies the involvement of the researcher.
>
> Rhodes, 2000, p.514

Human research takes place within relationships. My task is to find ways of writing from within those relationships which reflect aspects of the dialogical and relationally reflexive ways of being in practice relationships (Simon, 2014). Research into human experience takes place in different landscapes and, by locating 'as if' writing in a real townscape, for example, we can imagine Yuma imagining the other sitting next to her on the park bench throwing away their half-eaten lunch while she is hungry. We experience not only a 'transient convergence' (Anderson, 2009; Cornforth, Lang & Wright, 2011) as readers imagine Yuma in that space but also we witness the transient convergence of Yuma in the telling of her story alongside a stranger in a London square feeling peripheral to the claim on the space.

There are ways in which I render myself visible in '(Gail Imagining) Yuma' through my commitment to foreground her story, to amplify her voice. The title immediately oriented the reader in that it describes my role in imagining Yuma speaking. No-one is pretending Yuma wrote this piece. In it, I include an imagined reflection 'by her' on our relationship. The act of sharing and discussing this writing with her has some resemblance to Karl Tomm's and John Burnham's *Internalised Other Interviewing* (Tomm, in Burnham, 2006; Burnham, 2006; Epston, 2003) in which a therapist interviews a person 'as if' they were someone or something else and reflects with them afterwards on the experience. Speaking from within a first person position also connects with Jane Speedy's writing on witnessing in the use of definitional ceremonies as a form of research (Speedy, 2004).

Ethical and technical choices

> How do we create texts that are vital? That are attended to? That make a difference?
>
> Richardson, 1994, p.517

I think of this kind of writing as a 'fifth province dis-position' (McCarthy and Byrne, 2007, p.3). In their writing, 'Towards an Ethics of Imagination', McCarthy and Byrne make links between creativity and care.

> Imagining another calls for an ethic of care. To imagine the life of an other is to adopt a stance of ethical responsibility towards the other. Placing such a stance within a therapeutic domain, which features issues of social justice, is also a political act. Thus imagining a fifth province dis-position in systemic therapies is, for us, about occupying a borderline territory between one's own world and that of those we are in conversation with.
>
> McCarthy and Byrne 2007, p.330

Writing '(Gail Imagining) Yuma' presented me with both ethical and technical challenges. Actually, it is hard to separate out the technical from the ethical. Am I borrowing her voice to write with? I think so. I may be lending her my articulation of my imagining of her thoughts, feelings and bodily responses. I may be imposing my sentence construction and language. And it may be that in ‘imagining Yuma’, I am also writing my concerns. “I cannot dare to hope” and “I want to hear the word ‘yet’ on the end of my sentence but it doesn’t come”. I know those feelings. There are some overlaps in our language now. But this isn’t make-believe. Yuma is not a ‘made-up’ character. She is someone I know and am in moving conversation with, silent and spoken. She has often told me what she feels and thinks about her life, about the people she meets, the authorities, the place of her past in her waking and sleeping life. When I remember the conversations with Yuma, I hear her voice. It is the voice of an African woman. When I ‘transcribe’ some of ‘her’ thoughts about her life, I hear her voice. I try to write and read it with her accent, with a certain kind of African voice in mind but I am not in a position to write in her country's accent. Perhaps Yuma sounds quite English to people from her country. I write with my inner ears and read back with a listening for what I call ‘sounds enough like’ which I feel is the best I can hope for and offer.

I discussed all parts of this text with Yuma and asked her if this piece of writing sounded like her talking or thinking - or was it like hearing an English person speaking for her. She said it sounded how she thinks and she gave me an example. She made some dry and humorous remarks and she was moved. She says it is important for this piece of writing to be out there so others can know what is really going on. But there are complicating issues to do with power and resources which influence the exchanges between us and which may create a sense of indebtedness to me.

I have been likening writing choices to that of taking a professional stance. McCarthy and Byrne suggest ‘that a professional stance is never “innocent” [.......]. This is because professional discourses are shot through with normative and professional judgements, that inevitably collide with marginalised personal accounts.’ (McCarthy & Byrne, 2007, p.330).

Imagining the other is part of my everyday living ethics and practice as a counsellor and supervisor. As I write my imagining of her, I write in the hope that Yuma feels something important has been understood by me about the complexity of her experience. Perhaps my writing ‘as if’ Yuma was a form of ventriloquation, a way of creating distance between the speaker of the words and their writer (Tannen, 2009, 2010) while bringing her experiences and thoughts closer to a reflexive reader.

> The taking on of voices, then, is a resource by which speakers negotiate relative connection and power, because it allows them to introduce a persona, then borrow characteristics associated with that persona, to, for example, downplay the relative hierarchy between themselves and interlocutors or create closeness with interlocutors or with those whose personas they reference.
>
> Tannen, 2009, p.6

When Yuma says, "I think to myself '*I should write. I should write about... everything that has happened...*' I have so many things I could tell. But, I cannot write." I hear not so much a *lost* voice, as Visweswaran (1994) suggests in trying to account for the gaps in first person voices in ethnographic literature, but perhaps a censored voice or a person traumatised into silence. The word 'lost' sounds more innocent than 'censored', 'overwhelmed', 'silenced' or 'murdered'. I have found it useful to borrow from Burnham's practice of 'lending someone his imagination' (Burnham, 2003) in thinking about lending voice, courage or, indeed, borrowing their voice, courage or imagination with which to speak.

Rhodes suggests,

> research can be examined as a form of textual practice in which researchers create images of others and also enter those images... In such a practice, research can be understood as a dialogic process where researchers are never neutral in their attempts to write about the lives of other people. This then leads to a need for researchers to account for their textual choices and their role in producing accounts of the experience of others.
>
> Rhodes, 2000, p.511

This writing has done more than highlight issues facing many lesbian or gay asylum seekers or facing counsellors working with asylum seekers. It has provided material for Yuma and I to discuss in our conversations and she has said how important it has been for me to try to understand her situation through my writing.

Writing with a responsibility to a social justice agenda

This writing is not intended as finalised text or finished telling, not as "neat, Hollywood tales, but hard-fought, messy forays into the unknown" (Wyatt & Tamas, 2013, p. 7). My attempts to speak through writing had three main research objectives. The first was an attempt to offer Yuma and me a space for reflexive and collaborative inquiry about my understanding of her experience. The second involved a concern to find ways of exposing and making sense of the contradictions in what counts as truth between the worlds of counselling and immigration officers and immigration courts. Their dangerously ill-informed and methodologically weak means of establishing truth on which to base their decisions meant they had to rely on limited experience of the person and a belief in the power of their superior position to know better than a number of expert witnesses all in agreement. Detailed and meticulously prepared reports by expert psychiatrists, psychologists, lesbian and gay specialists, trauma specialists, scarring specialists (many re-produced by subsequent experts after the first report were thrown out by a judge on spurious grounds). Her life, her embodied evidence, her hard to speak history had been twice, thrice, four times struck through with deliberate cuts showing no care for her or for the other people whose life lay in photocopied reports on desks, in briefcases and filing cabinets, in the cars of professionals between workplaces while she – and others – had no freedom of movement or platform from which to speak. The third objective was to expose and discuss the complex workings of counsellors and counselling relationships by using writing to reveal and discuss inner dialogue, dilemmas, imagining and ethics in order to learn more about how we work as counsellors, our identities as people in the world and how we live our ethics.

Ghostwriting and ventriloquation can be used to expose forms of oppression by collaborating with those not able to tell their own stories. They are reflexive and collaborative forms of inquiry opening opportunities for sharing of reflection and furthering understanding. A commitment to heightened reflexivity and relational ethics reduces the risk of further exploitation to people who have already been oppressed. Ventriloquation makes it possible to render audible a range of voices within i) inner and internalised dialogue, ii) outer talk and iii) the insistent, pervasive presence in everyday life of oppressive dominant discourses and their embodied practices of power.

Acknowledgements

With respect and appreciation to all those within and beyond this paper who have helped it find a voice and a place and thanks to the Baltic Art Center, Gotland, Sweden for the writing residency.

References

Anderson, H. (2005). Collaborative Therapy Workshop. Harrogate, Yorkshire, UK. 27th May 2005.

Anderson, J. (2009). Transient convergence and relational sensibility: beyond the modern constitution of nature. *Emotion, Space & Society* 2.

Bakhtin, M. (1981). [2004 reprint] *The Dialogic Imagination and other essays.* Ed. M. Holquist. New edition (1982). Austin, TX: University of Texas Press.

Bennett, C. & Thomas F. (2013). Seeking asylum in the UK: lesbian perspectives. *Forced Migration Review. Sexual orientation and gender identity and the protection of forced migrants.* 42.

Burnham, J. (2003). Systemic Questions. Workshop. Harrogate, UK.

Burnham, J. (2006). Internalised Other Interviewing of Emotions: From Blame to Strength. *Context.* 2006: June.

Code, L. (1995). Questions of method in feminist practice. In *Changing Methods: Feminists Transforming Practice*. Eds. Burt, S. & Code, L. Ontario: Broadview.

Cornforth, S., Lang, S.W. & Wright, J. K. (2012). Writing ourselves in Waikawa: Bitter (sweet) waters. *Emotion Space & Society,* 5,3,156-163.

Epston, D. (1993). Internalized other questioning with couples: the New Zealand Version. In Gilligan, S. & Reese, P. *Therapeutic Conversations*. London: W. W. Norton.

Foucault, M. (1980). *language, counter-memory, practice.* Ed. D. Bouchard. Ithaca, NY: Cornell University Press.

Gergen, K. J. (2000). *Writing as Relationship*. Unpublished paper.

Gray, A. & McDowall, A. (2013). LGBT refugee protection in the UK: from discretion to belief? Special Issue on Sexual Orientation and Gender Identity and the protection of forced migrants. *Forced Migration Review.* 42, April 2013.

Jordan, S., & Morrissey, C. (2013). On What Grounds? LGBT Asylum Claims in Canada. Special Issue on Sexual Orientation and Gender Identity and the protection of forced migrants. *Forced Migration Review,* 42, 13–15.

Lather, P. (2007). *Getting Lost: Feminist Efforts Towards a Double(d). Science.* New York, NY: State University of New York Press.

McCarthy, I. C., & O'Reilly Byrne, N. (2007). A Fifth Province Approach to Intra-Cultural Issues in an Irish Context: Marginal Illuminations. In McGoldrick, M. & Hardy, K. (Eds.). *Revisioning Family Therapy: Race, Class, Culture, and Gender in Clinical Practice*. 2nd Edition. New York, NY: Guilford Press.

Reynolds, V. (2010). Fluid and imperfect ally positioning: Some gifts of queer theory. *Context.* October 2010, 13-17.

Rhodes, C. (2000). Ghostwriting Research: Positioning the Researcher in the Interview Text. *Qualitative Inquiry*, 6, 4, 511-525.

Richardson, L. (1994). Writing: A Method of Inquiry. In Denzin, N. K. and Lincoln, Y. S. (Eds.), *The SAGE Handbook of Qualitative Research.* London: Sage Publications.

Richardson, L., & St Pierre, E. (2005). Writing: A Method of Inquiry. In Denzin, N. K. and Lincoln, Y. S. (Eds.). *The SAGE Handbook of Qualitative Research.* 3rd Edition. London: Sage Publications.

Scott, D., Brown, A., Lunt, I. & Thorne, L., (2004). *Professional Doctorates: Integrating Professional and Academic Knowledge*. Buckingham: Open University Press.

Shotter, J. (1999). Writing from within "living moments:" "withness-writing" rather than "aboutness-writing". *Fourth National Writing Across the Curriculum Conference: Multiple Intelligences*, Cornell University, June 3rd-5th, 1999.

Shotter, J. (2011). *Getting It: With-ness Thinking and the Dialogical.... In Practice.* New York, NY: The Hampton Press Communication Series.

Simon, . (2013). Relational Ethnography: Writing and Reading in and about Research Relationships. *Forum Qualitative Sozialforschung / Forum: Qualitative Social Research,* 14, 1, 4.

Simon, G. (2014). Systemic Inquiry as a form of Qualitative Inquiry. In *Systemic Inquiry. Innovations in Systemic Practice Research*. Eds. Simon, G. & Chard, A. Farnhill: Everything is Connected Press.

Speedy, J. (2004). Living a more peopled life: Definitional ceremony as inquiry into psychotherapy 'outcomes'. *The International Journal of Narrative Therapy and Community Work,* 2004, 3, 43-53.

Tannen, D. (2009). Abduction, *Dialogicality and Prior Text: The Taking on of Voices in Conversational Discourse.* Plenary 84th annual Linguistic Society of America, Baltimore, 8/1/09. Georgetown University.

Tannen, D. (2010). Abduction and identity in family interaction: Ventriloquizing as indirectness. *Journal of Pragmatics*, 42, 2, 307-316.

Visweswaran, K. (1994). *Fictions of Feminist Ethnography*. University of Minnesota Press.

Wyatt, J., & Tamas, S. (2013). Intimate (Dis)connections: Research, Therapy, and "Real" Life. *Qualitative Inquiry*, 19, 1, 3-8.

TWELVE

Eight Criteria for Quality in Systemic Practitioner Research

Introduction

> red makes a kind of black
> makes a kind of black that blue doesn't
> it's a black that you see when you close your eyes
> it's something you know intimately
> and it's that sort of knowing
> that I feel is the real subject of the work
>
> Anish Kapoor 2009

> We live in a numbers dominated world. We know after a decade of critique in the health, welfare, and educational fields that the evidence-based measures of quality and excellence rely on narrow models of objectivity and impact. Researcher reputation, citation, and impact scores are not acceptable indicators of quality. They should not be the criteria we use to judge our work, or one another. They should not be allowed to shape what we do.
>
> Norman Denzin 2017, p.9

This paper introduces criteria suited to evaluating quality in systemic practitioner research. By using criteria for systemic practitioner research based on historical and contemporary systemic practice theory, we can validate and render transparent how we appraise what counts as quality in our practice and in our research. Systemically coherent criteria which honour professional knowledge and know-how support the development of qualitative research into systemic practice. The criteria are designed for research conducted from within the doing of relationally reflexive professional practice namely, *practitioner research*.

In order to evaluate quality in research designed to understand more about how systemic practice works, we need to step into the activities and relational spaces of professional practice to find ways of researching our practice which render visible the careful co-ordinations of everyday life. This requires criteria which reflect professional knowledge, knowing and know-how (Nowotny et al 2008; Scott et al 2004) which sit comfortably alongside the responsibilities of relational practice.

The criteria in this paper are a fusion of i) criteria for what counts as quality in qualitative research (Denzin 2003; Ellis 2000; Richardson 2000; Tracy 2010) and ii) systemic practice principles, values and theory (for example, Burnham 1992; Markovic 1993; McCarthy & Byrne 2007; McNamee 2004; Selvini Palazzoli et al 1980). They evolved out of a need to be able to demonstrate quality in systemic and dialogic practitioner research in the wider community and specifically for the Professional Doctorate in Systemic Practice at the University of Bedfordshire and former KCC. They are suitable for any relationally reflexive practitioner researcher needing to provide a framework for showing quality in researching their own practice.

Systemic practitioner research recognises the social constructionist principle that we construct realities with each other through our everyday exchanges, policies and legislation (McNamee & Gergen 1992; McNamee & Hosking 2012). Systemic social constructionist ideology supports a post-positivist paradigm which understands research as constructing realities and not a means of representing realities - unless hyphenating the word to emphasise the inevitability of subjective *re-presentation* of our realities (Fine 1994). Systemic social constructionist research renders visible the influence of our ideology on the production of information, on what counts as information and accepts that research material can be presented and interpreted in a number of ways, sometimes used for conflicting agendas.

In this paper, I offer eight criteria for assessing quality in systemic practitioner research and discuss how it is both useful and ethical for practitioner researchers to identify criteria by which they expect the quality of their research to be evaluated. The criteria include:

i) Systemic Practice
ii) Methodology
iii) Situatedness
iv) Relational Ethics
v) Relational Aesthetics
vi) Reflexivity
vii) Coherence
viii) Contributions

The criteria are described in more detail later but first, a few words on practitioner research and also on criteria.

What is Practitioner Research?

Practitioner research is research conducted by professionals as part of and from within their everyday professional practice. It is different from research *about* practice or about non-practice topics which could be undertaken by either practitioners or non-practitioners. Practitioner research is based on insider research principles which involve contextually responsive and interpretive research based on pre-existing professional knowledge, knowing and know-how which can be surfaced and included through first person inquiry. It aims to enhance the practitioner's professional knowledge and practice development, and to share learning for the benefit of clients, colleagues or communities.

Practitioner research is part of our daily practice (Anderson 2014; St George & Wulff 2014). Practitioner research methodologies arise out of the practice under investigation. They commonly involve a form of first-person ethnography (autoethnography, relational ethnography, performance ethnography), first person collaborative action research, various forms of dialogical inquiry, reflexive inquiry, phenomenological approaches, heuristic inquiry, writing in different forms as methods of inquiry, and arts-based research. All the above-mentioned approaches reflect methodological developments in post-positivist qualitative research as documented, for example, in the Sage Handbook of Qualitative Research (Denzin & Lincoln 1994, 2000, 2005, 2011, 2018).

Practitioner researchers are more likely to be conducting "process research". Practitioner researchers may not be as interested in evaluating an approach as in using research to expose and discuss a situation or an approach in order to generate understanding and share learning and usefulness for others. Consequently, in this kind of study, the research material is often described as *material* and less as *data*. The producer of the material is not seen as separate from the material but part of it – because they are part of what they are researching. They will not attempt to finalise an interpretation or produce conclusive findings. There may not be an expectation of analysing material so much as speaking from within complex, shifting practice in a deeply reflective and subjective manner. There may be more than a single speaker in the text. The practitioner researcher is likely to develop creative ways of writing ethically about and from within practice relationships, and offer a rich, critical discussion of the material, related theory and ethical matters. Relationally reflexive practitioner researchers need to produce reflexive writing which inspires reflexivity in their readers.

What are we good at? Inquiry! Reflection! Sense-making!

Let's pause for a moment to reflect on a few of the many things that we as systemic practitioners bring to the research picnic:

- Systemic therapists, leaders, trainers and consultants are trained to postgraduate level in methods of inquiry, communication skills, theory of knowledge, the philosophy of discourse, relationship theory, and systems theories. Professionals who are trained systemically are competent in an unusually extensive range of questions to explore complex aspects of human behaviour, beliefs and relational activity. Furthermore, we have an in-depth, critical understanding and appreciation of how inquiry can produce or overlook some truths over others.

- We are experts in setting up conversations with people on a wide and often difficult range of subjects. We are trained to be competent and ethical in engaging people, in establishing a dialogical culture and addressing inequality of voices in inner and outer dialogue.
- We are skilled in practically and ethically eliciting information and feedback from our conversational partners. We have ways of checking understanding, of sense-making with others and on our own. We explain context for conversation and check that our understandings and expectations match.
- We are natural collaborative action researchers. Negotiate > Act > Reflect > Negotiate > Act > Reflect> Negotiate > Act > Reflect.
- We are always involved in ongoing first-person inquiry on our own, with clients, with colleagues, with employers. We use self and relational reflexivity to navigate complex relational co-ordinations by reflecting in, on and after the moment of relational activity.
- We are critical thinkers and pragmatic actors who adapt, abandon or utilise theory to suit the needs of occasion. We are prepared to be surprised by what we learn and not marry our hypotheses or idealise our working methods.
- We have a preoccupation with ethics-led practice using continuous inner and outward accountability for decisions.

We adjust our ways of speaking, our words, our plans and actions to accommodate the hopes and abilities of our conversational partners and other stake holders.

- We are good at analysing our work, speaking about it, explaining what we are doing, why, how and to what hoped for effect. Through supervision, training, writing, and everyday conversation we develop new accounts, new theory. We ask, "What was happening here?" and "What else was happening there?" We encourage multiple perspectives. We are experts at describing relational space, ways of knowing, talking and creatively reframing or challenging restrictive ideas and practices.
- We have a philosophical and pragmatic understanding of the impossibility of objectivity and single "truths". We are critically reflexive about theory and practice. We are trained to prepare for the inevitability of prejudice and how to address prejudice - our own and that of others. We have a critique of how language works in spoken and unspoken ways to influence the social construction of knowledge in the context of imbalanced power relations. We are trained to anticipate the consequences of how we use our linguistic power to describe people and communities.
- We understand that "truth" is problematic and rarely exists with a consensus. We are pragmatists and work with what we have, with the resources available to us. We know that we live in a multiverse of stories and that some of these stories are more helpful than others.

Systemic practitioners are clearly not lesser relatives in practices of inquiry and knowledge generation! Academic researchers normally start their research with a fraction of this expertise. These points make a convincing argument for how established systemic knowledge practices can start to reframe relationally reflexive professional practice as a form of inquiry, as research.

Some Words about Criteria

Criteria are values which organise our thinking about what counts and about how we develop accounts. It is important to acknowledge that all criteria for establishing value are products of specific cultures, moments in time, trends in science, different paradigms – to meet the needs of differing contexts. Systemic criteria can support the development of new research practice and new professional practice by employing key systemic theories, values and practices as scaffolding.

If we accept that systemic practice is already using many methods of inquiry, and expects rigorous reflection on what counts as knowledge, we should play to the strengths of what, as practitioner researchers, we can bring to research and not simply expect to learn from academia.

Our gift to the qualitative research field is that i) we offer a relational perspective on criteria for quality in qualitative research and ii) we offer a systemic critique of the taken-for-granted narrative of the individual as a site for study and instead portray a relational perspective on the world (people, theory, events, experience, time and space).

The gift to the systemic practice field is the relationally oriented criteria for evaluating quality in systemic practice research. As a profession, we need systemic practitioner researchers to be sufficiently familiar with criteria for quality in research so they can critically identify, adapt or create criteria to use in each new research context.

There continues to be a rich debate on criteria in the qualitative research field. Criteria highlight the importance of writing texts that move the reader to learn or do something differently, which employ literary strategies to tell authentic stories well, and to always research with a social justice agenda (Ellis 2000; Denzin 2000, 2003; Bochner 2000; Richardson 2000; Liz Spencer et al, Cabinet Office, UK 2003; Tracy 2010; Cho and Trent 2009). In the fields of counselling, psychotherapy and organisational research, there are strong advocates for including research criteria arising out of professional practice such as reflexivity (Etherington 2004; Stiles 1993; Morrow 2005; Cunliffe 2009).

Post-structuralist writers who critique objective truth and scientific method (McNamee & Gergen 1992; Lather 1994, 2007) offer criteria for quality in research. Patti Lather proposes that any set of criteria arising out of a post-structuralist paradigm will inevitably be open-ended and context sensitive (Lather 1994). She introduces a playful array of definitions of validity such as ironic validity and rhizomatic validity which are relevant to systemic practitioner research (Lather 1993). As a practice community, we could use relational ethics as a basis to develop what Norman Denzin calls "moral criteria" (Denzin 2017). Rather than using criteria to support traditional ways of attempting to represent the world, we must offer a postcolonial and "complex set of questions, namely, who had the right to speak for whom, and how?" (Denzin 2017, p.11).

Research into the fluid and improvised collaborations of contextually responsive systemic practice requires new criteria that are designed to investigate the complexity of psychotherapeutic practice, organisational culture, relationships, training and supervision. The micro processes, visible, audible, sensible, imperceptible, in everyday practice need studying in ways appropriate to each context to develop meaningful learning for practitioners and which offer detailed and accessible description woven with reflexivity.

These eight criteria situate practitioner research within a context of critically situated reflexivity. All the criteria are reflexively linked and they will change and develop as we exercise critical reflexivity on encountering new contexts and cultures. The criteria serve several purposes. Firstly, we need to be able to participate somehow in the discourse of the first order worlds in which we live which expect clearly articulated outcomes, methodologies and generalisable quality standards. Secondly, we need to provide rigorous and imaginative criteria which are coherent with systemic theory, practice and ethics. Thirdly, unlike modernist expectations of creating criteria which will concretise quality standards, these systemic criteria are offered as stepping stones, subject to change, as signposts *for now.*

Eight Criteria for Quality in Systemic Practitioner Research

1. Systemic Practice

a) Research focus is on systemic practice.
b) Creative use of systemic theory and practice.
c) Rich detail of relational movements from within practice, inner and outer dialogue.
d) Professional judgement.
e) Accounting for unexpected and expected material, planned and improvisational co-ordinations, changes from original design.

2. Situatedness

a) The research asks and answers the questions: How come the researcher is doing this research? Why now? With what intentions?
b) The research topic is illustrated with examples from professional practice.
c) Critical knowledge and discussion of the literature relevant to
    i) the focus of the inquiry
    ii) systemic theory
    iii) philosophical or ideological context
d) The research is critically situated in relevant and comparative national and international literature and other material.
e) Discussion about what counts as knowledge, evidence or relevance to the subject.
f) Detail of how literature and other material are being sourced.

g) The practice research is critically situated within local and global contexts: e.g. human, technological, political, economic and environmental systems.

3. Methodology

a) The methodology arises out of the practice in focus and is supported by systemic thinking.
b) Discussion of philosophical and ideological premises, paradigmatic situatedness underlying the methodology, and explanations for coherence and incoherence.
c) Substantial, critical and reflexive discussion of the methodological framework, accounting for the choice of approaches, limitations and advantages of the approaches.
d) Critical reflection on the strengths and limitations of i) the design process, ii) capturing or creating research material, iii) the means of reflecting on the material, iv) presenting material and v) possible consequences for the researcher and others.
e) Methodological innovation, critical thinking, a balance of imagination and rigour, theoretical and structural irreverence.
f) An account of what the methodology adds to systemic practice research.
g) Identification of criteria by which the research can be judged and why.
h) All methodological terms are explained with an indication of how and why they are used in that way.

4. Relational Ethics

a) The research is ethics-led over method-led. Ethics is not an add-on.
b) Rich consideration of power relations, differences in lived experience, belonging and identity, and how these matters play out in the multi-systemic worlds of professional

practice inquiry, research relationships and wider socio-political systems.

c) Reflexive discussion and appreciation of ethical issues in the research study over the entire lifespan of the research study from initial planning; in connecting to other work in the field; throughout creating, collecting and collating material, reflection and sense-making activities; in presenting the research, reporting to stakeholders, and in wider publication or dissemination.
d) Critical discussion and evidence of how research has enhanced professional work and has not undermined it.
e) Clear description and critical discussion of how research activities and use of material have been negotiated with participants and how this complies with relevant research governance.
f) The research has a stated social responsibility objective, addressing real concerns for people, organisations and the communities in which they live, showing how the practice in the inquiry improves the lives of others.
g) Demonstration of how the research enhanced personal / professional learning or experience for participants.
h) The researcher writes in a dialogical style, anticipates the reader, and avoids finalising.
i) Researchers are visible throughout reports of the research, speak in the first person and from within lived experience and practice relationships.

5. Relational Aesthetics

a) The presentation of the research has aesthetic merit.
b) The researcher has chosen a style of writing and presentational format that works for them, for the participants, for the audience and for the subject.

c) The researcher has integrated the discussion of the literature and stories from other sources well in their chosen format.
d) Research writing is presented in a style which provides readers with an accessible and reflexive space to make their own meaning alongside the researcher's own reflections.
e) The researcher anticipates a systemic and non-systemic audience.

6. Reflexivity

a) Demonstration that reflexivity is present as an ethical way of being in relation throughout one's practice and research.
b) Sophisticated examples of self and relational reflexivity, local and global reflexivity.
c) An honest, transparent and reflexive account about the selection of material and interpretation and/or use of the material.
d) Critical and reflexive thinking about the literature incorporated in the texts and how it might apply across different socio-economic, cultural contexts or areas of life experience, identity or professional practice.
e) Evidence of transformation in the researcher's thinking and practice.
f) Sufficient detail about the presence and influence of the researcher including inner and outer dialogue, thoughts in progress, noticings, feelings, the concrete and the transient.
g) Critical and reflexive appraisal of the advantages and disadvantages of being a practitioner researcher.
h) Rich discussion of distinctions between systemic practice and systemic research, where or whether they occur.
i) Critical consideration of where and how voices of others are included in the research.

7. Coherence

a) All areas of research activity reflect the values and relational ethics of systemic practice: negotiations with participants, collection of material, engagement with literature, writing and presenting the research etc.
b) The suitability of approaches for reporting or sharing strategies with the research focus.
c) Sufficient coherence between the ethics submission and the reports on outcome and process of the research or explanation for incoherence.
d) Coherence between title, research focus and content.

8. Contributions

a) Evidence and discussion of how the research makes an original and impactful contribution to the field of systemic practice and systemic inquiry, to members of the public, or other professionals, communities or organisations.
b) The research offers useful and innovative elaborations of theory for systemic practice and systemic practice research.
c) The research takes the reader further in their relationship with the subject and/or methodology.

Becoming Systemic Practitioner Researchers (again)

We cannot not think systemically. We understand talk, especially that of an inquiring nature, as transformative. Systemic thinking has an ethical intention to ensure we are working with bias mindfully to promote equality and consider the best ways of responding in each unique situation. We need to study our existing systemic ways of knowing and seeing in order to find ways of speaking about our work and explore what constitutes quality.

The professions of psychotherapy and organisational practice were founded on the methodology of case studies and ethnographies. Early professional practice was also a form of action research, using experimental methods, reflexive inquiry and writing as a form of inquiry.

The rich and extraordinary body of systemic theory and practice arose out of different forms of collaborative and reflexive inquiry: team case discussion, video review of consultations, learning from client feedback, self and relational reflexivity, supervision, the Macy conferences, reading and discussion groups, writing papers, conferences and workshops, starting new journals, attempts at new relational co-ordinations with families and teams.

What are these relational co-ordinations? They involve ways of asking, responding, consulting, listening to inner and outer dialogue; maintaining an exquisite balance as one walks a risky edge between inner and outer dialogue aware of immediate and delayed consequences.

Where do relational co-ordinations take place? Between consultants and clients; between team and therapist; between hypotheses and unexpected twists; between emotion, embodied knowing and cognition; between referrer and service users; between policy and professional ways of knowing; between method and innovation; between greetings and endings; between ways of talking; between silences.

These are some of the places in which we practice balance, take risks, work with and despite mess and chaos, and inevitably discover new learning - whether by accident or intentionally. Meetings are rarely neat and formulaic. It follows that practice research undertaken by the practitioner will benefit from an approach that accommodates and shows processes of unpredictable, multifaceted movement and communication in everyday practice. This is not incidental to what happens but an integral part of the therapeutic, teaching, leadership or consultancy process and therefore inevitably part of a reflexive first-person research process. This research can only be done by the practitioner as a researcher from within and between the reflexive movements of inner and outer dialogue. Practice research conducted by an observer, trained or untrained in relational professional practice, results in the loss of important knowledge and information which is inevitably invisible, unrecognisable and insensible to such an observer.

Many areas of reflexive practice (counselling, osteopathy, acupuncture) are generating *practice-based evidence,* evidence which emerges out of practice through the knowledge practices of that profession. Robert van Hennik has taken this further by integrating research and systemic therapy in what he calls Practice Based Evidence Based Practice (PBEBP) in Feedback Informed Therapy in Systems (FITS) (van Hennik 2018; van Hennik & Hillewaere 2017). Other systemic practitioner researchers have also been developing many useful practice-based research methods: Dialogic Participatory Action Research (Olsson 2014); Relational Constructionist Research (McNamee & Hosking 2012); Praction Research (Simon 2012); Embodied Dialogical Inquiry (Vedeler 2011); Pragmatic Inquiry (Juhl 2012); Essay Writing as Dialogical Inquiry (Kebbe 2014); Discursive Qualitative Research (Borsca & Rober 2016); Phenomenological-Relational Study (Pedersen 2012); Reflexive Conversational Inquiry (Barge et al 2014); Performance Methodologies (Bava 2005); Relational Ethnography (Simon 2013); Feedback Informed Therapy (Tilsen & McNamee 2015); Collaborative-Dialogue Based Research (Anderson 2014); Research as Daily Practice (St George & Wullf 2014); Rich Portraiture (Day 2014); Responsive Temporally Framed Narrative Inquiry (Salter 2018).

Systemic social constructionist practitioner research is perturbing, disruptive, creative, generative, transformative and unexpected – and not homeostatic, representational, eliciting of a single truth. The history of paradigm shifts in family therapy shows how we are still on the move. The early Milan approach was an attempt to perfect a formulaic approach (Selvini Palazzoli et al 1980) in which relational ethics were subordinate to theory. The critique of supposed objectivity in family therapy by Black, Minority Ethnic, Feminist, LGBTQ practitioners showed the systemic community that there were all manner of prejudices and power imbalances in therapeutic and consultation relationships dressed up as theory or formulation (Boyd Franklin 2002; Goldner et al 1990; Hardy & Laszloffy

1995; Hoffman 1990; McCarthy & Byrne 2007; McGoldrick 1998; Simon 1998). The postmodern critique of scientific knowledge was embraced by our profession and "knowledge" was understood as fluid and emergent in the context of relationships and wider cultures. We broke the separation of observer and observed, understanding this as a philosophical and theoretical impossibility (Maturana & Varela 1979). Cecchin encouraged us to be irreverent about our relationship with taken-for-granted ways of inquiring and what we are being asked to perform.

> It is impossible to be neutral. You always have some opinions about what is going on and your opinions are going to have an influence. The big challenge is to the belief in reality; looking for scientific truth and what is really going on. What is the real story with the family? What is the real diagnosis? This is the medical model. What is the real reason behind what is going on? You think that what you observe is there. But we find what we look for. The recent change in the past five or ten years is the realisation that there is no reality to discover. You are not discovering the reality, you are inventing the reality.
>
> Cecchin 1996

Positivist and post-positivist practice and research

The term "post-positivist" is useful in the context of social constructionist systemic research as it is this that separates out some forms of knowing from others, not qualitative versus quantitative. Positivist qualitative and quantitative approaches subscribe to the idea that the researcher should stand well back from the research subject(s) and hold their breath while collecting the data so as to avoid contamination of the evidence and leave the scene of research as they found it, unchanged.

The recommendation to manage the self of the researcher through the practice of bracketing (Fischer 2009) is based on a modernist assumption that it is possible to separate out the self from the observed. In co-constructionist systemic practice, not only is bracketing the self considered impossible but also undesirable as it would result in the loss of the echo and synergy of a dynamic and interactional dialogical whole. Code challenges the positivist belief that, "knowers are substitutable for one another in the sense that they can act as 'surrogate knowers' who can put themselves in anyone's place and know exactly what she or he would know." (Code 1995, p.16). As Lincoln and Guba remark, "Objectivity is a chimera: a mythological creature that never existed, save in the *imaginations of those who believe that knowing can be separated from the knower.*" (2000, p. 181).

Post-positivist research recognises that you always affect the context you are studying, and furthermore, that you *should* set out to constructively and collaboratively change the site of inquiry through the doing of research. Post-positivist researchers not only declare their bias but put it to work and offer rich transparency as rationale, background and learning for the study. This is not simply a trend in research. It connects to concerns expressed by oppressed and colonised groups of people who have been researched and had all manner of falsehoods, intentional or otherwise, written about them which have often led to the development of policies which have served to oppress these groups further and render invisible issues of concern facing those communities (Clifford & Marcus 1986; McCarthy & Byrne 2007; Simon 1998; Visweswaran 1994).

In the positivist sciences, research into people's every day home and workplace practices has been understood as the application of theory to practice or as the evaluation of their practices in the light of an academic theory. In both these approaches to research, researchers are outsiders, usually academics, but not practitioners. When we aspire to positivist research, we take this position. This is not practitioner research.

Practitioner research is researching as a professional from within the everyday reflexive know-how of in-the-moment practice. As practitioner researchers we generate what has been identified as Mode 2 knowledge - *professionally produced knowledge and ways of knowing* (Scott et al 2004; Nowotny et al 2008). The theory of Mode 2 knowledge is used across the professional research field to recognise that i) knowledge is generated within the context of production; ii) professional practice often involves innovative trans-disciplinarity, using a socially distributed range of theoretical perspectives and practical methodologies; iii) form and content of knowledge are necessarily and reflexively linked, non-hierarchical and transient; iv) there is professional accountability and reflexivity; v) criteria for quality reflect broader, composite, multi-dimensional concerns.

In post-positivist systemic inquiry, research emerges from within the movements which make up relational activity between people, things and places, for example. This was influenced by many of the recent paradigm shifts such as the linguistic turn which advocated a social constructionist view of language, discourse theory and critical review of what counts as knowledge, knowing and know-how in our everyday lives (Andersen 1987; Anderson & Goolishian 1988, 1992; Anderson 1997; Anderson & Gehart 2007; Bakhtin 1984; Burnham 1992, 2005; Dewey 1925, 1934; McNamee & Gergen 1992; Shotter & Katz 1998; Shotter 1989, 2011; White & Epston 1990; Wittgenstein 1953). Relational practice is understood as an emergent co-construction, as a form of reflexive action research. Instead of seeing language as an already established, self-contained system of linguistic communication that sets out a set of rules or social conventions that people make use of in talking about things, we can see it as a much more dynamic, embodied, participatory activity closely related to how we communicate through gestures *which are still coming into being*.

To embrace this view of language involves a different ontological approach to the world. Knowledge is emergent in the doing of relational activities – and continues to develop. We live in a living, dynamic, indivisible world of events that is always coming into being. We understand another person's utterances in terms of the responses they spontaneously arouse in us *and* as their responses to us or others or something else (Vedeler 2011; Shotter 2016). This view supports other linguistic theory such as on the power of language to reinforce or challenge narratives which restrict or open up stories of possibility. When we use this view to inform how we approach an inquiry into professional practice, we are starting in a different place to that of an outsider trying to gather "objective" material, a thing in itself, outside of a relational context. The invitation to generate relational co-constructionist research opens up exciting opportunities to learn more about our relationships, our work and the communities in which we live and work.

There are some important ontological choices in doing process research. We can ask, "What are we doing here?" and "To what effect?" which are first order ontological questions. Asking "Why are we doing this?" is a first order epistemological question. Going on to ask a second order epistemological question, "How do we know what we are doing here?" evokes an examination of the basis of one's knowing. It introduces more reflexivity, more ethical engagement: "How am I making sense and what am I more likely to notice or overlook?". Third wave ontology is not so much about being or knowing but about being in a perpetual reflexive state of becoming and knowing, knowing through becoming through doing. Ontology and epistemology fluidly entwine in the mutually shaping and re-orientating relational activities of learning, understanding, acting and becoming (Vedeler 2011). We are always on the way to somewhere else, learning and responding as we go.

Systemic practitioner research encourages the development of new practices and is curious about accounts of the fluid and shifting connections between experience and explanation, between theory and practice. The stories we might find helpful could come from anywhere: contemporary and historical systemic theory, philosophy, communication theory, the arts, social sciences, the physical sciences – and, of course, from our lived experiences, stories people tell us and that we tell each other.

These methodological developments in systemic practitioner research echo post-positivist methodological movements in the wider qualitative research field which signal a new era in what systemic therapists can do when they turn to their existing ways of knowing and enlist the help of:

i) pivotal systemic thinkers who contributed to understanding complexity in communicating systems and developed critical systemic thinking about the relationship between first and second order accounting practices and their consequences (for example, Andersen 1987; Anderson & Goolishian 1988; Boscolo et al 1987; Burnham 1992, 1993, 2005; Cronen & Pearce 1985; Pearce 1989; Epston & White 1990; Hoffman 2001; McCarthy & Byrne 2007; McCarthy 2010, 2016; McNamee & Gergen 1992; Maturana & Varela 1979; Selvini Palazzoli, Boscolo, Cecchin & Prata 1980; White 1991).

ii) contemporary thought leaders beyond the systemic fields who have critiqued method-led ways of extracting what counts as knowledge about human life and point out the limits of what kinds of knowledge can be generated under colonial and patriarchal knowledge practices (for example, bell hooks 1994; Rosi Braidotti 2011, 2013; Karen Barad 2007; Patti Lather 1994, 2007, 2013; Donna Haraway 2015; Gilles Deleuze & Félix Guattari 1987, 1994; Cynthia Dillard 2000; Lorraine Code 1995; Wanda Pillow 2003, 2015; D. Soyini Madison 2012; Alicia Youngblood Jackson & Lisa Mazzei 2012; John Shotter 2011, 2016).

Research as intervention

Research in our field tends to contain a social justice or critical responsibility agenda in its intention to improve lives and promote equality. The aim of systemic practitioner research leans towards producing innovative and leading-edge systemic practice rather than attempting to *prove* something. The research task then is two-fold. We ask, "How can we do something here that matters?" and "How can we show them out there that what we do here matters?" – in that order. The how to show arises out of the practice relationships and activities in focus. In post-positivist qualitative research, the people or practices at the heart of an inquiry are situated within critical and reflective descriptions of the relationships between immediate and wider systems-in-focus, local and global systems and discourses, and political, socio-economic and cultural structures and discourses. This offers opportunities to highlight the significance of the reflexive relationships between different levels of context or spheres of influence (Simon 2012) when focusing on an area of lived experience or practice.

Karl Tomm's papers on interventive interviewing were pivotal for systemic inquiry in that he showed how asking questions was never innocent and never without consequence.

> Every question asked by a therapist may be seen to embody some intent and to arise from certain assumptions. Many questions are intended to orient the therapist to the client's situation and experiences; others are asked primarily to provoke therapeutic change. Some questions are based on lineal assumptions about the phenomena being addressed; others are based on circular assumptions. The differences among these questions are not trivial. They tend to have dissimilar effects.
>
> Tomm 1987, p.1

Systemic social constructionist practitioner research understands that knowledge is never separate from the circumstances of its production. Theory and research methods are not standalone, decontextualised, god-given approaches to the generation of knowledge. They are each products of their era, culture, professional, social, political and economic agendas. Somebody made up each research method for a particular purpose. The systemic community has also been innovating ways of speaking, understanding and checking understanding to suit particular contexts. We need to be proud of this heritage and critical of any method requiring our context to fit with it and ask, "How come some ways of speaking or researching in this world, or in this era, are accorded more validity than at other times or in other cultures?". This way we open up practical, ethical and creative space - and fresh confidence – to support how we can inquire into our practice and draw on core systemic methods of inquiry, values and principles. This form of *systemic* inquiry reflects the relational ethics of our professional practice. We, and the people with whom we are working, our co-researchers, become not simply the means through which data collection occurs but the knowers and knowledge producers from within the collaborative processes of doing something together.

Resisting the flip back to positivism: and navigating ideological disorientation

> For the master's tools will never dismantle the master's house. They may allow us temporarily to beat him at his own game, but they will never enable us to bring about genuine change.
>
> Lorde 1984

> As clinicians, we should accept linear explanations as long as we do not believe them, because this kind of cause and effect, descriptive orientation to the world does not help us to construct a frame of curiosity. Linear explanations, as Bateson has demonstrated, have the effect of terminating dialogue and conversations.
>
> Cecchin 1987

> My suggestion is that as practitioners, we should not rigorously subject ourselves to the words of theorists; we should not think or act within their frameworks or systems. For that would be to subject ourselves to their imagined world, to their theoretical scheme of things, and to alienate ourselves from the world we already share with those around us.
>
> Shotter 2011, p.106

It is perhaps important to note the influence of the recent compulsory diverting of systemic practice by allied positivist professions such as psychiatry, medicine, and to a degree, psychology, into manualised practices is a major threat to the profession – and has obvious implications for systemic research. The instruction to systemic practitioners to learn and use new imported techniques risks distracting us for long enough that we forget or are too worn down to protect our rich systemic heritage of robust academic theory, disruptive and constructive philosophy, innovative practice, dialogical ways of speaking, preoccupation with ethics, social justice and equality, and a commitment to challenge to unnegotiated practices of power and embodied expertise.

In addition, the systemic professions have lagged behind in the public relations that research has offered other professions who are more research generative and have been more prepared. This has resulted in an unusually long gap in the history of the psychotherapies in sharing learning *from within the doing* of everyday practice. The primary response within our profession has been to concentrate on i) the development of suitable tools for gathering a certain genre of evidence in order to ii) generate evidence that systemic therapy works (Stratton et al 2013; Stratton 2017). We have focused on outcome research in an era of efficacy studies. We have played the main game to show that systemic therapy works. There is now confirmation that these evidence-oriented studies have made a useful but limited impact in the case for systemic therapy in specific contexts, for example, eating disorders and psychosis (Stratton 2017). The drive to develop a strong evidence base has been necessary but has also had some secondary consequences and there are several problems that need addressing or redressing.

Firstly, systemic research has, in recent times, taken the shape of systematic outcome research. *Systematic* is very different from systemic in that the former is pre-planned with a road map to predict the course of a journey. *Systemic* involves preparation, not planning (Shotter 2016) in order to respond from within the midst of unpredictable needs and movements of participants in therapeutic or supervisory conversation. Both systematic and systemic have their own criteria for rigour. They each have associated methods of analysis which generate ways of learning from material. Systematic analysis attempts to generate data which are reproducible. Systemic research understands that data (meaning-making activities, storytelling, experimental co-ordinations, for example) are not separate from the context of its production. The outcome research studies *about* (conducted from outside of) systemic practice have relied on positivist and non-practitioner research criteria for evaluating quality of research designed for researchers taking a traditional "aboutness" perspective (Shotter 1999, 2011) in relation to their subject.

Secondly, the recent domination of positivist research in systemic training programmes and systemic journals has inadvertently implied that everyday systemic methods of inquiry are redundant in the search for evidencing or understanding practice. Practitioners have been implicitly encouraged to revert to first order thinking about their subject, about "information gathering" practices and about the framing of inquiry and "outcomes" of knowledge. Systemic therapists often feel pressure to become quasi social scientists, to step outside of their normal methods of inquiry and professional role to research a topic related to their work. The danger in training our practitioners to conduct academic research not directly connected to practice process is that we take practitioners away from their well-developed ways of knowing and doing, and in effect, deskill them. This produces poor quality research and leads to two outcomes: i) the suggestion that the profession needs to bring in "real" researchers from outside to do "proper" research well and ii) that we train our practitioners more thoroughly in traditional non-practitioner research methods. You may see the circularity in this problem. Systemic therapists are, not surprisingly, confused by this flip back into modernist methods of accounting and are discouraged by the tacit devaluing of existing systemic forms of inquiry and our critical postmodern thinking about what counts as "knowledge".

Thirdly, I have noticed in my teaching of systemic practice and in supervising systemic masters and doctoral research that smart and experienced systemic practitioners often feel they must now jettison all they have been taught, all that they have learned on the job as if it is irrelevant to the doing of research. It is as if they feel they have been asked instead to learn from scratch a foreign language called "research". And when teaching masters research to qualifying students, there is a risky moment at the beginning of the class when, as a tutor, I see eyes glaze over, shoulders give up, sighs make an audible Mexican wave around the room and everyone, me included, is wondering if they will make it to the tea break or the end of the course. Yet, by the end of this first session they feel inspired, engaged, energised and continue a such throughout the research process. How research is described to systemic practitioners and how it is taught is key to the success and continuation of the profession. We cannot afford to have more systemic practitioners switch off or feel deskilled in relation to research. It is important to note that most systemic research is conducted by masters students and most of that is not finding its way into the public domain.

Fourthly, a major concern is the neglect of process or practitioner research leading to a gap in the development of practice knowledge. Comparatively little qualitative research into systemic practice has been generated in recent times. This leaves the field with less opportunity for shared learning from the complex depths of practice and fewer systemic professionals feeling that they have a platform in journals to speak with colleagues about their practice through writing. There is an urgent need for systemic practitioners to be turned (back) on to knowledge generation arising out of practice know-how and practitioner knowing. Without this rich learning, our profession and our journals are in danger of losing their way. As a professional community, we risk becoming dissociated from knowing how to be with people in constructive, ethical ways, from being able to reflect on extraordinary and complex activities from within the doing of systemic practice.

Finally, there is a confusion about who the research audience is for systemic research. Practitioners often understand research as needing to be generated for people with decision-making power outside of the profession and not for practitioners themselves. The alienation from research felt by many systemic practitioners necessitates that we find ways of rehabilitating the story of research as directly useful to the professional community. We can be our own research audience.

Looking ahead - with confidence and systemic creativity

It is the case that systemic questions were not designed to elicit proof so much as open up reflection and information about how things are working between people and explore the presence and influence of some ideas over others. This is why it is important to understand systemic practitioner research as situated in a post-positivist paradigm which values this approach to knowing and knowledge generation. We need to be able to demonstrate how *new learning is continuously co-produced in systemic practice and* how we understand and live our ethics in transformative practice and in transformative research (Simon 2016). This learning is fluid and changing of all participants, including the practitioner researcher.

Consequently, it is vital that we use systemic practitioner research criteria as guidance, as reference points, so we can be clear about what we do and how we can generate and share learning safely and ethically from within practice. Criteria for systemic practitioner research can help colleagues from our own and other disciplines make informed decisions about the quality, ethics and viability of our research.

Research ethics committees or institutional review boards need to be assured that research conducted by practitioners from within the living moment of professional practice is safe and ethical. This is why we need to speak in the first language of ethics committee members whose professional knowing may be situated in positivist discourses and demonstrate clearly to them which criteria we are using, why and how.

Most of the outcome research points to the therapeutic relationship as the deciding factor in whether therapy is helpful or not. We need to keep exploring how systemic practice works and notice with a critical eye how and why it evolves. So how do we generate and share learning about how *we* work and resist the impatient and narrowing demand of positivist culture to generalise learning, finalise knowledge and create fixed ways of working with people?

There is a need for more research about *what happens between conversational participants in practice.* We could call it process research but practitioner research is a more precise term suited to our context. Depending on one's research aims, we don't need to prove anything. "Proof" is the language of cul-de-sac evidence ("case closed") – finalising practices from within positivist discourse. Shotter advises,

> We must teach ourselves, not only to act, intellectually, as best we can in relation to states of affairs in statu nascendi, that are still coming into being, but also, to accept that what we are trying to deal with can never in fact be fully finalized and must be left open to yet further development.
>
> Shotter 2016, p.177

We are so well equipped as a professional community to develop ways of using qualitative research and show the highly skilled workings within practice. We need to show how losing control, regaining balance, finding our way safely with others through uncharted territories is what we do well; that working with teams, families, individual and communities is not a predictable, formulaic exercise but one involving perpetual movement and re-orientation to ensure that the co-ordinations with all present are ethical and constructive. It is a challenge to show how we really practice, what really happens in our inner dialogue, in our bodies, in outer talk; how being lost or confused is inevitable and how skilled we are in managing the process of using orientational activities with our conversational partners. But as Laurel Richardson says, "a postmodernist position does allow us to know 'some-thing' without claiming to know everything. Having a partial, local, historical knowledge is still knowing." (Richardson 1994, p.518).

Systemic practitioners are systemic researchers. It is important that we remember our indigenous knowledge, ways of knowing and know-how when exploring our own practice. To restrict ourselves to only certain ways of researching practice will stifle the development of our profession.

Research, like supervision, offers the opportunity to widen a discursive space around often quite unseen practice. Michael White, drawing on Foucault, asks what other voices may be present but not yet heard? (1992). This is an interesting research question and not one which is answered through analysing outer talk alone. New learning is unlikely to arise out of constrained or prescribed ways of speaking/writing. John Shotter points out, "If our ways of talking are constrained in any way - if, for instance, only certain ways of talking are considered legitimate and not others - then our understanding, and apparently our experience of ourselves, *will be constrained also*." (Shotter 1989, p.141).

In conclusion

The eight criteria for quality in systemic practitioner research arise out of accepted qualitative research criteria and systemic practice theory and philosophy. The systemic practice community can use these to demonstrate the presence of quality in systemic practitioner research. Systemic practice is already a form of inquiry. The in-depth trans-disciplinary theoretical knowledge we possess and generate about human relational experience, communication, behaviour and emotion prepares us to study our subject and devise suitable methodologies for studying our practice. The extensive range of methods of inquiry which our profession has developed along with its practice of reflexivity, philosophical study of knowledge, knowing and know-how, establishes the systemic profession as highly equipped to conduct research using our existing knowledge and discursive practices. We need to pause and check the impact of stepping back into first order scientific ways of accounting, sharing knowledge and writing to avoid the loss of our own unique and sophisticated accounting practices. We especially need to take care of our training programmes to ensure we foster creative practitioner researchers and not simply academics dispossessed of their rich professional knowledge.

Research, in the systemic field, needs to improve its reputation starting with how it is taught, how it is conceived, how it is written for it to be experienced as engaging and relevant to the systemic communities. The narratives of what research can be need expanding to include and be led by practitioner research and practitioner knowledge. To be considered worthy of publication and influencing of policy, systemic practitioner research needs to demonstrate what the quality standards are for qualitative practitioner research. This can be done though using these criteria developed from both systemic practice and qualitative research within a post-positivist paradigm.

Acknowledgements

Many thanks to Peter Stratton, Sheila McNamee, Birgitte Pedersen, Liz Day and Joanna Michopoulou for their feedback and encouragement with this paper.

References

Andersen, Tom (1987). The Reflective team: dialogue and meta-dialogue in clinical work. *Family Process*, 26, 415 – 427.

Anderson, Harlene & Goolishian, Harold (1988). Human Systems as Linguistic Systems: Preliminary and evolving ideas about the implications for clinical theory. *Family Process,* 27, 371-393.

Anderson, Harlene & Goolishian, Harold (1992). The client is the expert: a not-knowing approach to therapy. In: Sheila McNamee & Kenneth Gergen (Eds.), *Therapy as Social Construction.* London: Sage.

Anderson, Harlene (2014). Collaborative-Dialogue Based Research as Everyday Practice: Questioning our Myths. In Gail Simon & Alex Chard (Eds.), *Systemic Inquiry. Innovations in Systemic Practice Research.* Farnhill: Everything is Connected Press.

Bakhtin, Mikhail (1986) [2007 reprint]. *Speech Genres and Other Late Essays.* Trans. V.W. McGee. Caryl Emerson & Michael Holquist (Eds.). Austin, TX: University of Texas Press.

Barad, Karen (2007). *Meeting the Universe Halfway: Quantum Physics and the Entanglement of Matter and Meaning.* Durham, NH: Duke University Press.

Barge, Kevin; Hornstrup, Carsten & Gill, Rebecca (2014). Conversational Reflexivity and Researching Practice. In G. Simon & A. Chard (Eds.), *Systemic Inquiry. Innovations in Systemic Practice Research*. Farnhill: Everything is Connected Press.

Bava, Saliha (2005). Performance Methodology: Constructing Discourses and Discursive Practices in Family Therapy Research. In Sprenkle, Douglas & Piercy, Fred, (Eds.), *Research Methods in Family Therapy*. [2nd edition]. London: Guilford Press.

Bochner, Arthur P. (2000). Criteria Against Ourselves. *Qualitative Inquiry,* 6, 2, 266-272.

Borcsa, Maria & Rober, Peter (Eds.) (2016). *Research Perspectives in Couple Therapy. Discursive Qualitative Methods.* Cham, SW: Springer.

Boscolo, Luigi; Cecchin, Gianfranco; Hoffman, Lynn & Penn, Peggy (1987). *Milan Systemic Family Therapy: Conversations in Theory and Practice.* New York: Basic Books.

Boyd-Franklin, Nancy (2002). Race, class and poverty. In F. Walsh (Ed.), *Normal family processes: Growing diversity and complexity* (3rd edition, pp. 260–279). New York, NY: Guilford Press.

Braidotti, Rosi (2011). *Nomadic Theory: The Portable Rosi Braidotti.* New York, NY: Columbia University Press.

Braidotti, Rosi (2013). *The Posthuman.* London: Polity Press.

Burnham, John (1992). Approach, Method, Technique: Making Distinctions and Creating Connections. *Human Systems: Journal of Systemic Consultation and Management,* 3, 1, 3-26.

Burnham, John (1993). Systemic Supervision: The evolution of reflexivity in the context of the supervisory relationship. *Human Systems: Journal of Systemic Consultation and Management,* 4, 3-4, 349-381.

Burnham, John (2005). Relational reflexivity: a tool for socially constructing therapeutic relationships. In Flaskas, Carmel et al. *The space between: experience, context and process in the therapeutic relationship.* London: Karnac.

Cecchin, Gianfranco (1987). Hypothesising, circularity and neutrality revisited: an invitation to curiosity. *Family Process* 26, 405-413.

Cecchin, Gianfranco (1996). Prejudiced about prejudice. Interview by John Söderlund. *The New Therapist*.

Cho, Jeasik & Trent, Allen (2009). Validity Criteria for Performance-Related Qualitative Work for Performance in/as Qualitative Inquiry. Toward a Reflexive, Evaluative, and Co-constructive Framework. *Qualitative Inquiry*, 15, 6, 1013-1041.

Clifford, James & Marcus, George E. (Eds.) (1986). *Writing Culture: the poetics and politics of ethnography*. Berkley, CA: University of California Press.

Code, Lorraine (1995). Questions of method in feminist practice in *Changing Methods: Feminists Transforming Practice*. Burt, S. & Code, L. (Eds.). Ontario: Broadview

Cronen, Vernon E., & Pearce, W. Barnett (1985). An explanation of how the Milan method works: an invitation to a systemic epistemology and the evolution of family systems. In D. Campbell & R. Draper (Eds.). *Applications of systemic family therapy: the Milan approach.* London: Grune & Stratton.

Cunliffe, Ann L. (2009). Reflexivity, learning and reflexive practice. In S. Armstrong & C. Fukami (Eds.) Handbook of Management Learning, Education and Development. London: Sage.

Day, Elizabeth (2014). *A rich portrait of the non-violent resistance multi-parent therapeutic programme.* Unpublished doctoral d*issertation, University of Bedfordshire.* http://hdl.handle.net/10547/582696

Deleuze, Gilles & Guattari, Felix (1987). *A Thousand plateaus: Capitalism and Schizophrenia* (tr. Brian Massumi). University of Minnesota Press.

Deleuze, Gilles & Guattari, Felix (1994). *What is philosophy?* (trans. H. Tomlinson & G. Burchell). New York, NY: Columbia University Press.

Denzin, Norman K. & Lincoln, Yvonna S. (Eds.) (2005). *The SAGE Handbook of Qualitative Research*. 3rd Edition. London: Sage Publications.

Denzin, Norman K. & Lincoln, Yvonna S. (Eds.) (2011). *The SAGE Handbook of Qualitative Research*. 4th Edition. London: Sage Publications.

Denzin, Norman K. & Lincoln, Yvonna S. (Eds.) (2018). *The SAGE Handbook of Qualitative Research*. 5th Edition. London: Sage Publications.

Denzin, Norman K. (2003). *Performance Ethnography: critical pedagogy and the politics of culture*. London: Sage Publications.

Denzin, Norman K. (2017). Critical Qualitative Inquiry. *Qualitative Inquiry* 23, 1, 8–16.

Dewey, John (1925/1958). *Experience and nature*. New York, NY: Dover Publications.

Dewey, John (1934/1980). *Art as experience*. New York, NY: Perigee Books.

Dillard, Cynthia (2000). The substance of things hoped for, the evidence of things not seen: examining an endarkened feminist epistemology in educational research and leadership *International Journal of Qualitative Studies in Education*, 13, 6, 661-681.

Ellis, Carolyn (2000). Creating Criteria: An Ethnographic Short Story. *Qualitative Inquiry,* 6, 2, 273-277.

Etherington, Kim (2004). *Becoming a Reflexive Researcher: Using Our Selves in Research*. London: Jessica Kingsley Publishers.

Fine, Michelle (1994). Working the hyphens: reinventing self and other in qualitative research. In Norman K. Denzin & Yvonna S. Lincoln (Eds.), *The SAGE Handbook of Qualitative Research*. London: Sage.

Fischer, Constance T. (2009). Bracketing in qualitative research: conceptual and practical matters. *Psychotherapy Research,* 19, 4-5, 583-590.

Goldner, Virginia (1988). Generation and gender: Normative and covert hierarchies. In Monica McGoldrick, Carol M. Anderson, & Froma Walsh (Eds.), *Women in families. A Framework for Family Therapy.* New York, NY: Norton.

Haraway, Donna (2015). Anthropocene, Capitalocene, Plantationocene, Chthulucene: Making Kin. *Environmental Humanities*, 6, 159-165 http://environmentalhumanities.org/arch/vol6/6.7.pdf

Hardy, Kenneth V., & Laszloffy, Tracey A. (1995). The cultural genogram:

Key to training culturally competent family therapists. *Journal of Marital and Family Therapy*, 21, 3, 227–237.

Hoffman, Lynn (1990). Constructing Realities: An Art of Lenses. *Family Process* 29, 1-12.

Hoffman, Lynn (2001). *Family Therapy: An Intimate History.* London: W.W. Norton.

hooks, bell (1994). *Teaching to Transgress: Education as the Practice of Freedom*. New York: Routledge.

Jackson, Alecia Youngblood & Mazzei, Lisa A. (2012). *Thinking with Theory in Qualitative Research: Viewing Data Across Multiple Perspectives.* Abingdon, Oxon: Routledge.

Juhl, Andreas (2012). *A multi-positional and pragmatic reflexive approach to organizational consultancy. Doctoral Dissertation, University of Bedfordshire.* http://hdl.handle.net/10547/265179

Kapoor, Anish (2009). *Imagine...* BBC Television Programme.

Kebbe, Lisen (2014). Essay Writing as Dialogical Inquiry. In Gail Simon & Alex Chard (Eds.), *Systemic Inquiry. Innovations in Systemic Practice Research*. Farnhill: Everything is Connected Press.

Lather, Patti (1993). Fertile Obsession: Validity after Poststructuralism. *The Sociological Quarterly*, 34, 4, 673-693.

Lather, Patti (1994). *Getting Smart: Feminist Research and Pedagogy within/in the Postmodern*. London Routledge.

Lather, Patti (2007). *Getting Lost: Feminist Efforts Towards a Double(d). Science.* New York, NY: State University of New York Press.

Lather, Patti & St Pierre, Elizabeth A. (2013). Post-qualitative research. *International Journal of Qualitative Studies in Education.* 26, 6, 629-633.

Lorde, Audrey (2004 [1984]). The Master's Tools Will Never Dismantle The Master's House. In *Feminist Frontiers*. Laurel Richardson, Verta Taylor & Nancy Whittier (Eds.). 6th Edition. (Originally in *Sister Outsider* 1984). New York: McGraw Hill.

Madison, D. Soyini (2012). *Critical Ethnography. Methods, Ethics, and Performance*. London: Sage Publications Ltd.

Markovic (then Radovanovic), Desa (1993). Prisoners of Identity: A Conversation with Dr Gianfranco Cecchin. *Human Systems: Journal of Systemic Consultation and Management*. 4, 1, 3-18.

Maturana, Humberto (1988). Reality: The search for objectivity or the quest for a compelling argument. *The Irish Journal of Psychology*, 9, 1, 25-82.

Maturana, Humberto & Varela, Francisco (1979). *Autopoiesis and Cognition: The Realization of the Living*. Dordrecht, Holland: Reidel.

McCarthy, Imelda Colgan & O'Reilly Byrne, Nollaig (2007). A Fifth Province Approach to Intra-Cultural Issues in an Irish Context: Marginal Illuminations. In Monica McGoldrick & Ken Hardy (Eds.). *Revisioning Family Therapy: Race, Class, Culture, and Gender in Clinical Practice*. 2nd Edition. New York, NY: Guilford Press.

McCarthy, Imelda (2010). A Traumatic Intrusion with Transgressive Possibilities: power as a relational and discursive phenomenon. *Context*, October 2010.

McCarthy, Imelda & Simon, Gail (Eds.) (2016). *Systemic Therapy as Transformative Practice*. Farnhill: Everything is Connected Press.

McGoldrick, Monica (Ed.). (1998). *Re-visioning family therapy: Race, culture, and gender in clinical practice*. New York, NY: Guilford Press.

McNamee, Sheila (2004). Promiscuity in the practice of family therapy. *Journal of Family Therapy*, 26, 3, 224-244.

McNamee, Sheila & Gergen, Kenneth (Eds.) (1992). *Therapy as Social Construction* (Inquiries in Social Construction series). London: Sage Publications.

McNamee, Sheila & Hosking, Dian Marie (2012). *Research and social change. A relational constructionist approach*. London: Routledge.

Morrow, Susan L. (2005). Quality and Trustworthiness in Qualitative Research. *The Counseling Psychologist*, 52, 2, 250-260.

Nowotny, Helga; Scott, Peter & Gibbons, Michael (2008). *Re-Thinking*

Science. Cambridge: Polity Press.

Olsson, Ann-Margreth (2014). The Impact of Dialogical Participatory Action Research (DPAR). Riding in the peloton of dialogical collaboration. In Gail Simon & Alex Chard (Eds.), *Systemic Inquiry. Innovations in Systemic Practice Research*. Farnhill: Everything is Connected Press.

Pearce, W. Barnett (1989). *Communication and the human condition.* Carbondale, IL: Illinois University Press.

Pedersen, Birgitte (2012). *Beyond talent management: a relational portrait of companies adapting to global financial downturns. Unpublished doctoral thesis. University of Bedfordshire.*

Pillow, Wanda (2003). Confession, catharsis, or cure? Rethinking the uses of reflexivity as methodological power in qualitative research. *International Journal of Qualitative Studies in Education*. 16, 2, 175-196.

Pillow, Wanda (2015). Reflexivity as Interpretation and Genealogy in Research. *Cultural Studies ↔ Critical Methodologies.* 15, 6, 419–434.

Richardson, Laurel (1994). Writing: A Method of Inquiry. In Denzin, Norman K. & Lincoln, Yvonna S. (Eds.), *The SAGE Handbook of Qualitative Research.* London: Sage Publications.

Richardson, Laurel (2000). Evaluating Ethnography. *Qualitative Inquiry,* 6, 2, 253-255.

Salter, Leah (2018). *Acts of resistance: A reflexive inquiry into narrative group work with women who have experienced abuse or oppression.* Unpublished doctoral thesis. University of Bedfordshire.

Scott, David; Brown, Andrew; Lunt, Ingrid & Thorne, Lucy (2004). *Professional Doctorates. Integrating Professional and Academic Knowledge.* Maidenhead: Open University Press.

Selvini Palazzoli, Mara; Boscolo, Luigi; Cecchin, Gianfranco & Prata, Giulianna (1980). Hypothesising - circularity - neutrality: Three guidelines for the conductor of the session. *Family Process* 19, 1, 3-12.

Shotter, John (1999). Writing from within "living moments:" "withness-writing" rather than "aboutness-writing". *Fourth National Writing Across the Curriculum Conference: Multiple Intelligences*, Cornell University, June 3rd-5th, 1999.

Shotter, John (2011). *Getting It: With-ness Thinking and the Dialogical.... In Practice.* The Hampton Press Communication Series.

Shotter, John (2016). *Speaking Actually. Towards a New 'Fluid' Common-Sense Understanding of Relational Becomings.* Farnhill: Everything is Connected Press.

Simon, Gail (1998). Incitement to Riot? Individual Identity and Group Membership: Some Reflections on the Politics of a Post-Modernist Therapy. *Human Systems: Journal of Systemic Consultation and Management*. 9, 1, 33-50.

Simon, Gail (2012). Praction Research: A Model of Systemic Inquiry. *Human Systems Journal of Systemic Consultation and Management.* 23, 1, 103-124.

Simon, Gail (2013). Relational ethnography: writing and reading in and about research relationships. *Forum Qualitative Sozialforschung/Forum: Qualitative Social Research*. [S.l.], 14 (1), Nov. 2012. ISSN 1438-5627.

Simon, Gail (2014). Systemic inquiry as a form of qualitative inquiry. In Gail Simon & Alex Chard (Eds.), *Systemic Inquiry. Innovations in Systemic Practice Research*. Farnhill: Everything is Connected Press.

Simon, Gail (2016). Systemic Practice as Systemic Inquiry as Transformative Research. In McCarthy, Imelda & Simon, Gail (Eds.). *Systemic Therapy as Transformative Practice*. Farnhill: Everything is Connected Press.

Spencer, Liz; Ritchie, Jane; Lewis, Jane & Dillon, Lucy (2003). *Quality in Qualitative Evaluation: A framework for assessing research evidence. A Quality Framework.* National Centre for Social Research. Cabinet Office.

St George, Sally & Wulff, Dan (2014). Research as Daily Practice. In Gail Simon & Alex Chard (Eds.), *Systemic Inquiry. Innovations in Systemic*

Practice Research. Farnhill: Everything is Connected Press.

Stiles, William B. (1993). Quality Control in Qualitative Research. *Clinical Psychology Review*, 13, 593-618.

Stratton, Peter; Lask, Judith; Bland, Julia; Nowotny, Ewa; Evans, Chris; Singh, Reenee; Janes, Emma & Peppiatt, Anneka (2013). Validation of the SCORE-15 Index of Family Functioning and Change in detecting therapeutic improvement early in therapy. *Journal of Family Therapy* 36, 1, 3-19.

Stratton, Peter (2017). The Evidence Base of Family Therapy and Systemic Practice. *The Association for Family Therapy and Systemic Practice.*

Tilsen, Julie & McNamee, Sheila (2015). Feedback Informed Treatment: Evidence-Based Practice Meets Social Construction. *Family Process*, 54, 1, 124–137.

Tracy, Sarah J. (2010). Qualitative Quality: Eight "Big-Tent" Criteria for Excellent Qualitative Research. *Qualitative Inquiry,* 16, 10, 837– 851.

Tomm, Karl (1987). Interventive Interviewing: Part III. Intending to ask lineal, circular, strategic or reflexive questions? *Family Process*, 27, 1-15.

Tracy, Sarah J. (2010). Qualitative Quality: Eight "Big-Tent" Criteria for Excellent Qualitative Research. *Qualitative Inquiry,* 16, 10, 837– 851.

White, Michael & Epston, David (1990). *Narrative Means to Therapeutic Ends*. New York, NY: Norton.

White, Michael (1992). Deconstruction and therapy. In *Experience, contradiction, narrative, & imagination: Selected papers of David Epston and Michael White*, 1989-1991. Adelaide, Australia: Dulwich Centre Publications.

Wittgenstein, Ludwig (1953). *Philosophical Investigations*. Oxford: Blackwell.

Van Hennik, Robert & Hillewaere, Bruno (2017). Practice Based Evidence Based Practice. Navigating based on coordinated improvisation, collaborative learning and multi-methods research in Feedback Informed Systemic Therapy. *Journal of Family Therapy,* 39, 3, 288–309.

Van Hennik, Robert (2018). *Practice Based Evidence Based Practice. Navigating complexity in Feedback-informed Systemic Therapy.* Unpublished doctoral thesis. University of Bedfordshire.

Vedeler, Anne Hedvig (2011). *Dialogical Practices: Diving into the Poetic Movement. Exploring 'supervision' and 'therapy'. Unpublished doctoral thesis. University of Bedfordshire.* http://hdl.handle.net/10547/223011

Visweswaran, Kamala (1994). *Fictions of Feminist Ethnography.* Minneapolis, MN: University of Minnesota Press.

THIRTEEN

Transmaterial Worlding: Beyond Human Systems

Gail Simon and Leah Salter

Introduction

I find a parking space under some trees. Opening the car door, I turn up my nose at the smell of my car's diesel fumes and feel lost about how I can afford a less polluting car.

Around the car the ground is flooded. I take a big step onto the grass and see gleaming new-born conkers lying among the leaves. I look up at the canopy to see how the horse chestnut tree is faring given the spread of the new species-threatening disease. Far fewer fruits than last year. Was last year's bumper crop a farewell? My stomach contracts. I bend down and pick up six or eight differently sized conkers, put them in my pockets and head for the café in the woods.

***

After talking with Callie for a while, she notices the conkers on the table by our mugs. I picked them up, I tell her, for us to use to see how you are all connected in your family. How you want to be connected. With her mother, we imagine configurations of Callie and her family when she is at home or at school and when she might want to move away from home. I want to move to a big city, she says and then adds, if I can afford to. What would the conkers have to say about that, I ask? Her mother answers: They would say come and live near us in the countryside or parks. We can clear the air for you so your asthma doesn't, um, make you ill. Callie interjects you mean so the pollution doesn't make me ill. My asthma is triggered by others, by the way we all live. It's good to meet in the park.

When we are ready to finish, I want to offer Callie the conkers. She hesitates about taking them. The world, she says, needs trees. Let's plant them, I suggest. Callie divides them up between me and her. I have soil and pots, her mother says. Callie puts them in her pocket. We are all trying to save the planet and live well.

****

As an example from systemic practice, this might feel familiar. Many of us will have worked with stones or leaves or other everyday objects from nature that we might use to represent family or workplace systems, human beings in relation to each other. These elements offer us useful ways of describing relationships between things or people or parts of the world but it also runs a risk of overlooking their own vitality, contribution and place in and of this world. Systemic living involves more than a focus on *human* systems.

In this paper, we propose a development on a key concept in the pivotal work "Human Systems as Linguistic Systems" by Harlene Anderson and Harry Goolishian (1988) to *transmaterial systems as communicating systems*. We may live in a relational world mostly thought of as mediated and manufactured through human communication but we also live in layers and entanglements of different kinds of materiality. As systemic practitioners and researchers, when we study human life, we cannot see it or investigate it as separate from all else around it and us, whether "man-made" and/or naturally occurring. We are in a world of worlding (Barad 2007).

Transmaterial worlding

Transmaterial worlding extends the notion of "social" in social construction to include human *and* non-human participants – animal, vegetable and mineral.

Transmaterial worlding is a reframe of social construction in emphasising the continuous process of intra-becoming within and between species and matter (Barad 2007). Transmaterial worlding describes processes we use to make sense of and create realities about human experience and the vitality of other matter, to show interconnectedness between humans and non-humans, to reframe life and death as not species specific but grounded in complex systems of animacies.

We are all involved in *worlding* processes (Barad 2007) – bringing the world into being as we respond within it. Stories we generate have consequences for human and non-human life, for our environment, for how we go on together. Systemic theories arise out of more than the practices of therapy or leadership, they reflect and resist everyday and dominant values and practices for living in and understanding complex transmaterial systems. We use the term "co-construction" (Tomm 1999) to describe joint, continuous meaning-making activities. We are always in the process of becoming-in-relationship and creating social worlds through our engagement with and as parts of the world, human and otherwise. We do not live *in* ecology, we *are* ecology.

Non-human parts of the world have their voices and experience interpreted by some more or less "expert" humans in many different ways which leaves most people perplexed about what counts as fact or how to use facts in a way that feels coherent with their lifestyles. The invention of terms such as "climate crisis" potentially connects and separates humans from the lived experience of their non-human co-inhabitants. As humans we have been taught to practice compartmentalised naming, selective hearing, selective processing and to decontextualise what we see, hear, eat, and consume. Living with not knowing what to do is no longer a practical or ethical option.

Yet we must hold an openness to develop better listening abilities – not just to grasp more fact in a world where fiction is promoted in the form of decontextualised truths – but to develop new comprehension abilities, to become translinguistic to hear our transmaterial family and see how we are making and unmaking this world together.

The idea that humans alone are able to develop stories about the world is anthropocentric, a man-made myth. Other parts of the "universe" also story humans. We need to learn to read responses from other material as communications of what we have been making. Together we create a multiverse of stories but human stories are what most people in advanced capitalism tend to tell and be told. Some of the most interesting and useful storying of the transmaterial world have come from Indigenous cultures. Most theories about how the world functions have side-lined this rich knowledge and promoted instead the unacknowledged ideological assumptions about the superiority of white people, particularly men and based on heterosexual, cisgendered, wealthy, male, westernised privilege. Stories, and those voicing them, from indigenous human cultures, have been systematically oppressed or erased but they have much to counter and extend the dissociative living of advanced capitalism (Braidotti 2019; Pillow, 2019; Richardson/Kinewesquao 2018; Rosiek & Snyder 2018).

The declaration in 2019 that Uluṟu (formerly Ayer's Rock) can no longer be climbed by visiting tourists is an example of how decolonial actions, however delayed and inadequate, can reform westernised human behaviour and potentially restore sacred living landscapes for human and non-human inhabitants: spirits, living histories, flora, fauna, indigenous people. Uluṟu, to Australian Indigenous people, is an animate, sacred landscape that is not just a *site* of Aṉangu knowledge and culture, it *is* the living of stories of knowledge, knowing and know-how. It is living and breathing. Our actions are communications which open or close possibilities. The message given to local indigenous people by the last minute rush of climbers to Uluṟu before the legislation came into force shows disregard for people and place, and disconnect between "me" and "we".

Several systemic therapists have developed ways of supporting the narratives of experience in response to concerns expressed by oppressed and colonised groups of people to counter falsehoods written *about* them, which have often led to the development of policies which have served to oppress these groups further and render invisible issues of concern facing those communities (McCarthy and Byrne 2007; Reynolds 2019; Salter, 2018; Simon 1998; Tuhiwai-Smith 1999; Visweswaran 1994). First person and co-constructionist research act as a counter-movement to decolonise research practice (Dillard 2000; Lather 1994, 2007; Madison 2012; Pillow 2019; Tuhiwai Smith, 1999; Wade 1997).

Reframing "me" and "us" and "them"

To extend this idea of transmaterial worlding further let's take some systemic questions, apply them in another professional context and step into a different ecology.

Let us imagine for a moment that we are in the mountains in The Himalayas, surrounded by clean, white snow, feeling the burning sun on our skin and the biting cold in our bones. We are researching the impact of mountain climbers on Everest. Educational and policy led innovations have had only a limited effect on the demand to climb Everest. We are experimenting with an intervention that we hope might go some way to protect the fragile ecology of the mountain Sagarmatha (Nepalese) or Chomolungma (Tibetan). The boundary between Nepal and the "Tibet Autonomous Region" runs across its summit.

We are curious about the human impact on the mountain and the impact the mountain has on humans. The relationship is more complex than a simple two-way model of interaction. We are in the realm of *intra-action* (Barad 2007) in which there is no separation of climber, mountain, photographer, competing economies, international power relations and air travel. Together they-we create a transmaterial ecology of all that is locally and remotely present in the material and narrative worlds. If, in this context, we were to ask transmaterial systemic questions about this, they might look or sound like this:

- *How could the snow at the bottom of Everest make its experience of being transformed by climbers heard in ways that climbers became more sensitised to the needs of the mountain over personal pursuit resulting in a change of climbing practice?*
- *How might we tell stories that move people about the tipping point between profit or gain of the individual, wellbeing of the mountain and its indigenous communities for human and non-human stakeholders in Everest?*
- *What kind of pre-booking preparation could there be for climbers to empathise with the mountain and its surrounding ecology before making a decision to book their trip?*
- *How does an international boundary between Nepal and now China affect the local exchange and practice of knowledge previously used by the peoples of Tibet and Nepal on the mountain, if at all?*

Palaeontologists have named this era the Anthropocene to witness how humans have affected the planet to such a degree that there is little left that is unaffected by humans. Philosopher, Rosi Braidotti speaks of the posthuman as a way of describing a shift away from anthropocentrism which allows for new ways of understanding and describing the implications of what it means to be human with the fast-moving sciences of biotechnologies, neural sciences, communication technologies, climate change and so on.

> The posthuman predicament is... framed by the opportunistic commodification of all that lives, which... is the political economy of advanced capitalism.
>
> Braidotti 2019, p.35

Art in 1995. Endangered species in 2019.

The artwork, *Moss wall,* by Icelandic/Danish artist Ólafur Eliasson is made up of reindeer lichen (Cladonia rangiferina) an important food source for reindeer in Iceland and Norway. It is now illegal for humans to pick in Norway as reindeer struggle to find food. The artist spoke at the opening of his retrospective exhibition at the Tate Modern, London in July 2019:

> The air that we breathe cannot be taken for granted as natural anymore. It is human, it is influenced by human activity. There's nowhere, not a rock in Iceland which has not been touched in some way or another by airplane pollution, or the change in temperature, the arctic moss that I photographed and documented so often, the rivers. Those glaciers for example. How different they are after 20 years. They really are unbelievably different. A whole glacier is just gone.
>
> Ólafur Eliasson 2019

Material-discursive practice

When we use language that says that we are *inter-acting* with someone or something, we are separating out parts of a relationship. The concept of "inter" assumes ontological distinguishability between entities: things or people, apparently separate *from* "one another", as configuring *of* "each other", as doing things *with* "each other". Karen Barad argues, "humans enter not as fully formed, pre-existing subjects but as subjects intra-actively co-constituted through the material-discursive practices that they engage in." (Barad, 2007, p.168).

What it means to be human has been changing. For example, humans can be understood as techno-humans. To say we "have" a phone perpetuates a distinction of separation, and ownership, between the human and the technological device. When we say, "My phone reminded me that..." or "I messaged..." these phrases still show phone and self as separate from each other and yet we have become fused with our gadgets (Haraway, 2004, 2015). Technology plays an increasingly significant role in how we interact in and with the world, how we communicate with others, in how our gadgets extend our memory, how we are remembered or lost by others, how we are identified by others, how we identify ourselves to our gadgets and remote systems, how we locate ourselves in the virtual-physical worlds, and how we are located by remote unknown others with or without our permission (Simon 2010; Allinson 2014).

The Guardian (October 2019) reports that a prototype phone has been developed by French scientists that is covered in a material that responds like human skin. You can pinch it, pull it, interact with it, as if your phone has skin, like you and I. Techo-human; human-techno. Where is the point of separation? Rosi Braidotti (2013) asks if prosthetic limbs are really "otherwise human". Gregory Bateson (1972) previously asked if the blind man, his cane, and the environment he moves about in are not all one entity or act as one. Bronwyn Preece speaks of the intersections in embodied theory between ecology and disability, explaining how she engages "with the other-than-human world as alive... I do not segregate biota from abiota, organic from non-organic, the trees from the forest, the ocean from the machines, the stone from mountain" (Preece 2019, p. 76). These questions invite us to consider if the phone can be seen as simply an implement (other to "us") to navigate the modern world (out 'there')? Or are humans enabling the phones to go about the business of remote corporations while the dominant narrative is of the phone enabling its owner? The mobile phone may not yet be a microchip under the physical skin of a human but proximity of humans and their devices is becoming increasingly intimate. Braidotti suggests that the relationship between human and technology has been extended to "unprecedented degrees of intimacy and intrusion" (Braidotti 2013, p.89).

If *knowledge* practices are inseparable from the contexts out of which they emerge, then we must accept that *language* is never innocent or neutral. Social constructionism reminds us of the power of language which we extend to include the role of all matter and power that takes material forms through legislation or profit, for example.

Recognising the presence of power relations and which realities have more influence over others is critical to transmaterial worlding as a form of inquiry. In transmaterial worlding, we understand researching linguistic practice as a form of mattering. There are no final conclusions – though there may be useful knowledge – and the need to attempt to describe journeys of knowing in which contextualised, situated ways of knowing extend or close down ways of accounting and the potential for transformation of participants. Transmaterial worlding is a process of moving, constructing, deconstructing, reconstructing and reviving stories which include the voices of those normally heard through privileged channels and the voices of marginalised, silenced or exterminated peoples, places, human and non-human, across many matters, across context, across time. Inevitably, material changes depending on where the describer is standing, how they are dressed, how the light is falling or arranged. Any "apparatus" in use, is part of the world that is being co-constructed (Barad, 2007). Discursive mattering is inevitably influenced by the limits of the describer's own apparatus - cultural lenses and filters which frequently result in a reproductive mattering of dominant white supremacist, patriarchal, heteronormative narratives and practices (Chen 2012; Pillow 2019).

How we *configure* "other" people, places or things can happen through taking an aboutness position (Shotter 2011) and become an act of colonisation in attributing meaning or interpreting meaning. Acts of colonisation separate the knower from their knowing and know-how leading us into binary constructions of "us" and "them", and stories of people who apparently know nothing. Histories are lost and communities fractured. This has resulted in catastrophic change such as loss of rainforests, sustainable communities, homelands, dunes, clean air, uncontaminated sites, the ozone layer and much, much more. So, it becomes an *ethical imperative* to ask, "What and who are in focus?" and "Why?" and "How can other silenced voices or erased matters be animated, rendered audible through our research?"

Transmaterial worlding evokes ecological and contextual curiosity and invites questions that pay attention to relational affect involving a more-than-human relating and a more-than-local focus. For example, a recently commissioned beach survey by Surfers Against Sewage (2019) found that Coca Cola and Pepsi Cola were together responsible for 25.8% of the plastic found on UK beaches (Pipeline 2019). In this example, so many major world issues (plastic waste and water pollution, dune conservation, advanced consumerism, violence towards workers in low paid countries, bio-diversity, sugar addiction, wealth inequality and more) are in the frame and it becomes difficult to see them as isolatable issues. They are connected. The shock of half a million "hermit" crabs living on "remote" islands dying from plastic pollution shows us that we need to deconstruct narratives of geographical remoteness and isolated entities. Though the branding of the litter is often more visible to our consumer eyes than the litter itself, this, too, is changing. Consumers are beginning to re-brand it for themselves as "single use plastic".

In the era out of which we are emerging, we are moving from recognising a "coke" bottle to seeing it as single use plastic or associated with workers' rights. This is the transitional material world in which we are living-transforming. Slowly, perhaps too slowly, humans are trying to change their habits and environment by researching these items, reading about them, picking up their own and other people's litter, to stop buying plastic, to learn to connect local and remote contexts. To become a consumer under advanced capitalism often requires becoming dissociated from the context of production of the material goods one is purchasing. The opposite of dissociation is relational reflexivity which is an ethical stance. Joining dots is a systemic activity. We are unlearning compartmentalisation. We have a choice of who we listen to, who we believe. Are we listening to the "silent" deaths of other creatures and glaciers, rain forests and fields of lichen or have we trained our ears to filter matters out that apparently do not matter to us in our human and immediate time-frame? How do we listen, how do we listen in order to witness, to live with shock and concern, to not become numb, to be moved instead to alternative action, and to look after "ourselves" (*and* check who is included in "we")?

Systemic therapy has produced a number of transdisciplinary questions which help bring forth others not present but who would understand the experiences of others such as internalised other questions (Burnham, 2000), outsider witness practice (White 1997), wider system questions used with hypothetical audiences (Simon 1998). These differing real life contexts and the threads that connect them can be understood as *transcontextual* material (Nora Bateson 2016) and form part of the rich tapestry of "what counts" as "worthy of study" within qualitative inquiry (Denzin 2017; Simon 2018). Victims of injustice, their advocates, professionals, academics the world over struggle for their truths to be taken seriously in a world which uses 21st century technologies to amplify dominant discourses and fan preferred truths to generate simplistic dismissals of what, in another era, would have counted as fact.

Systemic living and ethical mattering

We are using the term *systemic living* in lieu of systemic practice to emphasise systemic ways of being, doing, thinking, feeling, noticing and communicating. It includes systemic therapy and leadership and supervision and so on but systemic ways of thinking about things, conceptualising things go way beyond what takes place under the auspices of commissioned or employed professional practice. Systemic living means being alert to incoherence between stories lived, stories told, stories ignored and stories re-written (Cronen and Pearce 1999; McNamee 2020). These are not activities which are separable from each other, which take place chronologically in different moments. Systemic living is a commitment to fluidly attempting integration of changing positions. Transmaterial worlding describes philosophically based ways of systemic being-seeing-doing-becoming in and of the world. It is living onto-epistemological coherence: we learn as we go; we become as we reflect on what we are doing; we write and learn, listen and change. All the time. That is the systemic ethic.

We understand systemic living as a form of social activist inquiry. This goes beyond observing. It reframes participant-observation (Anderson and Goolishian 1988) as intentional, inevitably disruptive, preoccupied with social and environmental justice, and committed to collaborative transformation. Stasis is an illusory concept existing in a humancentric timeframe. Instead, we live in perpetual, hard-to-follow entangled movements for which we try to develop narratives depending on the ideological contexts affecting our investment in some theories of relational causality over others. The use of the term relational here is included purposefully, not superfluously, to render visible contexts for theories of causality. Theories do not randomly exist in isolation. They have their lobbies and investors expecting different kinds of return for distinct sections of the population.

Systemic living is guided by an ethical imperative to address practices of power by asking how stories are generated, why some truths are propagated over others, by whom, and to what end. Systemic practitioners are committed to understanding the relational effect of stories and how some stories carry more weight than others in different contexts.

Transmaterial worlding reframes professional, personal and academic activities as bringing into being a diverse but connected transmaterial world. Systemic practice and research become an opportunity to understand *and* disrupt power relations in order to challenge and reduce injustice. It is an opportunity to pay attention to who-what matters, who-what is directing and who-what counts as mattering.

In her book, "Staying with the Trouble. Making kin in the Chthulucene", Donna Haraway says,

> It matters what matters we use to think other matters with; it matters what stories we tell to tell other stories with; it matters what knots knot knots, what thoughts think thoughts, what descriptions describe descriptions, what ties tie ties. It matters what stories make worlds, what worlds make stories.
>
> Haraway 2016, p.12

As systemically informed people, we understand the power of fragmented or contradictory narratives and how to engage enquiringly in talk that exposes incoherence and helps to understand the context for why some narratives are problematic or enabling in dominant or subaltern discourses. We situate these challenges within relationships. Mainly within human relationships. But what if we don't think of externalising exercises (White and Epston 1999) or internalised other interviewing (Tomm 1998; Burnham 2000) as human relationship strategies but as opportunities to build more understanding relationships with non-human life in our world? How would it have been to ask Callie and her mother to speak as a conker or cluster of conkers and explore interconnections between their futures?

Systemic mattering practices draw on social construction and narrative theory to open dialogical spaces in which we can deconstruct taken for granted terms and cultural constructs. Matter and what matters - whose voices we listen to and how we respond - can include many parts of our "universe": trees, plants, mosses, plastic (and other) waste, drugs we pass through our systems and into the water table of the earth, chemicals which benefit, sedate or annihilate entire communities with growing medical punctuation of social and political problems. We are waking daily to long lists of interconnected environmental matters and in an ongoing state of shock or denial or compliance.

Deconstructing animacy and inanimacy

Definitions of what counts as alive and dead are changing and also the rights accorded to non-human matter. Some human communities are realising we are killing other life forms and that we need to act to prevent further death.

> "On 26 February 2019, a lake became human."
> Appalled by the lake's degradation, and exhausted by state and federal failures to improve Erie's health, in December 2018 Toledo residents drew up an extraordinary document: an emergency "bill of rights" for Lake Erie. At the bill's heart was a radical proposition: that the "Lake Erie ecosystem" should be granted legal personhood, and accorded the consequent rights in law – including the right "to exist, flourish, and naturally evolve".
>
> MacFarlane 2019

In Iceland, in August 2019, a hundred people gather at the funeral of a glacier. The Okjökull glacier was declared dead about a decade before but the symbolic funeral was arranged in 2019 and a plaque was erected entitled "A letter to the future" that read:

A letter to the future

Ok is the first Icelandic glacier to lose its status as a glacier.
In the next 200 years all our glaciers are expected
to follow the same path.
This monument is to acknowledge that we know
what is happening and what needs to be done.
Only you know if we did it.

19th August 2019
415ppm CO_2

This is a profound message that draws on a dialogue between present and future timeframes as a mechanism to evoke emotions that might lead to action, now. It is open about accountability, about cause and effect. Many things in our material world are linear albeit part of complex systems. But how we maintain or disrupt linearity is a systemic challenge. Perhaps this paper is written for a moment in time, this moment in time: it's message: let us take down the idea that systemic practice takes place within four walled spaces and bring systemic living into the streets, the mountains, the shopping centres and listen to other voices speaking back to us. We are still working on fighting for human rights. Now we have to extend this campaign to those living parts of the world who are not accorded human status but treat them as if they were a human with high entitlement for safety, survival and quality of life.

New materialist thinkers invite us to deconstruct the concepts of animate/living, and inanimate/dead (Bennett 2010; Chen 2012). These can be understood as socially constructed narratives which teach communities and their colonisers to disconnect their immediate local environment from remote global environments. Jane Bennett discourages the term "environment" in order to highlight what she calls "vital materiality"

(Bennett 2010, p.12). She points out that "We are vital materiality and we are surrounded by it, though we do not always see it that way. The ethical task at hand here is to cultivate the ability to discern nonhuman vitality, to become perceptually open to it." (Bennett 2010, p.14).

When Gregory Bateson and the Milan School of Systemic Family Therapy critiqued the notion of linear causality, they shifted their interest from how problems started to what maintained problems. The cybernetic theories of self-correcting systems and homeostasis proposed by Maturana and Varela (1992) and earlier by James Lovelock in relation to earth as a self-correcting system (1979) do not fully address what happens when the balance tips to the point that systems can no longer self-correct but are threatened with extinction (Braidotti 2008). Sometimes things end, people are displaced, territories lost to their dwellers or dwellers lost to their territories.

Extinction Rebellion protests that started in 2018 have demonstrated the relevance of humans using their bodies to visually represent their concern for the earth and its' dwellers and to symbolise the fear that our world might be lost, permanently. People putting themselves in the way of cars or aeroplanes is one way to do this; but we also need to acknowledge that it is human activity that has created this "wicked problem" (Nora Bateson 2016). The aeroplane and car (at this moment in time) are neither self-organising nor self-regulating; they are propelled by human activity. Human life is given more weight than other life forms including the earth itself as a living *entity,* not simply as a *resource*.

One consequence of the anthropocentric narrative is to categorise matter as *either* animate or inanimate (Bennett 2010). Rock is not inanimate, it is alive. It hosts life, it protects life. It provides a platform for life. In terms of the time frame in which plants, animals and humans live, rock offers stability. We humans have a short life span compared to rock. Rock grows or changes in mostly a much slower time frame to the life spans of humans, flora and fauna. We don't notice the parallel time worlds. We think rock and glaciers are dead because they are not moving in ways *we* can perceive with our eyes. We tell ourselves simple stories. We say they are frozen, immobile, inanimate. But it is we who are frozen in time. Our own timeframe. A human timeframe.

Transmaterial worlding requires that we re-think our relations *with-in* our environment, that we re-position ourselves from in-habiting the world or co-habiting (both separate us from other materiality) to *co-inhabiting.* Co-inhabitation emphasises not simply collaboration and intra-action (Barad 2007) but a humility to re-position humans as living *in* a vital-emergent-disappearing world, *alongside* and *as* vital-emergent-disappearing matter. We are all equal earth dwellers. Thinking in terms of co-inhabitation requires an active stance - to engage *in* and *with* our environment with an ethic of care and an assumption of having some responsibility. We are not sharing *our* planet with other forms of life; we are reconfiguring what it means to live, temporarily, alongside and with others, human and other material life forms.

In separating out human and non-human we recognise we are engaging in a particular way of viewing and storying the world. We have a long history of connecting with these ideas in systemic thinking. Gregory Bateson, in 1972, challenged the practice of categorising, and therefore separating, subjects and things; with the impact of creating a narrative that obscures relationality, highlights differences over similarities and foregrounds thingness over relational activity. New materialist thinkers might call this an epistemological error (Bateson 1972), critiquing the anthropocentric narrative of human as separate from the world around them. Karen Barad proposes that matter of *all* kinds is not separate but inevitably *entangled.* Barad explains,

> The very nature of materiality is an entanglement. Matter itself is always already open to, or rather entangled with, the 'Other.' The intra-actively emergent 'parts' of phenomena are co-constituted
>
> Barad 2007, p.393

Transmaterial, co-constructive questions

Transmaterial worlding as inquiry asks investigative, co-constructive questions such as,

- How can *we* show what matters, how it matters, and to whom it matters?
- How can *we* show others what is being constructed, how and with whom?
- How can *we* use our understanding of communication to show how relations in the world are being created?

The *how can we show* questions are not innocent or decontextualised research questions. Firstly, the "we" is a cynical we which needs critical and reflexive responsivity. The questions reflect some anxiety that facts and findings alone will not be accepted as evidence. They anticipate an increasingly sceptical audience. Members of the public see politicians fighting with scientists over who is telling the truth. Black, minority ethnic and Indigenous communities struggle to have their realities of systematic and institutionalised abuse taken seriously by those in positions of influence. Evidence using what was traditionally considered robust research methods is no longer enough. On the one hand, methods often reproduce colonising values which serve to reproduce material which does not reflect lived experience for example, of oppressed and minority peoples. On the other hand, approaches that do reflect experiences of minority or oppressed peoples are often critiqued for being too subjective and insufficiently rigorous.

Systemic questions, and the theory behind them, extend the new materialist understanding of worlding by attending to emergent relationality and living contexts.

These questions address the voices of human and non-human life forms:

- How is material being defined?
- Which voices are being included or excluded?

- What are the politics of representation?
- What negotiations are involved in the process of knowledge generation and knowledge sharing?

There are different kinds of power to consider in transmaterial worlding:

i) The power to influence how people configure realities through discourse and narrative
ii) The power to create structures which solidify and embody those realities
iii) The power to deconstruct and reconstruct material and linguistic structures
iv) The power to recognise that truths are not representative of one's own, other people's or the material environment's experience
v) The power to deliberately seek out first person experience and alternative truths

In order for systemic living to make a difference, we need to ask:

- What are the governing contexts that have given rise to the problem?
- How are imbalances of power maintaining this problem?
- How can systemic living disrupt the power relations that prevent social justice driven change?
- Which voices need to be heard and how can we extend what we can hear and see?
- Who-what is best placed to represent issues and how and with what support?

Transmaterial worlding needs to draw on systemic and posthuman understandings of context and power to explain:

i) why is change difficult to effect?
ii) Why is challenging the social construction of language in itself not going to result in systemic change - desirable, meaningful, sustainable change?
iii) how can we create change and why it might be difficult?

Here are two examples of transmaterial worlding which use a range of systemic questions to bring forth both human and beyond human knowledges, to explore narratives and act as transformational practice by inviting new and empathic ways of knowing.

Research driven by concern for young people at risk in their neighbourhoods could extend the framework of contextual safeguarding (Firmin 2018) to include human and non-human voices and understand research as transformative of people, places, discourses and power structures:

- If the voices of stairwells in housing estates were included as research participants, what would they say works well about them as spaces to allow effective intimidation of young people by people who lead them into trouble?
- How can research support young people to re-design the stairwells in their block of flats and empower them to make their views heard by those in power to make changes?
- How can research map where local people, landlords and local organisations say the threshold is between personal monetary gain and social gain? And how can research bring forth their ideas for what can be done where doing nothing is not an option?

An inquiry into how current residents are affected by illness and lost relatives through radioactive toxicity brought into their worlds by local factories or nuclear plants (see the moving ethnographic research by Cathy Richardson/Kinewesquao 2018) could ask:

- Do the spirits of your ancestors speak to you about their experience or yours? How do they communicate? What do they advise you to do?
- What are the languages that you feel local government officials are most likely to listen to when local people express worry about their sickness?
- How can research support local people to teach government officials local knowledge and practices of knowing?

- If local government officials understood your experiences and could listen to what the land has to say and took advice from your ancestors, what would persuade them to act on this understanding and knowledge? What would they see that convinced them that this had been a good thing to do?
- How have you managed to keep alive practices that give life and hope?

These examples of questions from practice remind us that questions are never neutral and are a contextual intervention for the person being asked a question (Selvini Palazzoli 1980; Tomm 1988). Some questions invite an "ethic of care" in "imagining the other" (McCarthy and Byrne 2007). Others are hypothetical questions (Tomm 1988), context setting questions, appreciative inquiry, hope oriented, narrative questions. Systemic therapy has a rich array of types of questions, and theories of transformation through dialogue and relational response-ability (for example, Burnham 1992, 2000; Fredman 2004; Hedges 2005; McCarthy and Byrne 2007; Tomm 1999; Waldegrave et al. 2003).

Summary

In this paper we propose how we can reframe systemic social construction to move away from a focus on human systems and human communication to transmaterial systems as communicating systems. This involves a fundamental re-think of who-what counts in decision-making and what counts as knowledge and know-how. Systemic living is a meta-position to *being* a systemic practitioner. It involves critically reflexive engagement in entanglements of *becoming-with* and has an eye or two for how power is present and to what effects. Transmaterial worlding is a process of becoming through learning. It takes place in and between human and non-human activity motivated by a concern for ecological survival and "social" justice where social is reframed to include a consideration of all peoples and ecosystems. This requires critically separating from anthropocentric ideology and moving into a new way of seeing oneself and humans in a world of vital matter with whom we are in communication.

Transmaterial worlding invites the development of fluid and shifting connections between experience and explanation, between theory and practice, language and matter, human and non-human relating. It extends social to include human and non-human matter; promotes co-construction as intra-action as onto-epistemological becoming with and through learning; co-inhabitation of a world of complex entanglements; and systemic living as a way of being open to and supportive of stories and experience that make a difference across transmaterial contexts. Co-construction is not just a systemic activity but a systemic ethic and a systemic reality. We recognise the power of co-construction and its consequences. Transmaterial worlding is an important discursive and political tool. Firstly, it promotes understanding and support of decolonial, new materialist strategies to show, extend and disrupt relationships between language and material structures. Secondly, transmaterial worlding locates human activity as co-inhabitation within a wider fluid sphere of human and non-human environmental context. Examples of systemic questions demonstrate transformative possibilities for generating new and old knowledges that impact on daily practice; and extend curiosity for the purpose of promoting social justice and developing better social worlds (Pearce 2007).

Acknowledgments

With respect and appreciation to those struggling to ensure some stories reach our ears. Thanks also to the care taken by our reviewers.

References

Allinson, Jodie (2014). Training strategies for performance and landscape: Resisting the late-capitalist metaphor of environment as consumable resource, Theatre Dance and Performance Training, 5, 1, 4-14.

Anderson, Harlene & Goolishian, Harold (1988). Human Systems as Linguistic Systems: Preliminary and Evolving Ideas about the Implications for Clinical Theory. Family Process, 27, 371-393.

Barad, Karen (2007). Meeting the Universe Halfway: Quantum Physics and the Entanglement of Matter and Meaning. Durham, NC: Duke University Press.

Bateson, Gregory (1972). Steps to an ecology of mind. New York, NY: Ballantine Books.

Bateson, Nora (2016). Small arcs of larger circles: Framing through other patterns. Dorset: Triarchy Press.

Bennett, Jane (2010). Vibrant Matter: A Political Ecology of Things. Durham, NC: Duke University Press.

Braidotti, Rosi (2006). Transpositons: On Nomadic Ethics. London: Polity Press.

Braidotti, Rosi (2008). In Spite of the Times: The Postsecular Turn in Feminism. Theory, Culture & Society, 25, 6, 1–24.

Braidotti, Rosi (2011). Nomadic Theory: The Portable Rosi Braidotti. New York, NY: Columbia University Press.

Braidotti, Rosi (2013). The Posthuman. London: Polity Press.

Braidotti, Rosi (2019). A theoretical framework for the critical posthumanities. Theory, Culture and Society, 36, 6, 31-61.

Burnham, John (1992). Approach, Method, Technique: Making Distinctions and Creating Connections. Human Systems: Journal of Systemic Consultation and Management, 3, 1, 3-26.

Burnham, John (2000). Internalized other interviewing: evaluating and enhancing empathy. Clinical Psychology Forum, 140, 16-20.

Chen, Mel Y. (2012). Animacies. Biopolitics, Racial Mattering, and Queer Affect. Durham, NC: Duke University Press.

Cronen, Vernon, E. and Pearce, W. Barnett (1999). Using CMM: The coordinated management of meaning. Accessed 7th September 2019. http://www.pearceassociates.com/essays/cmm_seminar.pdf

Denzin, Norman K. (2017)." Critical Qualitative Inquiry". Qualitative Inquiry, 23, 1, 8–16.

Dillard, Cynthia (2000). The substance of things hoped for, the evidence of things not seen: examining an endarkened feminist epistemology in educational research and leadership International Journal of Qualitative Studies in Education, 13, 6, 661-681.

Firmin, Carlene and Hancock, David (2018). Profiling CSE: Building a Contextual Picture of a Local Problem. In: H. Beckett and J. Pearce, (Eds.), Understanding and Responding to Child Sexual Exploitation. Abingdon: Routledge, pp. 107-120.

Fredman, Glenda (2004). Transforming emotion: Conversations in Counselling and Psychotherapy. London: Wiley.

Haraway, Donna (2004). "Cyborgs, Coyotes, and Dogs: A Kinship of Feminist Figurations" and "There are Always More Things Going on Than You Thought! Methodologies as Thinking Technologies". The Haraway Reader. London: Routledge.

Haraway, Donna (2015). Anthropocene, Capitalocene, Plantationocene, Chthulucene: Making Kin. Environmental Humanities, 6, 159-165.

Haraway, Donna (2016). Staying with the trouble: Making kin in the Chthulucene. Durham, NC: Duke University Press.

Hedges, Fran (2005). An Introduction to Systemic Therapy with Individuals: A Social Constructionist Approach. London: Palgrave Macmillan.

Lather, Patti (1994). Getting Smart: Feminist Research and Pedagogy within/in the Postmodern. London: Routledge.

Lovelock, James. (1979). Gaia: A new look at life on earth. Oxford: Oxford University Press.

MacFarlane, Robert (2019). Should this tree have the same rights as you? The Guardian. 2nd November 2019. https://www.theguardian.com/books/2019/nov/02/trees-have-rights-too-robert-macfarlane-on-the-new-laws-of-nature

Madison, D. Soyini (2012). Critical Ethnography. Methods, Ethics, and Performance. London: Sage Publications.

McCarthy, Imelda Colgan and O'Reilly Byrne, Nollaig (2007). A Fifth Province Approach to Intra-Cultural Issues in an Irish Context: Marginal

Illuminations. In M. McGoldrick and K. Hardy (Eds.), Revisioning Family Therapy: Race, Class, Culture, and Gender in Clinical Practice. 2nd Edition. New York, NY: Guilford Press.

McNamee, Sheila (2020). Relational Research (Trans)forming Practices. In M. Ochs, M. Borcsa, and J. Schweitzer (Eds.), Linking systemic research and practice – Innovations in paradigms, strategies and methods. European Family Therapy Association Series, Volume 5. Cham, Germany: Springer International.

Pearce, W.B. (2007). Making social worlds: A communication perspective. Oxford: Blackwell.

Pillow, Wanda (2019). Epistemic witnessing: theoretical responsibilities, decolonial attitude and lenticular futures. International Journal of Qualitative Studies in Education. 32, 2, 118-135.

Surfers against Sewage (2019). Research reveals Coca Cola and PepsiCo responsible for 25% of packaging pollution found on UK beaches May 14th 2019. https://www.sas.org.uk/news/research-reveals-coca-cola-and-pepsico-responsible-for-25-of-packaging-pollution-found-on-uk-beaches/

Preece, Bronwyn (2019). Performing Embodiment: Improvisational Investigations into the Intersections of Ecology and Disability. Unpublished doctoral thesis, University of Huddersfield.

Reynolds, Vikki (2014). A solidarity approach: The rhizome and messy inquiry. In G. Simon and A. Chard (Eds.), Systemic inquiry: Innovations in reflexive practice research. Farnhill: Everything is Connected Press.

Reynolds, Vikki (2019). Justice-Doing at the Intersections of Power. Adelaide: Dulwich Centre Publications.

Richardson/Kinewesquao, Catherine Lynn (2018). Relating to illness in therapy. Murmurations: Journal of Transformative Systemic Practice, 1, 2, 14-26.

Rosiek, Jerry Lee & Snyder, Jimmy (2018). Narrative Inquiry and New Materialism: Stories as (Not Necessarily Benign) Agents. Qualitative Inquiry.

Salter, Leah (2018). Acts of resistance: A reflexive inquiry into narrative group work with women who have experienced abuse or oppression. Unpublished doctoral thesis. University of Bedfordshire. Available at: http://hdl.handle.net/10547/623290

Selvini Palazzoli, Mara, Boscolo, Luigi, Cecchin, Gianfranco and Prata, Giulianna (1980). Hypothesising - circularity - neutrality: Three guidelines for the conductor of the session. Family Process, 19, 1, 3-12.

Shotter, John (2011). Getting It: With-ness Thinking and the Dialogical.... In Practice. New York, NY: The Hampton Press.

Simon, Gail (1998). Incitement to Riot? Individual Identity and Group Membership: Some Reflections on the Politics of a Post-Modernist Therapy. Human Systems: Journal of Systemic Consultation and Management. 9, 1, 33-50.

Simon, Gail (2010). Self Supervision, Surveillance and Transgression. Journal of Family Therapy, 32, 3, 308–325.

Simon, Gail (2018). Eight criteria for quality in systemic practitioner research. Murmurations: Journal of Transformative Systemic Practice, 1, 2, 40-62.

Simon, Gail & Salter, Leah (2020). Transmaterial Worlding as Inquiry. In the Sage Handbook of Social Construction. Eds. Mary Gergen, Sheila McNamee et al. London: Sage Publications.

Tomm, Karl (1988). Interventive Interviewing: Part III. Intending to ask lineal, circular, strategic or reflexive questions? Family Process, 27, 1, 1-15.

Tomm, Karl; Hoyt, Michael F. & Madigan, Stephen (1998) Honoring our Internalized Others and the Ethics of Caring: A conversation with Karl Tomm. In The Handbook of Constructive Therapies, (Ed. Michael Hoyt)

Tomm, Karl (1999). Co - Constructing Responsibility. In McNamee, Sheila and Gergen, Ken (Eds.) Relational Responsibility: Resources for Sustainable Dialogue. Thousand Oaks, CA: Sage.

Tuhiwai Smith, Linda (1999). Decolonizing methodologies: Research and indigenous peoples London: Zed Books.

Visweswaran, Kamala (1994). Fictions of Feminist Ethnography. University of Minnesota Press.

Wade, Allan (1997). Small acts of living: Everyday resistance to violence and other forms of oppression. Journal of Contemporary Family Therapy, 19, 1, 23–40.

Waldegrave, Charles, Tamasese Kiwi, Tuhaka, Flora and Campbell Warihi (2003). Just Therapy - a journey: A collection of papers from the Just Therapy team New Zealand. Adelaide: Dulwich Centre Publications.

White, Michael (1997). Re-membering and definitional ceremony. In M. White, Narratives of Therapists' Lives (pp.3-114). Adelaide: Dulwich Centre Publications.

White, Michael (2007). Maps of Narrative Practice. London: W. W. Norton.

White, Michael & Epston, David (1999). Narrative Means to Therapeutic Ends. London: W. W. Norton.

Everything is Connected Press Publications

Systemic Inquiry. Innovations in Reflexive Practice Research
Gail Simon & Alex Chard (Eds.)
ISBN 978-0-9930723-0-7

Systemic Therapy and Transformative Practice
Imelda McCarthy & Gail Simon (Eds.)
ISBN 978-0-9930723-2-1

Speaking, Actually: Towards a New 'Fluid' Common-Sense Understanding of Relational Becomings
John Shotter
ISBN 978-0-9930723-4-5

A Wild Impatience. Critical Systemic Practice and Research. Selected Papers.
Gail Simon
ISBN 978-0-9930723-6-9

Murmurations: Journal of Transformative Systemic Practice
www.murmurations.cloud
ISSN 2516-0052

www.eicpress.com

everything is connected

everything is connected

Made in United States
North Haven, CT
10 November 2026

22081992R00186